Improving Mathematics at Work

DISCARD

Improving Mathematics at Work questions the mathematical knowledge and skills that matter in the twenty-first century world of work, and studies how the use of mathematics in the workplace is evolving in the rapidly changing context of new technologies and globalisation. Through a series of case studies from the manufacturing and financial service sectors, the authors argue that there has been a radical shift in the type of mathematical skills required for work – a shift not yet fully recognised by the formal education system, or by employers and managers.

Examining how information technology has changed mathematical requirements, the idea of Techno-mathematical Literacies (TmL) is introduced to describe the emerging need to be fluent in the language of mathematical inputs and outputs to technologies and to interpret and communicate with these, rather than merely to be procedurally competent with calculations. The authors argue for careful analyses of workplace activities, looking beyond the conventional thinking about numeracy, which still dominates policy arguments about workplace mathematics. Throughout their study, the authors answer the following fundamental questions:

- What mathematical knowledge and skills matter for the world of work today?
- How does information technology change the necessary knowledge and the ways in which it is encountered?
- How can we develop these essential new skills in the workforce?

With evidence of successful learning co-designed with employers and employees, this book provides suggestions for the development of TmL through authentic learning activities involving symbolic workplace artefacts reconstituted with interactive software. Essential reading for trainers and managers in industry, teachers, researchers and lecturers of mathematics education and stakeholders implementing evidence-based policy, this book maps the fundamental changes taking place in workplace mathematics.

Celia Hoyles is Professor of Mathematics Education, London Knowledge Lab, Institute of Education, University of London, UK.

Richard Noss is Professor of Mathematics Education and Co-director of the London Knowledge Lab, Institute of Education, University of London, UK.

Philip Kent is a Research Officer, London Knowledge Lab, Institute of Education, University of London, UK.

Arthur Bakker is a Research Officer in the TmL project, currently at the Freudenthal Institute, Utrecht University, the Netherlands.

Improving Learning TLRP

Series Editor: Andrew Pollard, Director of the ESRC Teaching and Learning Programme

The Improving Learning series showcases findings from projects within ESRC's Teaching and Learning Research Programme (TLRP) – the UK's largest ever co-ordinated educational research initiative. Each book is explicitly designed to support 'evidence-informed' decisions in educational practice and policy-making. In particular, they combine rigorous social and educational science with high awareness of the significance of the issues being researched.

Improving Literacy by Teaching Morphemes
Terezinha Nunes and Peter Bryant

Improving Workplace Learning
Karen Evans, Phil Hodkinson, Helen Rainbird and Lorna Unwin

Improving Schools, Developing Inclusion
Mel Ainscow, Tony Booth and Alan Dyson

Improving Subject Teaching: Lessons from research in science education
Robin Millar, John Leach, Jonathan Osborne and Mary Ratcliffe

Improving Learning Cultures in Further Education
David James and Gert Biesta

Improving Learning How to Learn: Classrooms, schools and networks
Mary James, Robert McCormick, Paul Black, Patrick Carmichael, Mary-Jane Drummond, Alison Fox, John MacBeath, Bethan Marshall, David Pedder, Richard Procter, Sue Swaffield, Joanna Swann and Dylan Wiliam

Improving Learning through Consulting Pupils
Jean Rudduck and Donald McIntyre

Improving Learning, Skills and Inclusion: The impact of policy on post-compulsory education
Frank Coffield, Sheila Edward, Ian Finlay, Ann Hodgson, Ken Spours and Richard Steer

Improving Classroom Learning with ICT
Rosamund Sutherland

Improving Learning in College: Rethinking literacies across the curriculum
Roz Ivanic, Richard Edwards, David Barton, Marilyn Martin-Jones, Zoe Fowler, Buddug Hughes, Greg Mannion, Kate Miller, Candice Satchwell and June Smith

Improving Learning in Later Life
Alexandra Withnall

Improving Learning by Widening Participation in Higher Education
Edited by Miriam David

Improving Research Through User Engagement (forthcoming)
Mark Rickinson, Anne Edwards and Judy Sebba

Improving What is Learned at University: An exploration of the social and organisational diversity of university education (forthcoming)
John Brennan

Improving Inter-professional Collaborations: 'Multi-agency working for children's wellbeing'
Anne Edwards, Harry Daniels, Tony Gallagher, Jane Leadbetter and Paul Warmington

Improving Mathematics at Work

The need for techno-mathematical literacies

Celia Hoyles, Richard Noss,
Phillip Kent and Arthur Bakker

Routledge
Taylor & Francis Group

LONDON AND NEW YORK

OAKTON COMMUNITY COLLEGE
DES PLAINES CAMPUS
1600 EAST GOLF ROAD
DES PLAINES, IL 60016

First edition published 2010
by Routledge
2 Park Square, Milton Park, Abingdon, Oxon, OX14 4RN

Simultaneously published in the USA and Canada
by Routledge
270 Madison Avenue, New York, NY 10016

Routledge is an imprint of the Taylor & Francis Group, an informa business

© 2010 Celia Hoyles, Richard Noss, Phillip Kent and Arthur Bakker

Typeset in Charter ICT and Stone Sans
by Keystroke, Tettenhall, Wolverhampton
Printed and bound in Great Britain
by CPI Antony Rowe, Chippenham, Wiltshire

All rights reserved. No part of this book may be reprinted or
reproduced or utilised in any form or by any electronic,
mechanical, or other means, now known or hereafter invented,
including photocopying and recording, or in any information
storage or retrieval system, without permission in writing from
the publishers.

British Library Cataloguing in Publication Data
A catalogue record for this book is available from the British
Library

Library of Congress Cataloging-in-Publication Data
Improving mathematics at work : the need for techno-
mathematical literacies / Celia Hoyles . . . [et al.]. — 1st ed.
        p. cm.
     Includes bibliographical references.
     1. Communication in mathematics.   2. Communication of
technical information.   3. Mathematical ability.   4. Workplace
literacy.   I. Hoyles, Celia, 1946–
QA41.4.I47 2010
510—dc22   2009040066

ISBN10: 0–415–48007–8 (hbk)
ISBN10: 0–415–48008–6 (pbk)
ISBN10: 0–203–85465–9 (ebk)

ISBN13: 978–0–415–48007–9 (hbk)
ISBN13: 978–0–415–48008–6 (pbk)
ISBN13: 978–0–203–85465–5 (ebk)

Contents

Illustrations

Figures

Tables

Boxes

Acknowledgements

We gratefully acknowledge funding of the research described in this book by the United Kingdom Economic and Social Research Council's Teaching and Learning Research Programme (www.tlrp.org), grant number L139-25-0119, October 2003 to June 2007.

We especially thank the companies and organisations that allowed us to make observations in their factories and offices, and the many employees who made time to show us their workplaces, and to be interviewed.

We are also grateful to SEMTA (the Sector Skills Council for Science, Engineering and Manufacturing Technologies) and the Financial Services Skills Council for providing key networks of employer contacts in several industry sectors.

We owe a special thanks to Chand Bhinder, who made an exceptional contribution to the project during his 12-month working with us as a designer and programmer. With his background in financial services and mathematics, he made a central contribution to the design of the software tools ('TEBOs') developed in the research, and was entirely responsible for the superb coding of the Flash-based visual TEBOs.

Megan Craig at the London Knowledge Lab was the administrator for the project. Mark Moors and Linda Timmer at Utrecht University provided graphical expertise in creating final versions of many of the figures.

David Guile at the Institute of Education was a consultant to the project providing key expertise in social and educational studies of workplaces. Professor Alan Brown, from Warwick University and deputy director of the TLRP with responsibility for workplace research projects, was always ready to offer expertise and support to our research, and became a co-researcher with us in an additional research project on 'technical and communicative skills' in the workplace (funded by the TLRP Technology Enhanced Learning programme in 2006).

We are grateful to the members of the Project Advisory Group for continual support throughout the project: Professor Alan Brown (Warwick University and TLRP), Dr Neil Challis (Sheffield Hallam University), Sybil Cock (Tower Hamlets College), Professor Neville Davies (Royal Statistical Society Centre for Statistical Education), John Harris (SEMTA), Sarah Jones (Association of the British Pharmaceutical Industry), Professor Ken Mayhew (Oxford University), Karen Spencer (Kingston College), and Gordon Stewart (The Packaging Society).

Chapter 1

Introduction

This book presents a report on a three-and-a-half year research project, 'Techno-mathematical Literacies in the Workplace', that was conducted by the authors between October 2003 and June 2007. This chapter introduces the key ideas and aims of the project and some of the main theoretical and practical approaches adopted. Chapters 2 to 5 of the book present the body of research findings from the different industry sectors that we studied: manufacturing (Chapters 2 and 3) and financial services (Chapters 4 and 5). Each chapter consists of ethnographic observations of companies, and accounts of the design and development of new learning materials undertaken with companies. Chapter 6 concludes the book by bringing together key findings and observations across all the industry sectors covered in the research, the challenges of researching the workplace and the implications for improving 'techno-mathematical' learning at work.

New demands on commerce and industry

This book is about understanding and improving mathematical skills in the workplace. We begin by describing the shifts that are occurring in the mathematical skills required in UK workplaces, set against the broader picture of business and employment in companies in the manufacturing and service sectors.

Globalisation and free market competition have become commonplace ideas that are used to account for the changes that are occurring in economics and business, and the working lives of individual employees. We do not propose to comment on the effectiveness of these concepts in explaining current trends, and it is well beyond our remit to analyse globalisation as a broad phenomenon: we are neither economists nor sociologists. What we can certainly say from our direct experience is that the forces of globalisation do exist: every company that we worked with during the research project reported in this book (between 2003 and 2007) told us how its products and practices were changing significantly as a result of global markets and competition, the associated ubiquitous use of computer systems to improve efficiency of production and quality of products, and how these two phenomena shaped the mathematical skills required by employees.

An example of these trends involved a company making plastic films (see Chapter 2: Filmic) which had closed down production of the most basic polythene film because it could not compete on price, the only market factor in that case, with competitor manufacturers in Eastern Europe. Packaging does have some unique characteristics that affect costs and support localised production: given its nature as a protective container, packaging is mostly empty space, so long-distance shipping costs are generally prohibitive, although not for the most basic types of film. For Filmic, manufacture of complex films continued to be profitable, since higher technical skills were demanded of employees and a high market price could be achieved.

A second example, concerned with the price of labour, was expressed by a senior training manager from one of the top five financial services companies in the UK. He acknowledged that the need for mathematically based technical skills in customer services was increasing, in order to understand and sell products more effectively. His company intended to satisfy this need by large-scale outsourcing of its customer service work to other countries, with UK-based call centres handling only low-level administrative tasks. At that time the customer service work was being done in India, though in the future it would be moving to the Eastern states of the EU, where there was an expected growth in English-speaking, technically capable and relatively cheap graduate employees.

This latter example illustrates a key concern in this book: the perception amongst employers and policy-makers of a serious 'skills gap' in the UK workforce for understanding and dealing with technical information expressed in symbolic form. In our observations, some companies avoided this skills gap by outsourcing – as above; some hired specialists to set up and operate their IT systems (who inevitably lacked the knowledge and practical experience of the business). Others recruited graduates directly into management positions rather than, as in the past, allowing employees to progress in a 'time-served' manner. Both these tendencies have worrying implications for the career and development prospects of time-served employees, and for companies who fail to achieve an optimal balance of graduate and time-served employees in management teams. In this book, we will describe, for different industry sectors, how we sought to understand the nature of this skills gap, and explored ways of developing skills through in-work training.

Another key driver of change is that the nature of the relationship between manufacturer or service provider and customer is changing – from mass *production* to mass *customisation*, where it is possible for automated processes to produce single items that are customised to the needs of particular customers (Victor & Boynton, 1998). As with globalisation, there is a tendency in the business and management literature to over-simplify arguments about the nature and the speed of change. But mass custom-isation is certainly happening, as we witnessed in several companies. In the manufacturing context, one example was Classic Motors (Chapter 3), where production lines had been modified to produce more than one type of car at the same time, so that each car could be customised to a particular buyer's order. In this situation, production-line employees had to do far more than repeat the same basic sequence of actions (with the repetitive work increasingly done by robots).

Another example, in the financial services context, occurred where the shift to mass customisation was connected to a business perception that competitive advantage came from offering customers a greater degree of flexible communication. For example, much customer service work in the pension and insurance business had been production-focused: employees were given targets to process a certain number of cases per day, moving enquiries through the system, largely irrespective of the needs of customers. In the emerging way of working, under slogans such as 'customer focus', straightforward customer enquiries were, if possible, resolved immediately on the phone, requiring employees to work as a team with distributed know-ledge, rather than passing the case on to specialist, technical employees (cf. Chapter 4).

A result of these new ways of working was that employees at many levels in a company needed to understand some elements of what is behind the interface of the IT system with which they interacted on a daily basis, so that they could communicate with other employees in different parts of the workplace, and (in some sectors) with customers who were demanding more information and more transparency. Increasingly, these elements involved the quantitative or symbolic data processed by IT systems. A key finding from the project's ethnographic work was that new skills were needed in IT-rich workplaces that are striving for improvements in efficiency and customer communication; that is where management and employees were under pressure to move beyond routines to cut down wastage of time and product and advance the quality of products or services.

This book focuses on these new skills, what they are and how they might be developed to improve working practices.

Information technology and the changing nature of work

The introduction of information technology into workplaces, in the form of computers or computerised machinery, is one of the most important trends of the past 25 years. Nowadays, a computer running more or less specialised workplace software is the central desktop tool of every admin-istrative or service employee. In manufacturing companies, every new machine introduced to the shop floor will have a computer-based control and monitoring interface (whether this is a standard computer monitor and keyboard, or a specialised machine interface). Dealing with the inputs and outputs of this interface is becoming part of the job role of an increasing number of shop floor and middle-management employees.

Some broad statistics for the UK, based on large-scale employer surveys conducted by Felstead *et al.* (2007) between 1986 and 2006, are suggestive of this IT trend (Table 1.1).

Despite the increasing presence of IT in workplaces, the extent of actual changes to workplace practice is often less marked. For example, one major survey (Nathan, Carpenter, & Roberts, 2003) reported that 75% of employees surveyed were using a computer or other IT equipment at work, and 70% saw the computer as essential or important to the job. Yet, the ubiquity of IT was not matched by corresponding changes in the 'organisation, management and style of work' (2003: 2). From a US perspective, more evidence is provided by Handel (2003, 2004).

A major issue for organisations is to decide how to exploit IT-based systems to enhance the efficiency of the work process. In both industry and commerce, there are enormously complex software systems for information management and process control – a trend that first began in companies whose business was abstract 'information', such as financial services, but has spread more and more into manufacturing industry and beyond. Wherever the introduction of information systems takes place, decisions need to be made about different users' relationships with the information system. Among these are two addressed in this book: (1) what is the relationship between the interface of the computer's model of the workplace and the workplace's actual operation and how is this relationship perceived

Table 1.1 Trends in the use of IT in workplaces

Percentage of employees using computerised or automated machinery	1986	2006
All employees	40%	77%
Administrative and secretarial	61%	97%
Plant and machine operatives	28%	53%
'Use of PC or computerised equipment in job is essential'	1997	2006
All employees	31%	47%
Administrative and secretarial	57%	82%
Plant and machine operatives	15%	22%

Source: Felstead *et al.*, 2007

by different groups of employees? And (2), to what degree and, specifically, *which* employees are required to possess some model of the internal workings of the system in order to use it?

Zuboff (1988) usefully depicts these issues in terms of the dual potential of information technology to *automate* and to *informate*: on the one hand, the potential of technology to replace human work, and on the other hand its potential to inform human work by making information more accessible and usable. Computerisation therefore requires choices to be made about which processes to automate, and to what degree, and which processes will benefit (in terms of efficiency or productivity) by 'informating' the employees involved. This is not an either–or choice, it is a matter of striking a balance for any particular process. It is important to note that informating is not something that only depends on IT – it is arguably an attitude towards the management of processes and process information. The idea of informating is inherent to process improvement methods, as we describe in Chapters 2 and 3.

Zuboff provides detailed case studies of IT implementations during the 1970s and 1980s, and notes how the importance of informating was often missed, leading to alienation of employees and flawed implementations. Similarly, Mathews (1989) provides an interesting overview of IT trends in service industries during the 1980s, and describes how some bank IT systems became highly automated in the name of efficiency, but were extremely sensitive to input errors made by 'de-skilled' bank clerks that could rapidly propagate through the IT system.

In our own observations of workplaces, it was evident that companies were increasingly careful in the design and scoping of IT systems, and in seeking to marry IT development with employee development; none of the companies with which we were involved was undertaking developments on the large scale which, for example, Zuboff describes in her case studies. However, it is still the case that many companies do not seem yet to have achieved a satisfactory balance between automation and information, leading to tensions and 'skills gaps' which companies come to live with, yet which can become acute problems and potential sources of breakdowns in work processes. For example, we have observed cases of situations (e.g. in automotive manufacturing and mortgage retailing) where a company had recognised a training need to informate its employees, but decided that it did not have the resources to deal with it. Our contention in this book is that achieving this required balance is indeed challenging, not least since it requires some appreciation at some level of the mathematical models relevant to each case. This appreciation we will term *techno-mathematical* since, for the majority of employees, the mathematical models are never dealt with in isolation from the IT system that executes them. (See below for an expanded discussion of this point under 'techno-mathematical literacies'.)

It is useful to consider the implementation of IT systems in terms of *models*; that is, systematic descriptions of the relationships between inputs, outputs and controlling parameters, which are used inside IT systems to calculate, control and analyse processes. To automate or to informate requires different models of the process to be constructed by different actors. The designers of an IT system must create a computational model of the process that can be implemented. At the same time, different users of the system must develop *mental models* of the system in order to engage with it. Such models are inevitably mediated by the artefacts of the IT system, the explicit operating procedures of the workplace, and the tacit knowledge of workplace practices of individuals and teams. Designers are largely mathematically educated professionals who deploy mathematical techniques and ideas in the development of models. Intermediate-level users, in contrast, will generally be expected to build their mental models from a basis of relatively limited mathematical education, but combined with a great deal of workplace experience, and knowledge of the IT systems in use. This leads to the development of personal models that we call techno-mathematical, and it is the characterisation of these models that will form a basis for our discussion throughout this book.

Background to the research

Mathematics in the workplace: evidence from educational research

In many countries, mathematics is widely considered a problematic subject in workplaces, and employers have for a long time been reporting 'skills deficits'. In the UK, a month seldom passes without the publication of another survey that shows that some large fraction of the UK adult population is 'incapable' of dealing with basic mathematics (and usually also, to a lesser extent, basic literacy). National governments in many countries, the UK included, have put forward waves of policy and curriculum innovations to address the problem of 'numeracy' in the school and vocational education system as well as in lifelong learning (see, for example, FitzSimons, Coben & O'Donaghue, 2003).

We do not wish to underestimate these challenges. The crucial point, however, is to establish a more nuanced understanding of what skills are involved, and which of these are or are not problematic – that is, to question the prevailing arguments about 'numeracy' (see Noss, 1998, for an extended critique of the concept of numeracy). Our starting point is the work of educational researchers since the 1980s, who have developed a rich strand of enquiry under the broad heading of 'situated cognition' (Lave, 1988; Lave & Wenger, 1991; Nunes, Carraher & Schliemann, 1993). This involved many detailed studies of adults' behaviour in workplaces and everyday situations: for example, research with dairy workers (Scribner, 1986), carpenters (Millroy, 1992), carpet-layers (Masingila, 1994), automotive industry workers (Smith & Douglas, 1997), civil engineers (Hall,

1999), glassware design and manufacture with computer-aided design (Magajna & Monaghan, 2003). These have led to a fundamental reappraisal of the different forms of mathematical reasoning.

The broad conclusion of these studies is that most adults use mathematics to make sense of situations in ways that differ quite radically from those of the formal mathematics of school, college and professional training. Rather than striving for consistency and generality, which is stressed by formal mathematics, problem-solving at work is characterised by pragmatic goals to solve particular types of problems, using techniques that are quick and efficient for these problems. For example, in our earlier research (Hoyles, Noss & Pozzi, 2001; Noss, Hoyles & Pozzi, 2002), we observed nurses calculating drug dosages in hospital wards, often in life-critical situations. They had been taught general calculation methods that trainers regarded as 'efficient'. In practice, however, these were not used, being replaced by drug- and patient type-specific rules that derived meaning from the situation, such as the nature of the drug, the volume of the phial in which the drug was stored, while working within its constraints.

This corpus of research has shown the need to characterise more precisely the nature of mathematics used in the workplace. It leads us to argue that much of the discussion around 'skills gaps' and the non-transferability of school mathematics misses the essential characteristics of the knowledge required in technology-mediated work where there has been a shift in requirement from fluency in doing explicit pen-and-paper calculations, to fluency in using and interpreting outputs from IT systems in order to informate workplace judgements and decision-making. But even before the recent demographic and organisational shifts engendered by IT, concerns were expressed about the characterisation of mathematics used in work and its tendency to be 'invisible', which we briefly describe in the next sub-section.

The invisibility of mathematical knowledge at work[1]

The invisibility of knowledge required in modern work has been much investigated by researchers in sociology and management studies (see, for example, Nardi & Engeström, 1999). From this perspective, invisibility is considered mainly to apply to working practices, such as cleaning or maintenance, rendering the individuals and communities concerned unnoticed, ignored and (often) silenced. While questions about the legitimacy of these kinds of work are important, our concerns are primarily with the *visibility of knowledge* held by persons or communities, rather than of persons themselves or the products of their labour and the ways that knowledge in general, and mathematical knowledge in particular, is transformed in the modern workplace. For an overview of research about this, in mainly non-technical settings, see Bessot and Ridgeway (2000).

Mathematical knowledge is judged to be invisible in many situations as it tends to be deeply embedded within the representational infrastructures of the models, tools and artefacts of the workplace (see, for example, Hall *et al.*, 2002). Our own work with bank employees, nurses and engineers evidenced this invisibility and showed, first, how mathematical knowledge in use is characterised by fragmented and pragmatic strategies intertwined with meanings of the mathematical knowledge and situational 'noise'; and second, that mathematical knowledge was transformed when it crossed boundaries between different situations or settings (Hoyles & Noss, 1996b; Hoyles *et al.*, 2001; Kent & Noss, 2002; Noss *et al.* 2002; for a summary see Noss, 2002). Others have reported similar outcomes following research in technical workplaces, such as structural engineering (Hall & Stevens, 1995, and Hall, 1999) and industrial chemistry laboratories (Wake & Williams, 2001; and Williams & Wake, 2002). It must also be noted that the invisibility of mathematical knowledge is compounded by the general perception that mathematical and technological competencies consist of de-contextualised skills or techniques, disconnected from each other, and from their context of application (see, for example, Smith & Douglas, 1997; Clayton, 1999). The knowledge that is mobilised in practice is mainly not codified knowledge (Eraut, 2004), in the sense that it is readily available in published sources. It is knowledge that exists through an intimate connection with practices and artefacts of the workplace, specifically with the technologies that perform and monitor the work process.

All these studies have had to face the methodological challenge of making visible the embedded mathematics of the practice in order to study and analyse it. Most have undertaken ethnographies, often focusing on 'disruptions' in the routines of work or on communication across different representational infrastructures (Hall, 1999; Noss *et al.*, 2002). We will describe later how our research methodology addressed this phenomenon of invisibility.

Pedagogy and mathematics

A perennial concern in mathematics education is the relationship between mathematics and the contexts in which it is used. Traditional pedagogy in school mathematics has tended to highlight general techniques devoid of any context, and then require students to apply these techniques to problems drawn from contextual situations. Proponents of other pedagogies (e.g. Realistic Mathematics Education, Treffers, 1987; Gravemeijer, 1994) start from contexts and 'real' problems, to motivate the mathematics needed for problem-solving.

We would argue that the situation for teaching and learning mathematics in the workplace should be very different from that of school. There are a multitude of meaningful contexts and typical problems with which employees engage that may usefully motivate mathematical thinking. Yet a disturbing observation of this research has been how workplace technical training involving mathematics remained dominated by the delivery of general techniques out of context, which employees were invited to apply to their work-based problems. This approach runs the risk of evoking negative reactions among those who might have been alienated by school mathematics (especially amongst the non-graduate workforce). But more importantly, we will argue that the kinds of techno-mathematical knowledge and skills involved are not easily or effectively developed by this strategy.

Also disturbing was the highly didactic nature of much of the workplace technical training that we observed, with its focus on content and little opportunity for employees to discuss issues and examples, or express their tacit knowledge of problem-solving at work. One course that we observed (see Chapter 3) consisted of several hundred PowerPoint slides, with every hour of the course organised in terms of the number of slides to be 'got through'. In addition, algebraic formulae were often used to introduce mathematical concepts in terms of definitions, which although precise and correct, were inaccessible to the majority of the employees.

There is clear evidence (see, for example, NCETM, 2008) that mathematics learning becomes meaningful when learners (whether young people in school, or adults in workplaces) are given the space to express, share and develop their own ideas (see Noss & Hoyles, 1996a) and teaching becomes effective if, for example, it builds on the knowledge learners already have, and develops appropriate mathematical language through communicative activities and higher-order questioning.

We are convinced that workplace training for mathematics can be more effective if some of these messages about teaching and learning mathematics are taken on board and combined with insights from researching learning at work. The approach we propose and have researched is summarised in this chapter and elaborated in the following chapters.

Antecedents of this research study and the emergence of key ideas

Our research on mathematics in workplaces dates back to 1994, when two of us (Hoyles and Noss) were invited by the directors of a large investment bank in the City of London to investigate the mathematical skills of employees in the administrative departments of the bank; the perceived problem was that many employees lacked an effective understanding of the mathematical models on which their financial instruments were based.[2] There was a general discomfort with mathematical ideas, and a consequent reluctance to think mathematically about financial transactions, and indeed for employees to talk mathematically among themselves. The results of all this were that employee mistakes were common, costing the bank many millions of pounds each year.

The banking research presented two challenges. The first was to understand what kind of mathematics was at stake for the bank employees. The second was to find a valid and effective way to run a training programme for employees to enhance their understanding of the relevant mathematics, given that it was widely recognised that some kind of formal 'banking mathematics' curriculum would not adequately achieve this goal. (For a full account of this work, see Noss & Hoyles, 1996b.)

Looking back to that work, we see an early indication of the wider business trend to come, of the use of IT systems and the problems of invisible mathematics and mathematical communication that result. We can also see a method of investigation that we have refined over the years through a sequence of projects, which combines workplace ethnography, usually focusing on situations of breakdown, controversy or doubt, followed by the iterative design and testing of learning interventions with employees. Subsequent projects investigated mathematics in the work of nurses and pilots (Noss, Hoyles & Pozzi, 2002), and professional engineers (Kent & Noss, 2003). These studies all involved professional workers for whom mathematical knowledge is explicitly prescribed and assessed through qualifications. Even so, as in the nursing study referred to earlier, the *situated* rather then formalised nature of mathematical reasoning in practice was the most common observation, with prescribed general mathematical techniques often rejected in favour of particular techniques tuned to particular types of workplace problems.

The workplace-based project conducted immediately prior to the 'Techno-mathematical Literacies' research, 'Maths Skills in the Workplace' (Hoyles, Wolf, Molyneux-Hodgson & Kent, 2002) was commissioned by a UK national training organisation and a number of regional development organisations, to make a review of mathematical practices in a range of industrial and commercial sectors (seven sectors, and 22 companies). This project had a somewhat different character from the studies just mentioned, for several reasons. First it was required to reach conclusions that could shape policy, and second, the focus was on *intermediate level* jobs, that is, jobs for which the expected employee level of qualification was above the level of 'basic skills' but below degree-level qualifications.[3] Most research that has been done on mathematics in workplaces has looked at professional workers (notably engineers and scientists), or manual workers. Intermediate-level employees, in contrast to professional workers, rely on qualifications and experience gained whilst working. A typical case of the intermediate level employee is the first-level manager (sometimes called 'team leader' or 'group leader') on the factory shop floor, who manages a team of manual operators, and is usually an experienced operator who has been promoted to the management role.

The scope of the Mathematics Skills in the Workplace project did not allow for in-depth study of any of the companies: researchers spent only a few hours in each workplace and most of the research data was based on interviews with managers at various levels. Somewhat to our surprise, given the indicative nature of the research findings, the summary report (Hoyles *et al.*, 2002) turned out to be influential amongst policy-makers and politicians. All the findings seemed to resonate with readers. We note a few of relevance here.

First, team leaders needed to manage and communicate information much more than in the past. As one senior manager told us:

> We're data-driven much of the time, and it is clearly our strategy to push a data-driven approach right down through the organisation. Now, team leaders have to come and present to me a lot of analytical data about what happened in their shift.

The required ability for team leaders was characterised as 'to be able to interpret data, to transform it into a trend or a problem-solving analysis . . . to use the information in a well-constructed argument'.

The second finding concerned a marketplace that was more competitive, with profit margins much leaner than they used to be, and clients demanding higher quality and more complex contractual arrangements. Managers thus needed to determine realistic performance criteria that formed part of complex models of production, including for example, product output as a function of 'man-hours', and productive machine time. They then needed to use these data to assess performance against criteria and targets. Fluent manipulation of variables, some of which were not directly visible in the work process, was therefore crucial. Thus managers, including team leaders, needed to see data both as a concrete representation of what the company produced, and, at the same time, as an abstract representation that identified the implications of the data in terms of general trends that had both historical and predictive significance.

Third, team leaders were identified as playing a pivotal role in the operations of the factory, 'reading in' information to an abstract model of the workplace (such as performance data in a spreadsheet) for upward communication to management, and 'reading out' information from the model for dissemination to operational workers. To fulfil the latter purpose, data were often displayed on factory floors, in the form of graphs, which also depicted output related to given targets. Team leaders also often had to identify poor performance, and recognise anomalies and erroneous input data. Apart from the vertical metaphors of upward and downward communication, such information also often had to be channelled *horizontally* within a project team to communicate among people with different skills, and *outwards* to customers.

Fourth, another finding with considerable resonance was the report's claim that mathematical skills were becoming increasingly inter-related with IT skills:

All the sectors exhibit the ubiquitous use of Information Technology. *This has changed the nature of the mathematical skills required, while not reducing the need for mathematics.* On the contrary, in many cases, a competitive and IT-dependent environment means that many employees are using mathematics skills that their predecessors, or they themselves in the past, did not require.

(Hoyles *et al.*, 2002: 10; emphasis in original)

This was further characterised in terms of *mathematical literacy*:

Mathematical literacy is framed by the work situation and practice, and, in many cases, by the use of IT tools. . . . Alongside the modelling side of mathematical literacy, there is also the need to know how to calculate and estimate and to have a feel for numbers, percentages and proportions. Mathematical literacy is, however, much more than a set of simple and disconnected skills; and it goes well beyond a command of number or basic numeracy. It is anchored in real data (often in the form of data output from spreadsheet models), and set in the local and global context of the work. It involves an appreciation of the thresholds and constraints of a model (such as the limitations on factory output, the costs of machinery, or throughput of production lines), flexibility in understanding different representations of the model (the columns of a spreadsheet; charts or graphs, or, less commonly, symbolic forms), and being able to modify the model to improve the simulation of work-place practices and outcomes. *Though it is often hidden, we maintain that mathematical literacy is of increasing importance.*

(2002: 11–12; emphasis in original)

The distinctive point about intermediate-level work is that the mathematics involved often has a sophisticated nature, unlike the 'basic mathematics' typical of manual work – it is much more than simple arithmetic. Yet, this mathematics is very likely to remain implicit and invisible within the worker's engagement with workplace documents (production schedules, record charts, etc.) and computer systems – unlike the mathematics encountered by the professional that tends to be based on explicit engagement with mathematical symbolism.

Reich (1992) described professional workers as 'symbolic analysts' compared with 'routine producers' who follow a standardised, repetitive set of procedures for the manufacture of a product or the delivery of a service. According to Reich, more and more professional workers would tend towards being symbolic analysts, who solve, identify and broker problems by manipulating symbols (1992: 178). The key point about symbolic analysts is that they model the processes of work into abstractions that can be communicated to other specialists. Our question, however, is not only to understand what the symbol-analysers need to know to develop useful symbolic representations of the workplace, but what the implications are for those who 'consume' the results of the symbol-analysers – many, if not most of whom will fall into the intermediate rather than professional category. In particular, in the years that have elapsed since Reich proposed his analysis, the relationships and intersections between different layers of the workforce have shifted in significant ways. Part of our research agenda was to seek to reshape our understandings of who needs to know what, and the ways in which the knowledge takes on a different character in relation to the sub-communities of practice within workplaces.

Our starting point in this research was that intermediate-level work roles increasingly entail a technical-mathematical sophistication that goes beyond 'routines'. We shall describe in the following chapters how the boundaries of the intermediate level are imprecise: we have witnessed situations in manufacturing industry where manual workers exhibit a rich knowledge of implicit mathematical relationships in workplace systems (see, for example, the insights of the shop floor manager, Jim, in the company Filmic in Chapter 2) and situations where higher-level, and professionally qualified, managers have lacked mathematical insight into workplace systems and processes (examples are reported at Classic Motors in Chapter 3). These data add to the considerable evidence that the language of skills policy that organises competences into divisions of skills hierarchies, does not adequately deal with the problems of understanding the intermediate-level skills problem in the UK (see Westwood, 2004). It needs to be replaced by an acceptance that skill hierarchies, however important, do not do justice to the complexities of working practices, particularly those that are IT-rich and that the divisions between skilled and unskilled, intermediate and professional, require a more detailed appreciation of what is to be communicated between different employees, and how.

A description of key ideas

In this book we will make use of several terms that we now describe. We introduce them because each expresses a potent idea, or set of ideas, and taken together we believe these terms form an outline for a language that describes and helps to make sense of mathematics as it is used in the workplace. (For comprehensive details of the sources of all these terms, see our annotated list of research publications in the list of further reading at the end of this book.)

Techno-mathematical literacies

What is the general form of skills that we are trying to describe? Neither 'numeracy' nor the apparently obvious term 'mathematics' do justice to our task. We have already criticised numeracy as an impoverished and narrow concept that fails to address the richness of mathematical needs required[4] (see Noss, 1998). And mathematics, which should imply all the breadth and richness of mathematics as a domain of knowledge, is for many in workplaces, both managers and general employees, not perceived as relevant to their day-to-day work.

We therefore decided to introduce the term *Techno-mathematical Literacies*, developing from the idea of mathematical literacy that was used in our previous research (see the previous section; also see Coben (2003: 15) for a relevant review). A literate person is someone who is competent in using language, both written and verbal, across different contexts and working with different rules and conventions. We are convinced that this core idea of literacy is crucial to emphasise for mathematics as well: individuals need to be able to understand and use mathematics as a language that will increasingly pervade the workplace through IT-based control and administration systems as much as conventional literacy (reading and writing) has pervaded working life for the last century. This literacy involves a language that is not mathematical but 'techno-mathematical', where the mathematics is expressed through technological artefacts. It is the particular nature of mathematical skills in workplaces, where IT is pervasive, which distinguishes our techno-mathematical approach to the idea of literacy from other approaches, which have taken a general perspective of the education process as it is experienced by young people – see for example the Quantitative Literacy movement in the USA (e.g. Steen, 1997) – and the OECD's Programme of International Student Assessment (PISA) defines it as follows:

> Mathematical literacy is an individual's capacity to identify and understand the role that mathematics plays in the world, to make well-founded judgements and to use and engage with mathematics in ways that meet the needs of that individual's life as a constructive, concerned and reflective citizen.
>
> (OECD, 2003: 24)

Noss (1998) and diSessa (2000) offer extensive discussion of the idea of mathematical literacy, showing how the new forms of computational technology that are used for doing mathematics are connected with new 'mathematical literacies'.

Symbolic boundary objects and boundary crossing

The term *boundary object* originated amongst sociologists studying the nature of collaboration in various kinds of workplaces, particularly where diverse types of people must establish a common ground in order to share information (see Lee (2007) for a recent review of the use of the idea); they noted that problems of communication, and solving those problems, often focused on the documents and physical tools that formed the material basis of the collaborative work: 'boundary objects are those objects that both inhabit several communities of practice and satisfy the informational requirements of each of them' (Bowker & Star, 1999: 297; Lee, 2007). *Boundary crossing* occurs when meanings are successfully communicated across community boundaries.

An example of a boundary object as described by Star and Griesemer (1989) concerns the heterogeneous nature of scientific practice in the curious case of the study of insects in the State of California in the 1930s. In this work, the interests of professional scientists frequently clashed with the interests of enthusiastic, but often poorly informed, amateurs living in the state. Star and Griesemer recount how the director of a zoological museum managed to bring these two communities into mutual collaboration through the development of new boundary objects, in the form of data-recording forms for collecting field information on insects, which guided amateur naturalists to collect the kind of information the scientists needed, and led to the scientists coming to regard the amateurs as valued collaborators instead of a source of trouble.

In our research, we add the important descriptor *symbolic* to the term boundary object since our work has a very particular focus – on how techno-mathematical knowledge is negotiated and transformed across boundaries within workplaces, as it is at the boundary that ideas may be contested, disruptions may occur, and different languages of description have to be aligned. In modern workplaces, it is the symbols generated by computers in the form of numbers, tables, charts and graphs that are frequently supposed to support communication between employees across boundaries, and thus serve as putative boundary objects.

We identified a common phenomenon in companies where symbolic information was understood by some (usually but not always lower level) employees as *pseudo-mathematics* – as labels or pictures with little if any appreciation or attention about the underlying mathematical relationships. Two cases in point are the interest rates and graphs associated with selling mortgages in Chapter 5: the interest rates were not used by employees as numbers that could be calculated with (and hence compared), but as labels for products (a '5.5% mortgage', a '1.5% per month credit card'), and the graphs of mortgage repayments were treated as expressions of different 'customer lifestyles' rather than actual mathematical calculations for how the mortgage could work for a customer.

We will illustrate some of the problems of communication involving symbolic artefacts by reference to our early research observations in a national retail company that provided credit to customers through store cards and credit cards. The company used data about its customers' spending habits in order to target customers for the marketing of new financial products or to encourage customers periodically to spend more using their cards. This targeting involved drawing samples of say, 50,000 or 100,000 people from the database of several million customers in such a way as to maximise the response rates on a mail-shot to the chosen sample. This process of 'data mining' was undertaken by a dedicated team of people in the company, working at the request of the marketing groups who designed and managed product launch and promotional campaigns. The data miners were generally highly qualified mathematically (post-graduate qualifications in statistics were typical), whereas the marketing officers generally had rather little exposure to formal mathematics beyond the age of 16. This may seem a sensible division of labour: it is the maths types who do the hard sums to get results for the marketing people to use.

Yet there were growing problems of communication, a 'grey area' in which marketing needs had to be expressed as analytical questions, and the results of statistical analysis had to be interpreted to make business decisions. The problem was that there were not enough marketing officers with a well-developed facility for mathematical interpretation, and at the same time there were not enough analysts with an ability to communicate their analyses in a non-technical way appropriate to marketing. The situation was characterised by the absence of an effective symbolic boundary object to support communication between the two groups.

We take the position that a well-designed symbolic artefact can serve as a boundary object for the productive sharing of information between different communities. A key design criterion is that the symbolic representations can be interpreted with some degree of shared knowledge of problem context and analytical technique.

The reverse case is that badly designed symbolic artefacts can result in a breakdown of communication, as several workplace examples will demonstrate. We will describe how the notion of symbolic boundary object helped to focus our attention in both phases of our research: in our ethnographies in workplaces and also in the design of our learning interventions. We will describe our observations of workplaces where we saw many problems arising from lack of communication of techno-mathematical information, often because of poorly functioning symbolic artefacts. We will show how we worked with companies to design and re-design technology-based and interactive symbolic artefacts to support boundary crossing – the development of shared meanings across communities. This takes us to the next key idea in our research: that of the *technology-enhanced boundary object*, or *TEBO*.

TEBO: a technology-enhanced boundary object

The idea of a TEBO was motivated by trying to find a means of developing employee understanding through interacting with relevant mathematical models – not necessarily the same model that might have been used by expert employees in developing products or IT support systems, but nevertheless a model that exposed enough layers of the expert model to foster engagement with the key ideas.

TEBOs are software tools that adapt or extend symbolic artefacts identified from existing work practice, that are intended to act as boundary objects, for the purposes of employees' learning and enhancing workplace communication. A key characteristic of a TEBO is that it involves symbolic information, typically a graph, a model expressed in algebraic symbols, or even a single numerical measure. In all the cases the meanings of the symbolic information are rendered more visible and manipulable, and therefore more accessible, by the use of interactive software tools.

Analytic articulation work

The idea of *articulation work* was developed originally by the sociologist Anselm Strauss (1993) to account for the under-valued and often invisible forms of work (particularly, for him, the work of women at home and at work) which are nevertheless critical to the completion of tasks in everyday life, or in workplaces. Suchman (1996) presents the striking example of a legal office in which the attorneys (almost all male) regarded the work of their (almost all female) 'document coding' support staff (i.e. doing the preparation of the database index of the hundreds or thousands of documents involved in each legal case) as 'mindless'. Yet upon investigation, the work was seen to involve many aspects of judgements based upon knowledge and practical experience; moreover, it was judged that the support staff were sufficiently skilled to be capable of doing some of the work done by junior attorneys, but this was not recognised by the attorneys. Suchman's example shows a feature of workplaces that we also observed, that capacities do exist amongst 'ordinary' employees that could be developed or enhanced through appropriate learning of teacher-mathematical literacies and engagement with appropriate mathematical tools in the workplace, redesigned as TEBOs.

In Strauss' terms (see Suchman, 1996; Hampson & Junor, 2005), articulation work is the coordination and integration that must occur so that organisational arrangements between the 'social worlds' inhabited by people are established, maintained and revised. Strauss (1993: 212) defines a *social world* in terms of there being a primary *activity* (or more than one); *sites* where the activity occurs; *technology* that is involved; and *organisations* that evolve to further one or more aspects of the world's activity. Here 'organisations' refer to both formal organisational structures of a workplace, but also the informal structures and culture that evolve amongst employees to maintain the practice. Informal structures like these, perhaps hardly recognised by senior managers, can be very important. Our focus is on how analytical data is articulated within organisations: in one customer service department that we observed (see Chapter 4; and Kent *et al.*, 2007) the employees maintained their own 'library' of information relating to different types of customer queries, and they wanted to be entrusted by managers to do more such information organisation.

'Interactional' processes are central to articulation work, including negotiating, compromising and educating. Social worlds intersect along 'fluid boundaries' that are continually negotiated. Our interest is in the symbolic artefacts, reconstructed as TEBOs through which these boundary negotiations take place.

Coordinating key ideas

Symbolic artefacts from a workplace can serve as boundary objects operating at the intersections of social worlds. Our intention is that these boundary objects, and their enhancements in the form of TEBOs be adapted into roles within the organisation to support more effective communication between employee groups (particularly technical and non-technical), to support training and (in the case of customer services) practical engagement with customers.

If extending the capabilities of employees through learning interventions can be seen as an exercise in developing analytic articulation work in which employees attempt to integrate the results of learning into their existing practices, we identify the following three ways by which symbolic boundary objects and their mediation of articulation work played a central coordinating role in our work:

- as an analytical description of how techno-mathematical literacies can become integrated within working practices;
- as a methodological strategy for conducting workplace research into the nature of mathematics as used in workplaces; and
- as a principle for the design of software-based mathematical tools to support mathematics learning in workplaces.

The second way is particularly pertinent: it implies that we as researchers are also doing articulation work, as we bring our social world into conjunction with the social worlds of the workplace. In some sense, it is obvious that researchers must do this, but we would like to stress how necessary we found it to think of ourselves in this way, adopting the position of co-developers and co-teachers with company trainers and technical experts, rather than as outside educational experts who 'objectively' observe the situation and deliver a learning 'solution'. Indeed, we have found that the 'why' of the context is as crucial as the 'what', and that 'mathematical experts' should not expect to understand what matters mathematically in the context, without doing the detailed articulation work of negotiation with the social worlds of the context.

Aims and methods

We reiterate the aims established at the outset of the project:

- to understand the techno-mathematical literacies – the coordination of mathematical, IT and workplace-specific competencies – required by employees at different levels to operate in workplaces in at least three different industrial and commercial sectors;
- to design iteratively, evaluate and disseminate – in collaboration with companies, sector organisations and training organisations – a set of software-based learning opportunities to help employees acquire appropriate techno-mathematical literacies; and to evolve a set of measures for evaluating the learning outcomes of the learning opportunities;
- to work with UK national sector organisations and training organisations to address issues concerning the forms of qualification and accreditation that should be made available to employees for developing techno-mathematical literacies, and to strengthen existing forms of work-based training.

Our research consisted of case studies in different companies in four industrial sectors, and in each sector the research was divided broadly into two phases: an *ethnographic* phase and a *design* phase (see Figure 1.1). The main aims of the ethnographic phase were to understand how different companies deployed IT-based systems, and the forms of (mathematical) knowledge required by employees to operate with these effectively. For the design phase, we aimed to develop, with companies as partners, prototype computationally enhanced learning materials to develop TmL, which would address skills gaps that we had observed in those companies. We further hoped that the prototypes could be developed as learning resources for the industry sector concerned, and we attempted to work with sector organisations to promote this. Figure 1.1 also summarises how the research was operationalised. Following the ethnographic phase, we developed case studies in the different companies and wrote a report that was discussed at meetings with relevant company personnel. We also summarised and presented the reports at sector-specific meetings and consultations, in order to validate the findings and disseminate them more broadly. The development of learning opportunities was based on these earlier findings and followed by cycles of implementation and evaluation. Finally, learning opportunities were disseminated through the sector and more broadly.

The sectors that we researched were:

- automotive manufacturing;
- financial services;

- packaging manufacturing, and manufacturing companies that are intensive users of automated packaging systems;
- pharmaceuticals manufacturing.

Three or four companies were involved in each sector. Full details of the companies involved and the research fieldwork we carried out are given in the appendix to this book: Details of Fieldwork. The data from the fieldwork are not represented equally in this book – in particular, there is relatively little about pharmaceuticals – but a wide range of results have been published in our research papers (see the Further Reading list at the end of this book).

The sectors covered by the research represent a reasonable sample in terms of the range of sophistication in the use of technology – financial services and pharmaceuticals companies are all heavy users of computer-based systems, and both sectors have strong cultures of employee training and development to support these systems. Packaging manufacturing is a diverse sector in which some companies operate highly automated, computer-controlled production lines and have operational cultures in which efficiency and process improvement are central concerns. However, others (especially smaller companies making simple paper or plastic packaging) are using older and less automated technologies and processes. Automotive manufacturing is also a diverse sector, in which vehicle manufacturing companies in the UK are becoming highly automated and using process improvement techniques to increase efficiency (following the lead set by Japanese automotive manufacturers decades ago), but different factories are at different stages of development.

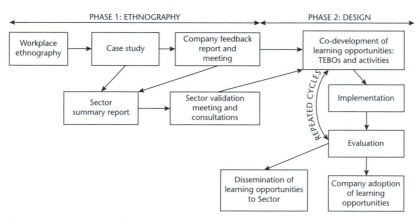

Figure 1.1 Diagram of the research process

The ethnographic phase: characterising the TmL and the boundary objects at stake

Our ethnographic research involved extended visits to three or four companies in each sector (sometimes two sites – factories or offices – of the same company), during which we conducted semi-structured interviews with employees ranging from senior management to junior roles of machine operators on the manufacturing shop floor, or telephone agents in financial services. These interviews were broadly structured around issues we knew we wanted to probe from our previous research, although we often allowed them to take unexpected directions that seemed promising. We also undertook work-shadowing, document analysis, and observations (usually using audio recording, as video was considered too invasive by many companies, though sometimes it was possible to take photographs), focusing on the symbolic artefacts that arose from the use of IT in generating computer displays, or documents used to communicate information to employees and to customers. Where relevant training courses existed, we attended these as participants or observers.

As we came to understand how work was carried out and organised, we progressively focused our interest on probing the meanings held by different groups of employees in the work process for those putative symbolic boundary objects (paper or computer-based) for which our ethnography indicated that communication between groups was problematic – that is, where the symbolic artefacts were broadly failing to convey information between groups within and beyond the workplace. We saw these problematic boundary objects as strong indicators of where techno-mathematical literacies for employees were necessary and lacking.

We describe our methods as ethnographic, by which we mean that we spent many hours in workplaces, observing and talking with people there. We did not (and could not) attempt the kind of engagement that characterises ethnography amongst professional anthropologists and sociologists, typically involving immersion in a culture or community over periods of months or years. We did not present ourselves to companies and employees as neutral observers, but shared our specific interest in what employees did in relation to processes involving mathematics, and how teaching and learning of both mathematics and technical knowledge was enacted.

An important detail of our ethnography is that we did not regard the findings from the initial ethnographic observation as definitive – as we set out into the second, design phase of the research we subjected our findings and interpretations to further triangulation and revision, following discussion with company managers and trainers. The iterative and collaborative nature of the design phase was particularly effective for this process, since at this point of design, we realised that some of our initial perceptions of workplace situations were inadequate. A key factor here was that we learned that our mathematical perspective gave only a partial view of how problems could be effectively solved within the workplace.

The design phase: learning opportunities and TEBOs co-designed and implemented with employer-partners

The ethnographic results fed into the second phase of the research, in which we worked in collaboration with companies and industry sector experts to carry out *design experiments* (Cobb *et al.*, 2003), which were characterised by design cycles of preparing, designing, testing and revision of prototype learning interventions that we called *learning opportunities*. These comprised sets of tasks incorporating interaction with TEBOs that could flexibly support formal and informal learning of teacher-mathematical literacies. This research method has typically been used by educational researchers to investigate novel types of learning in schools while generating theories as to how these types of learning might be supported. Hence we believed the method would be an effective way to establish collaborations with companies in order to generate novel activities and software for the development of workplace-based skills, as well as a more nuanced theoretical understanding of how teacher-mathematical literacies could be developed.

We called our interventions learning opportunities rather than 'training', since training has strong connotations of 'delivery'. In addition, we wanted to emphasise the interventions as opportunities for employees, trainers and managers to experience new ideas and methods, and that these might be adopted and developed by employer-partners as they felt appropriate. Box 1.1 summarises the design principles on which we based our work.

Box 1.1   Principles for designing learning opportunities

1   Use familiar symbolic artefacts (i.e. documents and tools) from the workplace in order to develop TEBOs to reveal relevant mathematical structures; provide appropriate preparatory activities for employees to be able to engage with these artefacts.

2   Take seriously employees' own (possibly incorrect) ideas and interpretations about the symbolic artefacts they encounter (for example in the company IT systems). Create opportunities for them to connect work-related and mathematical reasoning. Allow for ample discussion to foster 'bi-directional' learning, so that the mathematical experts can learn from the employees' ideas, as well as vice versa,

and provide support for employees to situate mathematical concepts in their own work context, and in the articulation work that they do.

3   Invite participation and provoke argumentation, by developing learning opportunities derived from workplace practice that evoke surprise, disagreement or doubt, or problems of communication. Such problem situations require systematic and explicit reasoning and appropriate articulation that can usefully draw on a mixture of techno-mathematical literacies and contextual knowledge.

The learning opportunities for the different industry sectors were piloted in companies, redesigned one or more times and re-piloted in the same or another company. The pilots typically involved five to ten employees for a period of half-a-day or a day; all participated voluntarily. In some cases, these employees had already participated in our ethnographic studies, hence there was a useful mutual familiarity.

Alongside TEBO development, we designed sequences of activities around the TEBO that invited employees to explore the ideas behind the symbolic boundary object, often starting with simple cases and then building up to more complex realistic situations (see Chapter 4 for examples in the financial sector). In all cases, although the TEBO was a simple software implementation, the benefit of its use for employees was often dramatic. For example, in the financial sector, employees were able to calculate pension values that were very close to those generated by the company's IT systems[5] whose operations had previously been completely unknown to nearly all of the employees.

The evidence of learning that we looked for in each company was exactly these changes in how employees thought about their work, and how they carried it out. It is not simple to identify and measure this evidence, since the timescales for this kind of learning to become fully evident, even to employees themselves, are quite long. Standard forms of evaluation measurement (such as written mathematics tests set to employees before and after a learning intervention) look only for short-term changes in an artificial context. They would not measure the effects that we sought, which we judged were meaningful in the workplace. After discussion with employers and experts in the sector, we used multiple methods of evaluation: evaluation forms following the learning opportunities (some designed by the companies themselves), follow-up interviews and questionnaires with participants and their managers, observation (where possible) of participants' work one or two months after our intervention, employees' self-reports of changes and collecting any information of how and where the TEBOs were being used.

Chapter 2

Manufacturing 1

Modelling and improving the work process in manufacturing industry

This chapter reports our findings in different manufacturing settings on the conduct of process improvement (PI), that is, using systematic techniques of different levels of sophistication to measure manufacturing processes, analysing the possibilities of improvement (often involving some form of cost benefit analysis), and implementing these improvements. This part of our research emerged from initial ethnographic work in companies that indicated that TmL are more apparent in IT-rich workplaces striving for improvements in efficiency and customer communication; for example, where management and employees are under pressure to move beyond established routines to cut down wastage of time and product and improve the quality of products or services.

This chapter looks at case studies of companies where PI was still formative, and not yet moved to a mature stage of using statistically based methodologies. In the next chapter, we present several case studies where the methodology of Statistical Process Control (SPC) was well established.

The key issues for examination in this chapter are:

1 How did employees understand the manufacturing production process?
2 What was the role of symbolic artefacts in the communication of the production process?
3 What models did employees have of the process?
4 How might employees' models be developed to support more effective working?

PI methodologies are applied to a wide variety of situations, industrial and non-industrial, and accordingly 'process' is understood in very general terms, as the transformation of a set of inputs (materials and methods) into outputs (products, services, information), which satisfy the needs of customers (see Caulcutt, 1995: 7). For our purposes in Chapters 2 and 3, however, process will refer to a physical, mechanical transformation of raw materials into a physical product (packaging material, food, cars, pharmaceutical tablets, etc.).

PI projects are often conducted by multi-level teams formed of managers, engineers, and shop floor employees, based on the principle that each level possesses essential, and distinctive, knowledge about the manufacturing process under investigation. As will be seen, symbolic artefacts (graphs, tables, charts, computer control systems) were instrumental in such projects, aiming to provide a means of reflection on the work process and act as boundary objects facilitating communication between different groups. All of the companies involved in our research were concerned with reducing costs and improving quality by making their processes more efficient, and regarded employee development at all levels as integral to this endeavour. All the companies were manufacturing sites operated by multinational (in one case, national) parent companies, so that the pressure to improve was often coming from a parent company, and involved being in direct competition on cost and quality with other company sites in the UK or abroad.

This chapter reviews the research undertaken in collaboration with three companies:

- *Master Cake*: a very large bakery with automated baking and packing systems; part of a large national food company;
- *Top Generics*: a pharmaceutical packaging factory, where already manufactured tablets are packaged into blister-packs; part of a multinational generic pharmaceuticals company;
- *Filmic*: a packaging manufacturer of special-purpose wrapping films, originally an independent UK company that had been bought out by a large US-based multinational packaging manufacturer.

We report the findings from the ethnographic research in each company and summarise what we identified as the TmL needed for PI to be effective. We then give an account of the design, implementation and findings from a set of learning opportunities co-developed and piloted several times at one company, Filmic, which aimed to develop employees' model-based understandings of the manufacturing process.

All of the companies reported in this chapter are involved with *packaging*. Packaging is a large and underacknowledged area of manufacturing activity in the UK, with an estimated 13,000 companies and 250,000 employees (see PACKMAP Project, 2003). Until recently, packaging was not a recognised sector for employment data collected by Government, with no national skills development organisation. In our research, we worked extensively with the UK Institute of Packaging (now part of the Institute of Materials, Minerals and Mining), who provided us with contacts to companies to do ethnographic fieldwork, facilitated access to industry experts for the validation of our results, and participated in discussion of our research outcomes in relation to packaging sector skills requirements as well as the development of national qualifications for UK packaging companies.

Process improvement in manufacturing

PI techniques in manufacturing are often based on the practices of Japanese companies, since Japanese and other East Asian companies are recognised as the leading exponents of such methods; methods include the Toyota Production System, Total Productive Maintenance, Lean manufacturing, and Six Sigma (Nakajima, 1989; Womack *et al.*, 1991; Deming, 2000; Bicheno, 2004; Montgomery & Woodall, 2008).

All PI methods involve technical complexities that will not concern us in detail. Our focus was simply that PI involves *the promotion of a workplace culture for all employees in which decisions are based on abstractions of work processes in the form of shared, and often computationally represented, symbolic data.* Employees involved in PI are therefore faced with the need to participate in the procedures of data collection and the interpretation of the charts, tables and graphs, and statistical indices derived from these data; and this applies to production and shop floor employees who previously had not been required to engage with symbolic information of this kind. Companies are therefore faced with the question of what skills and knowledge their employees needed in order to participate effectively in such activities.

Process improvement projects

Problem-solving projects are at the heart of PI activities, with multi-level teams identifying which parts of a process to improve, and carrying out improvements. In the case of the Master Cake bakery, below, we present a detailed description of one PI team project.

The 'DMAIC' process (Bicheno, 2004; George *et al.*, 2005; Montgomery & Woodall, 2008), part of Six Sigma methodology, gives a good illustration of the principles:

- *Define* a target problem: the team reaches agreement on the scope and goals of the project, and its financial and performance targets. This is rather complex (certainly compared with how modelling is conventionally taught in formal school or university education), since problems are rarely clear-cut and choosing the right problem requires quantifying time and budgetary, as well as technical, constraints;
- *Measure*: determine what to measure and how to measure it, and how to validate the measurements;
- *Analyse*: find the root causes of the targeted problems;
- *Improve*: develop and implement solutions to each problem, and gather statistical evidence that the solutions are working;
- *Control*: to maintain the improved outputs, by having controls in place, possibly using statistical process control (see Chapter 3).

The essential point about DMAIC or similar approaches is the necessity to track down problems and inefficiencies, as well as introduce greater levels of precision to the measurement of inputs and outputs, so that workers are able to form a better mental representation of the process as a whole. Different companies we worked with were at different stages of development of PI activity. Filmic was still following an older style of PI in which professionals were carrying out projects, with shop-floor workers hardly included. At Master Cake, shop-floor workers were involved, but there was a struggle to maintain any 'C' activity of DMAIC – Control – after the team projects had finished. And in Top Generics, work was at an early stage with priority accorded only to defining and measuring, with the other elements only being undertaken informally by managers and supervisors.

The use of numerical indicators

Modelling and measurement of processes is a central activity for PI. Many of these measurements will be, of course, detailed measurements of the behaviour of different machinery. From our research point of view, as well as exploring the role of symbolic representations as abstractions of the whole work process, we also became interested in the use of 'numerical indicators', such as measures of efficiency, which attempted to quantify the process under investigation. Such measures are common because, in the face of a complex production process involving many sub-processes and machines, models of the process are required that are quick, inexpensive to develop, and simple enough (preferably a single number) for all employees to think with and talk about. The point is to measure something that can lead to realistic targets and measurable improvement in process performance over short to medium time scales. As we shall describe, these abstract measures were not so easy for most intermediate-level employees to appreciate.

One common type of measure is the Key Performance Indicator (KPI). These are quantified measures of production (in general, business performance) that reflect critical success factors for a company, and can be used to set targets for outcomes and for improvement. Not surprisingly, KPIs are often about efficiency of production – the amount of product produced in a certain time period relative to target amounts, amount of good/reject product relative to targets, etc. An important interest for us was how far such measures involved *a negotiation between an abstract model of production and the physical production itself*. Suppose one part of a process is achieving a 78% quality rating, and the target for the whole process is 85%, then the question is how to improve the process to get closer to the target. As an abstraction, the KPI in itself does not prescribe how to achieve improvements; the numbers 78 and 85 may have no intrinsic meaning with regard to the process, and the gap of 7 is likely not to be 'linear', so that the effort and/or cost necessary to achieve a change from 82 to 85 say, may be much greater than to achieve a change from 78 to 82. Yet the KPI becomes a central means of communication amongst employees at the different levels of a factory about process performance and PI. However, a numerical indicator used without some appreciation by employees of the model from which it was derived, will simply be seen as a pseudo-mathematical label; worse, it comes to be viewed as a management tool for targeting employees' individual performance, rather than to support a collaborative improvement of the whole process. This was, to some extent, the situation we encountered in Top Generics and Classic Motors (see next chapter).

An exemplar of a numerical indicator: OEE (Overall Equipment Effectiveness)

OEE is a good example of an abstract numerical KPI, quite widely used in practice (Ishikawa, 1990, was the pioneer of the idea). It deliberately ignores the specific nature of a process by taking the form of a product of three generic variables in the production process: *Availability*, *Performance* and *Quality*. *Availability* is the percentage of time a machine is up and running, relative to the total available up-time; this might be 20 hours out of an expected 25 hours, or 80%. *Performance* is measured in terms of the rate at which the machine is expected to produce; whatever a machine could produce ideally represents a Performance of 100% (60% is a common target). *Quality* concerns what it is producing when it is working, that is, of the items made, what fraction are of merchantable quality; typically 95% might be expected. A key purpose of OEE is to prevent employees from only focusing on Performance outcomes: as we found at Top Generics, operators would run machines as fast as possible to meet their production target, but with a cost in terms of reduced quality or wear and tear of the machines (see later for detail).

The OEE is the product of these three generic numbers:

Availability × Performance × Quality × 100 = OEE %

for example:

$0.8 \times 0.6 \times 0.95 \times 100 = 46\%$

According to the managers we spoke to in several companies, and several industry consultants, 85% OEE is considered typical for a 'world class' business. One expert we consulted stated:

OEE is intended to be a hard measure of how effectively a process is being operated. The ultimate measure is, in effect, 'What did we get from the process compared to a perfect day, where a perfect day is the process running all available hours, at rated speed, producing perfect quality? The value in the OEE number comes from analysing why we do not achieve a 'perfect day'. That is, by asking the question 'Where do the losses come from?'

(PI consultant)

OEE gives a way of balancing key and often competing variables, and presenting the result in a single number that can both represent the process, and improve it, leaving, as we were told, the workers and the company with 'nowhere to hide':

> The beauty of OEE as a measure is that it is very difficult for a company to lie to itself and hide from its problems. If we were to just measure availability we would hear arguments about why 'maintenance time shouldn't be counted because we do it at the weekend instead of during the "normal" working week', or 'major breakdowns shouldn't be counted'. If Speed [i.e. Performance] were the main measure, people would be tempted to lie about the utilisation time to make it look like the process was operating faster, and if Quality were measured on its own, people would be tempted to discount set-up scrap or other product losses as 'set-up material, not lost production'. By multiplying the three factors, *we leave nowhere to hide*.

(PI consultant, emphasis added)

What would it mean for a manager of a production line to increase its OEE from 71% to 81% within 12 months? The OEE must be 'unpacked', looking for ways to reduce the different losses in each part of the production. Bicheno (2004: 58) points out that OEE can be improved in good and bad ways: 'Good ways are to reduce minor stoppages and decrease the length of a changeover. A bad way is simply to do fewer changeovers.' In other words, your OEE would be significantly improved by making too much of the wrong product. Alternatively, neglecting proper machine maintenance keeps machines working for longer – thus boosting OEE – but the machines break down from neglect. (This misuse of OEE as an indicator has similarities to the case of the process capability indices in Chapter 3.)

Modelling the work process

As mentioned earlier, the manufacturing companies involved in our research were at different points along the path of PI. The companies also varied in terms of the embedding of information technology, food production rating relatively low in technology use, and, unsurprisingly, pharmaceuticals rating very high. There is a tendency to equate capacity to do PI with availability of IT around the production process. However, one production manager (interviewed in the 'Maths Skills' project – see Hoyles *et al.*, 2002) cautioned against this interpretation and stressed the importance of employees' skills and ways of working:

> IT processing power is much better than it was ten years ago, but you could get the data manually, and companies like Toyota have been working in this way since the 1950s. So good companies have been using analytical techniques. Computers make it cheap and easy, but good companies have been doing PI anyway.
>
> (Interview with production manager, packaging company; data from the Maths Skills in the Workplace Project [Hoyles *et al.*, 2002])

This interpretation makes sense, as recognised by most recent PI methodologies such as Six Sigma, where employee development and clear lines of responsibility are integral to the methodology. None of the techniques involved in PI require high levels of technology support beyond a calculator with statistical functions and a means of generating graphs (although there are some specialised statistical techniques used, which would be carried out by professional engineers/statisticians). It is still common for PI charts to be constructed by hand: hand calculation and graphing were preferred in several companies (for example, Classic Motors and Sporting Motors, Chapter 3) because these were felt to encourage employees to have more direct engagement with data, which most software does not routinely encourage. As our examples will show, employees typically did not participate in the analytical aspects of PI and this lack of engagement could have implications both for the individuals concerned and for the operation of the work.

All the companies where we undertook our case studies were involved in modelling the production process with different levels of sophistication. Typically, only a minority of employees were prepared for such a 'systems approach' (engineers, managers), while some others (working in production) came to develop it through their own self-learning (see the examples in Filmic and Top Generics). Our learning opportunities set out to use the insights from the ways of thinking of the self-learned employees to design activities to engage the majority of shop-floor employees in the analytic aspects of process modelling through interacting with TEBOs.

'Black art' in the work process

We noticed that when any company sets out to model the work process they often came up against the idea of 'black art' for running a process, meaning that some individual machine operator or team could get better performance than others from the same machine/process by using black art – expertise that could not be explicitly described. Some interviewees could see no rational basis for this expertise, suggesting that better performance was simply due to a higher attention to detail and overall care. Other interviewees did think that subtle features of the working could not be codified: judgements in the timing of operation steps that affected overall speed, and fine-tuning ('tweaking') of machines during change-overs between runs for different products. It was certainly the case that these sorts of actions were better done by some operators, who were more sensitive to how machines and/or raw materials behaved, and who could tweak machines accordingly (in Top Generics, there was a recruitment focus on people with mechanical aptitude for this purpose).

The bakery manager at Master Cake was convinced that any art in a process was the sign of a poorly controlled and poorly managed process: where all parameters are systematically understood, and machines are capable of performing to required specifications, then the process should be predictable within specified limits.

Workplace observations of process improvement

We now turn to detailed descriptions of PI in three different companies.

Master Cake (a bakery with automated lines including packaging)[1]

This site was a very large cake bakery producing and packaging 400 different cakes (i.e. basic types multiplied by different sizes, fillings, flavours, etc.) in 12 plants, with the overall output in the order of several hundred thousand cakes per 24-hour day. Each plant is a continuous, semi-automated production line about 500 or 600 metres long that begins with raw ingredients, which are deposited into baking trays or sometimes continuous 'belts' of sponge, through baking, cooling (this is why the plants are very long physically, because the cake has to be baked for 15 or 20 minutes whilst it moves along by about 100m), forming of the cake (e.g. cutting and rolling of sponge layers), and packaging of finished cakes ready for dispatch.

Box 2.1   Company summary: Master Cake

Type of business: Very large automated cake bakery. One of the production sites of a national food company.

Number of employees: Total staff of 1,000, about 800 working in production; 50% of production workers are part-time.

Profile of employees: 75% of production workers classed as unskilled (jobs only 'requiring dexterity'), quantitative reasoning tests (as published by Saville and Holdsworth) used for job roles where this is required (e.g., first level managers).

Current use of PI methods: PI team projects on production lines.

Current training in PI: Training included within PI team project. Background skills development in 'basic skills' of literacy and numeracy being promoted for all employees.

Participation in the TmL research: Ethnographic observations of manufacturing activity and PI team work.

Our initial interest in the site was in the use and design of packaging, but it emerged from our early investigation that it was not possible to consider the packaging aspects of production separate from the baking of the cakes, since in some cases, the packaging was a carrier for the cake through the baking process. Also, the work being done on improving the production process throughout the bakery, and the implications of this for workers and their skills development, emerged as an interesting situation worthy of detailed investigation.

The following comment by the recently appointed general manager of the bakery indicates the direction of change:

> We are an engineering business that happens to make cakes, that's how I look at it . . . . It has been very much about touch and feel – the intuitions of key operators and team leaders to adjust the valve and change the deposit rate, because something has been observed to go out of specification. We want to sort out that black art, so that anyone can be brought in to a particular operation and be trained, so that we can get consistency 99 times out of a 100. Right now, it is people's long term experience which keeps the factory making good quality product, which is not right.

It is probably not a coincidence that this manager's background was as an engineer in the pharmaceuticals industry.

A long-term programme of activities to improve production efficiency (higher output and lower wastage) had been recently established by this bakery manager, with a focus on preparatory work for a systematic methodology:

1   dealing with obvious process deficiencies (as the detailed example on the PI team below will describe);
2   building a culture amongst employees of thinking about PI – the PI team was a key aspect of this, and overall it was understood to be a difficult development for a workforce dominated by unskilled and part-time workers;
3   installing electronic sensors to monitor 'critical control points' in the process.

Observation of a PI team project

The bakery PI teams were assembled to spend several weeks working full-time on an investigation of one particular production line. Each team con-sisted of volunteers drawn from different roles across the company. The PI team observed had the following members:

- night shift supervisor (third-level manager);
- team leader (first-level shop floor manager);
- four operators (two from the plant under investigation);
- fitter (mechanical engineer);
- electrician (electrical engineer);
- cleaner;
- two facilitators (PI managers for the bakery).

The idea was twofold. First, to exploit the operators' in-depth experience of the production line; second, to give operators a stake in the PI process. We describe the work of this PI team in reducing waste, and the symbolic artefacts (graphs, diagrams and data) used.

The PI team method was based on a 'package' which the bakery had bought from an external consultancy firm. This provided training materials, procedures and diagrams/charts/tables for problem-solving techniques, and consultants who visited the site initially to 'train the trainers' (i.e. the two PI managers for the site). From our point of view, the key activity in the PI exercise was a kind of *modelling*: making relationships between the elements and variables of the work process visible by physical measure-ments and representing these measurements in different types of symbolic artefacts.

The PI team that we observed looked at the production line producing a sponge sandwich cake. Schematically, the process was as follows:

1   sponge mixture deposited into a baking tin;
2   sponge baked;
3   baking tin removed and sponge sliced into two parts;
4   two parts separated – jam and cream deposited onto the base part – and 'lid' replaced onto base;
5   cake wrapped and packaged.

The PI team began with several days of classroom training. The train-ing sessions consisted of discussion, after which the team had to collect data about the whole production line and assemble it into a single chart, known as the 'capacity profile chart' (Figure 2.1). Since the meanings of different groups of employees drawn from reading this chart proved far from unproblematic, the chart became the first focus of our attention as a potential symbolic boundary object. The intention of this chart was to reveal any bottlenecks in the production process, so that the PI team could

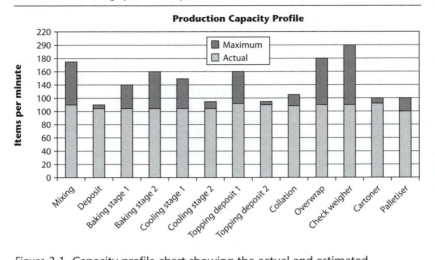

Figure 2.1   Capacity profile chart showing the actual and estimated maximum possible speeds of the different stages in the baking process

prioritise a programme of tasks to remedy the most important sources of inefficiency. Thus the chart was supposed to provide everyone with a comprehensive overview of the whole process. However, many operators could not see how 'their piece' fitted into the larger system:

> The operators run a packaging machine far faster than the production specification so that misalignments are very likely – so the machine will miss cartons and pile up, and if you say 'why don't you turn it down a bit', they've already accumulated stack work because of the pile-ups, so they say 'we can't turn it down we've got to deal with this stack work'. They get into a cycle of running the machine faster than needed, which creates a problem, which creates stack work to deal with.
>
> (Engineer in the PI team)

The capacity profile chart also served as a boundary object between us as researchers and the PI team. As mathematical experts we experienced some confusion as we tried to make sense of the chart, which looks like a bar chart of the different components in the baking process. Yet it is not a conventional bar chart: implicit in the horizontal axis is a time dimension: the sequence of baking and packing stages in the factory. Thus the chart must be read from left to right through the baking process (mixing of raw ingredients, baking, cooling, adding toppings, packaging of the finished cake). Further, we expected that the heights of all the 'actual' bars would be the same through the process (there is, after all, only one overall production rate). The fact that they were not, as we learnt by talking about this chart to employees, was in part due to the approximate nature of many of the measurements taken, and in part due to the fact that the process was not continuous in practice (there are breaks between stages where cakes may be removed from the process for temporary storage).

One further curiosity of the chart is that the operating throughputs are not capped by the main bottleneck – the 'deposit' – and later machines were allowed to run faster. The reason for this was that some machines were connected together and had to run at identical speed, whereas others worked in batches – a set of cakes was processed at a higher speed and then the machine went idle for a time. The PI team found that many operational speed settings were too high, in the sense that operators were running machines faster than required, and this caused pile-ups of cakes which had to be 'trayed off', that is, taken off the line onto storage trays whilst the breakdown was dealt with. Then the operators believed they had to keep the machine running fast in order to catch up on the backlog. This state of affairs had become standard. Apparently it had not been recognised before discussion of these charts that these problems could be fixed by simply running different machines and conveyor belts at optimal speeds to handle actual throughputs – a positive outcome of the analytical articulation work undertaken by the PI team, and stimulated by the chart.

On the basis of this initial analysis, the team identified the 'deposit' area as the major bottleneck, but the cost of fixing this bottleneck was so high that it would have required a high-level management decision that could not be made within the time frame of the PI exercise. Consequently, the team decided to shift its attention away from bottlenecks, to dealing with sources of waste in the production line judged to present a manageable set of problems within the project timespan of several weeks. A detailed measurement exercise was carried out, consisting of counting reject items from each sub-step of the process, which contrasted with standard procedure where all waste items from the whole line were dumped together; this quickly showed one area as the dominant source of waste, the 'topping depositor', where jam and other toppings are deposited onto cakes from a set of nozzles. The problem was that the toppings did not 'stick' cleanly, leading to waste. The model of this process, and its key variables, was not definitively known by anybody at the outset.

Focusing on this area, the team developed a 'cause and effect diagram' with clear analytic characterisation of the variables in the process and how they were interrelated. This was the second symbolic artefact serving as a putative boundary object to reveal the sub-problems that led to the overall waste problem (Figure 2.2).

This diagram was used as a dynamic tool by the PI team; it was drawn on a whiteboard and revised daily as the work progressed. Each day, sub-teams of two or three people were assigned to look at different problem areas, with a feedback meeting held at the end of each day. The version of the diagram shown here comes from partway through the work; we have added divisions into 'first-level', 'second-level' problems, etc., in order to

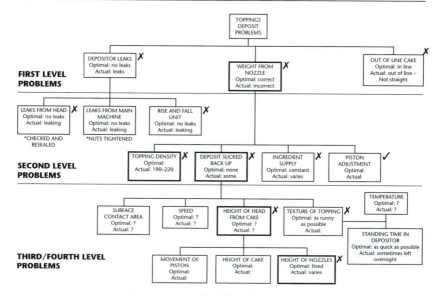

Figure 2.2 Cause and effect diagram of the topping deposit problems. The bold boxes show the line of investigation described here

make the diagram more readable. There are three main problem areas (first level), which had been broken down for investigation into sub-problems (second level), and several of these had been further broken down (third/fourth level). For each problem box, the optimum and actual states are indicated (many of these are shown incomplete, since they had not as yet been investigated); a tick indicates problem solved; an X indicates that the problem was still unsolved and problems without X or tick were still to be investigated.

We were able to observe directly the work of the team as it tackled the 'Deposit sucked back up' and 'Topping density' sub-problems:

> [W]e are looking at one aspect of [waste] . . . the deposit head, which is trying to stick topping onto the cake . . . it is the surface area of contact between topping and cake which determines if the topping stays on or gets sucked back up again . . . so we are trying to increase that surface contact area. . . . The team are trying to reduce the density of the topping, so that the same weight will deposit at a lot higher volume. At the moment they are gradually introducing more air into the topping to see if they improve the surface contact.
>
> (PI facilitator)

As part of this work, two operators had been given the task of trying to work out both an optimum height of the delivery of toppings onto the cake, and the density of the topping material, controlled by the amount of air injected into it (these were both sub-problems as identified in Figure 2.2). There was a significant complexity regarding the meaning of optimum in this situation: there are multiple variables to consider – height of delivery nozzles, density of topping ingredients and temperature of the ingredients – and we suspect that even the more expert members of the team did not have a good understanding of what the overall optimal solution would be.

We were struck by the fact that operators – in seeking some kind of optimal value – did not adopt a consistent way of measuring the height of the nozzles. For instance, they measured from the top of the cake to the ring of the nozzle in some cases, but from the bottom of the cake in other cases. This, of course, made it very hard to make reliable judgements on the data. Moreover, the operators recorded their data using very rough and loosely organised pen-and-paper notes of their numbers, scribbled on paper: consequently the numbers soon became disconnected from what they had measured.

One interchange between the operators and facilitator concerning the optimum density of the cream indicates the tension over data and what is considered good practice on the shop floor. Air is pumped into the cream to reduce its density, which is measured by the 'AMW value', the weight of a standard volume of substance. This needs to be as low as possible to reduce costs:

F[acilitator]: And your cream AMWs? Do you think that is as low as you can get for chocolate?

O[perator] 1: We did air to spec 225 AMW plus or minus 5, for air set at 0.2, so we did three alterations of that, air at 0.4, we got 191, 0.5, we got 187, and we did a check-weigh with that, and then we altered it to 0.6 and it came to 183.

O2: Which was too low wasn't it?

O1: And our waste went down to 35, 32, 37.

F: Could you turn it up to get the right weight?

O1: Yes.

F: So there is still enough adjustment – we need to try tomorrow.

O1: The operator says she doesn't like to run at that – she likes to run at 200.

F: Why – because the spec says so? We can get that changed if we think it's better. We need to carry on with that, find out how low we can get. Carry on with chocolate at 190 and keep going down.

Our assessment of the impact of the PI team was that the numbers generated had, as yet, little effect on practice and the graphs were not very successful in their intended role as boundary objects. We speculate that the measuring and recording tasks would have been more successful if the operators had access to software such as a spreadsheet, to organise their data and thus be able to explore any relationships between variables. This, however, was explicitly ruled out by the PI facilitator:

> We [the facilitators] do the number crunching part, and use graphs to communicate. . . . It would be helpful if everyone could design and use their own spreadsheets, but they can't so we do it – it would save us a lot of time and we could get more done in the time available. We try to keep things simple so everyone can progress at the same speed – it is really bad to have people left behind and lose interest.

Apart from this choice in division of labour, it obviously would not be enough to give spreadsheets to operators: there would be a need to spend time to develop a deeper understanding of systematic measurement, through using the tools and techniques that a spreadsheet provides. Nevertheless, we saw this as a missed opportunity, and it sharpened our view that the design and implementation of TEBOs where the relationships could be explored, would have been a promising direction for this company.

We did note learning benefits of the PI team experience: the two operators based on the production line that was investigated did develop a sense of the process, even to the point where they were anxious about returning to work on the line:

> They have been converted, looking at it in a different way, and they were worried about going back to the plant, working with people who don't want to think about what they are doing, not bother about what type of cake goes through, so long as it goes through – just worry about their own section where they work.
>
> (PI team colleague)

Continuous improvement on production lines

After the PI team finished its project on a line, PI work continued by way of a 'continuous improvement' team consisting of six people, meeting on a weekly basis to develop and carry out PI ideas originally proposed by the PI team, and subsequently to continue to look for and implement improvements. The members of the continuous improvement team would either have participated in a PI team, or they would be put through a shorter, one-week, training programme in the PI techniques (two days in classroom, three days problem-solving exercise on the production line).

A 'continuous improvement noticeboard' was put up beside the line to communicate efficiency information and status of problems being worked on. The continuous improvement manager said that there were weekly meetings on each plant: 'It is trends we are looking for – if it's going up we are happy that the work is going well, if going down, we'll be looking for

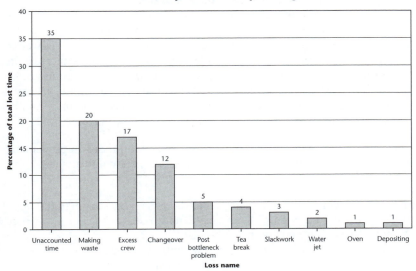

**MASTER CAKE 'S line': Pareto chart of top ten
losses by duration as a percentage**

Figure 2.3 Continuous improvement chart at Master Cake. The Pareto chart
is a frequency chart of causes for a particular phenomenon, in
this case it is lost production time; the idea is to use data to
identify the most important causes and to prioritise the
improvement work to be done. (This is a simplified and re-drawn
version based on actual charts used at the bakery.)

reasons why'. The following figure (Figure 2.3) shows a display chart, a
symbolic artefact intended to communicate the important causes of
particular phenomena identified by the team.

Alongside the charts, a 'continuous improvement action plan' detailed
aspects of the production line being investigated for improvement, the
status of each action, person responsible, and next steps to be taken.
Despite the continuous improvement manager's claims, our observations of
employees working on the lines showed mixed outcomes: on one line there
was confusion about why the charts were displayed, what they were
displaying, and who was responsible for them. The line manager had not
participated in the previous PI team exercise, and had not been informed
of the continuous improvement process.

In contrast, another line manager who had participated in a PI team
had become enthusiastic about continuous improvement and had participated in some complex projects, the most significant of which was to
reduce the baking time of the cake on his line from five minutes to four
minutes, and re-calibrating machinery and reorganising people to achieve
this goal:

My manager initiated that, when I first went onto 'P' Line. They originally tried a 3.6 bake – that was too fast for the operators to achieve, so we went back to trying for a four-minute bake. The Recipe Development Team helped us to achieve a consistent sponge, and our job was to get machinery up to spec. . . . We achieved that six weeks ago: 156 per minute instead of 125 per minute – so a big increase in throughput per minute. Now we are trying to do a four-minute bake for [larger-size cakes], but there is a constraint of machinery, we have no machine fast enough to pack them – we have put in a capital proposal for that, £167,000 for a new layout, new machines.

However, this manager was critical of the way continuous improvement work was implemented, mainly because employees could not read the symbolic data:

M: The problem with the PI team is that there is no backup – I'm too busy with my own plant now to go back and assess what we did – is it continuing, is it making things better? . . .

Researcher: I saw on 'S' Line there is a continuous improvement notice-board, but the manager did not know much about it.

M: If you are putting something on view for people to read, they should be able to read it. That is the same as what happened with the PI team that I worked in: the general operatives understood why the team was there, but after we left they haven't seen what came out of it. On S Line, yes they have speeded it up, but people don't know what has been achieved. Some people don't want to know, but some do. Yes, there is an information board, but *people don't know enough to understand it.* [emphasis added]

This manager was an interesting case: she saw the benefits of the work but recognised that the workers had not reached ownership of the process and the symbolic information that was posted was not read or not understood.

Summary of observations at Master Cake

We observed a successful PI initiative that was yielding considerable benefits to the company. Yet it was strongly evident that a lack of TmL among the production employees was limiting the results of PI, particularly in the long-term, continuous improvement of each baking plant.

We saw a considerable scope for learning opportunities to improve this situation. We had noticed for example that the operators in the PI teams were able to assist the managers and engineers in problem-solving, but did not seem to take away from the experience an ability to solve problems for themselves using the ideas and techniques they had encountered. They kept few records on which to ponder and discuss. The point is that problem-solving is not easily mastered in a short time, so there were outstanding issues about: (1) how to improve the PI team process so that operators might become more deeply involved in the problem-solving strategies; (2) how to continue and reinforce the learning experience after the PI project when people returned to their day-to-day production work; and (3) how better to communicate the outcomes of the PI work. Following our ethnographic work, we wrote a report to the management of the bakery and made a presentation of our ideas in the factory. We followed this up with the following suggestions as to how we might develop the work together:

- as part of their 'communication' course with a focus on graphs as communicating information and looking for trends;
- as part of the PI team to join discussion of systematic measurement and the use of displays such as driver trees and other charts;
- as part of a 'training event' (maybe with a video) that would publicise the work of the PI teams and encourage new recruits and show how more information could improve effectiveness; and
- as part of the induction of new recruits where we could co-design a short intervention around a simulation of the model of the whole work process at the bakery, again with a video.

In the end, the bakery decided not to follow up the work, maintaining that they had found our collaborative work interesting and informative, but believed that it was not the right time to expand employee involvement as major changes in production were happening at the site.

Top Generics (pharmaceuticals)

Top Generics is a multinational company that manufactures and distributes 'generic' drugs, that is, drugs for which the original patent has expired, and the 'recipe' is freely available to be used by any manufacturer. Prices for generic drugs are extremely competitive, profit margins are small, and efficiency of production is a critical issue.

We made observations in one of Top Generics' UK packaging factories. Manufactured tablets are delivered in bulk quantities, in order to be sealed into 'blister packs' (i.e. press-out plastic packaging) and packed into cardboard boxes, using automated machinery. The output of this quite small factory was phenomenal: eight packing lines operating on a 24-hour basis, each staffed by one employee working a 12-hour shift, would pack a total of 5.7 million tablets in each shift, equal to 4 billion tablets per year: 5 billion was a future target. This scale of output illustrates the challenges faced by the company, to continue to make a profit when sales profit margins are small and global manufacturing competition increasingly fierce.

The company had undergone radical restructuring several years previously in terms of investing in the best-quality automated machinery (costing about £1.5 million per packing line):

. . . literally you pour tablets in one end and feed it cartons, film, foil, leaflets – and out of the other end comes a sealed pack, and groups of packs boxed and labelled – all automatically; all the operator does with that is to stack it on the pallet . . . the main thing is the ability to be able to tweak the machine to keep it going at the optimum speed we require.

A further goal was to replace teams of six or seven people per line, typical of pharmaceuticals packaging, with just one person per line, classed as a 'technician', and required to be multi-skilled and take responsibility for quality, efficiency, set-ups and cleaning, and machine maintenance. In addition, fully-skilled engineers worked in each shift to deal with any complex problems. Each shift had one supervisor to oversee production and paperwork, monitor the computer systems for problems and make sure targets were reached.

Box 2.2   Company summary: Top Generics

Type of business: Pharmaceutical packaging – already manufactured tablets are sealed into blister packs and packed into cardboard boxes, in an automated process. One of the UK sites of a multinational generic pharmaceutical corporation.

Number of employees: About 100, including 50 packaging line technicians (two or three recruited per year) and four supervisors.

Profile of employees: Job applicants are tested in reasoning skills using standard psychometric tests; mechanical aptitude and interest was given greater weight than test results or formal qualifications.

Current use of PI methods: Introduction of real-time monitoring of production based on the OEE performance index. Use of OEE to identify and solve production problems.

Current training in PI: None.

Participation in the TmL research: Ethnographic observations of manufacturing activity.

The selection process for new technicians was quite intense, and included psychometric tests for mechanical aptitude and written and verbal reasoning. Yet common sense was paramount:

In this area there is not a lot of industry, so we take people on with mechanical and non-mechanical backgrounds – common sense comes into play a lot of the time, people with the most common sense seem to do best.

(Senior manager)

Manual dexterity (tested with a 'nuts and bolts' test: a set of nuts and bolts has to be unscrewed and re-screwed in a different location, within a certain target time) and curiosity about machines had also been found to be among the most effective selection criteria:

> [W]e scan CVs for hobbies and interests that will show a spark of what interests us ... we look for things like DIY, fixing motorbikes – something using the hands and their brains – or someone who likes electronics – we can develop that.
>
> (Senior Manager)

In the year prior to our observations, the company had begun to take efficiency to even higher levels: a centralised data recording system had been installed on all the packing lines, and this was used to monitor production and to generate OEE indices for every shift, packing line and packing job on the line. The system generated symbolic artefacts and numerical indicators that were becoming increasingly familiar on the shop floor. We therefore focused our observations around the use and interpretation of the outputs from this OEE-based production monitoring system, and how these computer displays of data served as boundary objects to facilitate communication between technicians and management.

Using automated data collection and OEE to monitor and improve production

When OEE was introduced into the factory, an 'events engine' computer terminal had been installed on each packing line that recorded data about the line: output, efficiency, stoppages and causes. The technician had to input a standard code for the cause of each stoppage, which had to be identified by hand, as a stoppage could occur in one place due to a cause elsewhere in the machine and it was straightforward for the technician to identify this cause but not for the machine to do so. A 'standard operating rate' was specified for each product – but setting those levels appropriately was still being worked on at the time of our case study. The events engines had been running for more than 12 months, but they had been initially unreliable, running efficiently for only a few months. It was intended that supervisors (middle management) would eventually take responsibility for managing the information in the events engines – but at the time of our observations it was the production manager who was dealing with the data, and developing specifications of supervisors' responsibilities.

Top Generics' version of OEE had three elements as follows:

- Rate to plan (*Performance*): the percentage of what was produced to what was planned for a product (by the production manager). This should be 100%, but since the plan was an estimate, the number could be more than 100%, and then needed to be adjusted for future runs of that product;

- Yield (*Quality*): good quantity divided by total quantity in per cent (target was 100%);
- Utilisation (*Availability*): running time divided by total time. Planned downtime such as breaks was always factored in, so that 10.5 hours of the 12 hour shift was the optimal running time. Utilisation could therefore never be 100%.

In the pharmaceuticals industry, downtimes are long, as thorough cleaning and checking of lines between product runs is vital and can be unpredictable; so OEE values lower than the 85% targets are acceptable but improvement is necessary:

> Currently we average 20% OEE across the lines. The focus for the next year is going to be on changeover times, which is the biggest cause of downtime – a changeover that is supposed to take four hours can take 24 hours, if different problems occur. Some technicians will do it in four hours every time, others will take 12 hours.
>
> (Production manager)

The production manager was very proud of the events engine data system, and showed us examples of how he was using the system. One tool we were shown was a chart of stoppages that automatically ranked the machine areas where stoppages had occurred:

> I've got a stoppage reasons pie chart . . . I can go in and pick a certain product or a certain line, crew or shift. And then I can select the top ten problems in the last seven days. Our approach is to work on reducing the top five problems, and [as we fix those] keep going back [for new ones]. The data helps to prioritise what to do. For example, I can quickly go in here [he demonstrates] and say 'Line 1 closing station' has cost 905 minutes. So I knew the closing station was a problem that justified shutting down the line for the engineers to work on. A year ago that would not have happened, no one would have known how long the closing station had been a problem. It's good that the data now makes things easy, visible – I can stick it on the engineer's desk to show them the problem. And for the technicians, they can see that they logged that problem with the closing station and it has been fixed.
>
> (Production manager)

In comparison, therefore, with Master Cake's charts, the new stoppages chart acted as an effective boundary object to communicate the causes of problems. A second useful tool was the 'line rate against time' chart, showing the output speed of a line:

I can look at the line rate for a given person for 48 hours, and I can see things like, at seven o'clock in the morning [time of handover from night shift to day shift] the machine has been turned up. So I know that people [in the night shift] have turned machines down to produce less, to have an easy day. Now I can say to people, why did you turn the speed down? And if they tell me there was a problem on the line, I can ask them why they have not logged it in the system. The problem is happening less now, because people know *we have a visible system.* [emphasis added]

(Production manager)

The manager's hope for using OEE data was to 'harmonise' production across the four shifts (technician teams), and to move thinking away from high rate as the only goal:

I think to be honest at the moment people are only looking at their rate, to get as much out as possible. We have a record set of 200,000 blisters in 12 hours, that is what they are aiming for . . . .. We have got four shifts competing against each other, and my role is to harmonise their working as a packaging department. That is difficult on a 12-hour shift pattern because people do not see each other. We do see people not helping each other out – slowing down a machine at six o'clock before the shift changeover. The last two years, we have had rapid growth, we've pushed people to focus [on rate] to achieve that but – you can run at 300 blisters per minute, but if you run at 250 you will pack more. That concept is just getting through now – we've known this principle for years: if you run your car at top speed all the time, it will be in the garage more and more often.

We were interested in how far the manager thought the OEE and the way data was displayed would help to change the practice on the line. The manager showed us the new display (Figure 2.4), designed to encourage technicians to take responsibility for recording causes of problems:

We have designed this page [Figure 2.4] for the technicians, so they have this display of best, worst and average – balancing that to get a better number here.
    . . . They will need to . . . understand what we are trying to do: why it is important to record the downtimes and assign it to the right cause – we can't make them do that, but if they can see the problems they record being fixed, and then they can turn up on a line and nothing will break that day. That will take time. We want people to compete over the OEE, not competing between shifts.

We paid attention to this symbolic display and sought to find out how the technicians interpreted its output and how these interpretations were negotiated with managers.

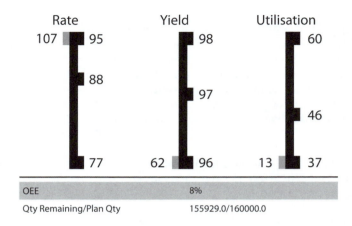

Figure 2.4 Part of an OEE information screen displayed by the events engine terminal on a packaging line. Numbers to left of the bars are values achieved for this product run; numbers to the right are the previously highest ever, average and lowest ever values. 'It is to give them a guide, if the best-achieved OEE is only 10%, they know it is how that tablet runs, it is not their fault' (Production manager). This screen shows OEE = 107% × 62% × 13% = 8%. (The 107% rate is due to the 'optimal' rate recorded in the system being incorrect, which was the case for most products.)

We noted that technicians were generally reluctant to engage with the OEE system. They did not enter accurate data for durations of stoppages, which meant that OEE numbers were often incorrect which, in turn, did not encourage the technicians to be more accurate. Also, we noticed that there were many mistakes and educated guesses in the rate and yield parameters entered by the production manager (hence the 107% rate shown in Figure 2.4).

Our ethnographic evidence indicated that there was little appreciation among operators of how each variable in the OEE system might be adjusted to improve the product or reach a target for the product: for example, if a target OEE of 12% is set, what value should a technician aim for in each of the three parameters? The OEE numerical indicator largely functioned as a pseudo-mathematical label, just a target with no structural underpinning. The reluctance we noticed among the technicians may also have had to do with their resistance to what they judged as workplace control, rather than with the complexity of the idea: some technicians felt that the system existed to measure their individual performance ('Big Brother'), the length of their tea breaks and mistakes they had made, rather than the overall performance of the packaging lines. For the managers, on the other hand, OEE evidently was a helpful summary measure.

We suggest that for an OEE data system to act as a symbolic boundary object facilitating communication between management and technicians, the OEE measures would need to be perceived as an abstract model of the *whole* production process. The system design only gave technicians access to information about their own line, not the broader data about the whole production process, which the manager and supervisors could access. To us at least, this broader view seemed important as a means for technicians to view OEE as something they could control and improve, and not merely as a management statistic.

We proposed to co-design and develop a TEBO based on the display shown in Figure 2.4 so that technicians could simulate their work practice by, for example, building in stoppages that they knew would happen and manipulating the software to see how to achieve a given OEE and of course checking if this could be done in practice. Sadly, although we had been given considerable access and time at Top Generics and our work had been very well received, there was a re-organisation of responsibilities at the factory and this second phase work proved impossible.

Filmic (packaging manufacturer)[2]

Filmic is a manufacturer of sophisticated, multi-layered plastic films, used primarily in the food industry. There are several major factories in the UK, and across East and West Europe. East European production was expanding, given skilled workforces and lower wage costs, but also due to the fact that packaging is best manufactured close to the expanding consumer markets of Eastern Europe (packaging is bulky, so transport is expensive).

The company was, until the 1990s, owned by a British multinational company. It was then taken over by a US-based multinational. One of the significant consequences of the takeover was a change in wage structures: pre-takeover, the policy was to pay employees at above local market rates; post-takeover, people in the same jobs were being paid only at average local rates. One consequence of this appeared to be that turnover of lower-grade, less-experienced employees went from virtually zero to relatively high.

Another change of policy post-takeover was that there was little interest in technical training of shop floor workers, unlike managers – who were expected to gain experience by working in different UK and other European sites. It was reported that a significant amount of in-house training was done in the 1980s – for example, a large training programme in SPC was carried out. Over time, training staff had moved on and had not been replaced and the training function was no longer a company priority. New employees received training directly 'on the job' by their colleagues and supervisors.

Box 2.3   Company summary: Filmic

Type of business: A packaging manufacturer of special-purpose wrapping films, originally an independent UK company that was bought out by a large US-based multinational packaging manufacturer.

Number of employees: About 500; 30 in the extrusion production area that was observed in detail.

Profile of employees: In general, prior experience of similar manufacturing work was valued more than qualifications. Mathematics and literacy tests at interview for new shop floor employees; no specific external qualifications required ('In the interview there is a maths test and a literacy test, which has some weight in the final decision – definitely if someone makes a lot of errors in maths, because we do use some maths in the department', manager, Extrusion department). Most of the senior, skilled shop floor employees had been in place for 20 or more years, so skills requirements had not really been identified.

Current use of PI methods: PI is a global company policy, but at the site observed PI activities had limited implementation and had not been brought within the responsibility of shop floor operators.

Current training in PI: None at the observed company site.

Participation in the TmL research: Ethnographic observations of manufacturing activity; co-development of learning opportunities and TEBO, and three learning trials.

The extrusion process

The area of production that we looked at in detail was the 'extrusion' production lines. There are four of these running continuously, making a thin (10 to 20 micrometres thick, i.e. thousandths of a millimetre) multi-layered plastic wrapping film. The process starts with granules of plastic which are melted into an initial thick tube (it is called 'tape' in the factory) which then goes through a complicated sequence of heating and stretching stages to reach a final required thickness of 13, 15, 19, etc. micrometres; the variability in thickness was of the order of plus-or-minus 0.2 micrometres. The machines are set to output different thicknesses depending on current customer orders and materials in stock. The most sensitive stage of the extrusion process was at what is known as 'the bubble', like an inflated balloon, where the tape is inflated with compressed air and its surface area increased by a factor of about 25; the bubble can be up to 1.5 metres wide and about 6 metres high in the largest machine. After inflation the tape is called 'film' and at the top of the bubble the tube of film is slit into two halves and rolled onto rollers, yielding the final wrapping film. If the bubble bursts (due to many possible causes) the line has to be stopped and it can take many hours to identify the problem and restart. So keeping the machines running at their highest possible speeds whilst maintaining the stability of the bubble was crucial to efficient production.

Each extrusion line is controlled by a computer system that monitors, controls and records numerous process parameters – typical display screens (see Figure 2.5) present 'flow diagrams' representing actual quantities and flows such as the temperatures and pressures at different points in the line, or the amounts of raw materials in input hoppers. The system has several feedback loops that kept the process stable despite variations in input parameters. Production employees were at best vaguely aware of these loops and how they worked – they could not manually influence what each loop was doing so the process parameters were largely invisible. For a change of film thickness, all the machinery in a line could be automatically adjusted by calling up a recipe in the computer system's memory. Process data for the past several months were accessible via a 'Historical Data' menu in the computer interface. Additionally, the supervisors recorded

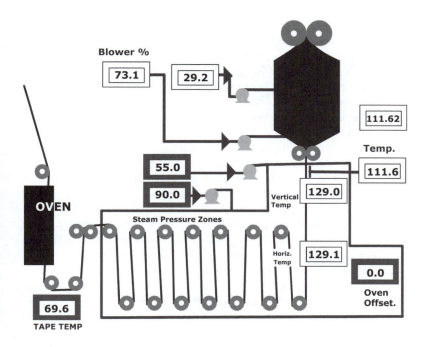

Figure 2.5 Part of the extrusion computer control system at Filmic. Black 'thread' shows the flow of the film through various production stages, with temperatures, pressures, etc. displayed. The bubble is represented as the hexagonal black area in the centre of the screen. (This is a simplified and re-drawn version based on the computer screen observed at the factory.)

individual jobs – known as 'MOs', Manufacturing Orders – moving in and out of the department using a separate administration computer system (job times, amounts of materials used, etc.).

A shop floor operational team in the extrusion department consisted of six people, working a 12-hour shift: a supervisor in charge for the purposes of team management, three shift leaders, who were all experienced operators (in some cases more than 20 years) and two operators. Technical process problems were dealt with across the team. The department was overseen by a Department Manager (daytime only), and there was a Process Engineer (chemical engineering graduate) resident in the department to deal with technical issues (process engineers were developed for senior management roles by working in different departments for about three years). The process engineer, Carol, became our principal contact with the company. She was an invaluable source of information about the extrusion process, and later during the development of learning opportunities, joined with us as a co-designer of the tools and activities, as well as a co-teacher for the trials with employees.

We took particular interest in how the operational team engaged with the computer control system as an obvious symbolic artefact that was intended to communicate information about the extrusion process. What TmL did operators need to interpret the system output? What kinds of mental models did the team have of the production process, given their day-to-day engagement with it? How did these personal models relate to the technical model built into the computer system?

When we looked at the computer system, it became clear that it had not been set up with the operators in mind; the computer tools available were 'engineer's tools' that assumed significant technical knowledge about the extrusion process. However, the historical data were a valuable resource for monitoring and understanding the process. Carol inspected these graphs (e.g. Figure 2.6) as part of her routine work, allowing her to become aware of the 'shapes' of the graphs during normal conditions so she could detect abnormal shapes as possible problems. The historical data were accessible to everyone, but shift leaders and operators rarely engaged with them. We will look later at the case of one shift leader, Jim, who did use historical data, and how this came about.

The ignoring of this data by the majority was not surprising given the complexity of the presentation – see Figure 2.6 for an example: up to eight different quantities are displayed simultaneously, each one having its own vertical scale. It was not company policy for the operational team to make use of process data, beyond the routine tasks of taking samples and recording the results, although Carol was convinced that it would make a difference to the overall performance and efficiency of the extrusion department:

> There are four guys who use the historical data significantly, and they all have 15-plus years experience. The youngest shift leader is willing

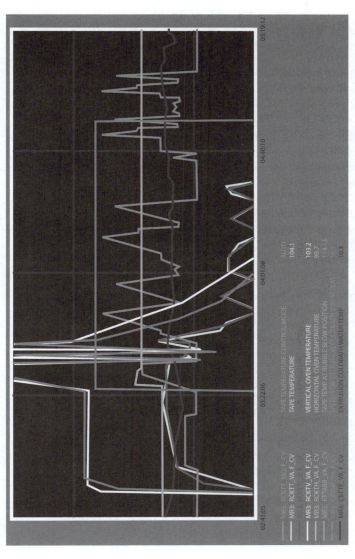

Figure 2.6 Graphs of 'historic data' displayed by the computer system. This information is extremely dense: eight different graphs are displayed simultaneously, each with its own vertical scale. (This is a simplified and re-drawn version based on the computer screen observed at the factory.)

to learn, but I'm sure he doesn't use the historical data – if there is a problem he will ask me, and I will look at it. The older guys, perhaps out of pride, prefer not to ask and will look at the historical data first. I think only four [out of 30 in the department] people use that data, the rest don't use it at all . . . I would like to sit with each supervisor and show them how to look things up. In a way I'm lazy, I'd prefer them to look up the history and work out a problem for themselves than asking me to do it. It's difficult to know how to fit that in-between all the other things that they and I have to do. . . . There is definitely an opportunity that we are not exploiting – when shift leaders have been looking at the data and seen something anomalous, they want to know why – because they pride themselves on knowing the process. So if more shift leaders at least know how to access the data, they would be happier overall – at the end of the shift they could not only look at a pallet full of film rolls, but also look at the coloured charts showing how well they had controlled things, instead of one with lines all over the place.

(Process engineer)

These comments pointed us to the historical graphs as an important potential symbolic boundary object, the interpretation of which became a focus of our study.

Controlling the thickness of extruded film

A basic problem at the time of our observations was that operators generally did not produce film at the thickness target required by management. Operators produced film at significantly higher thickness than the target of, for example, 14.5 micrometres, up to 15 micrometres and higher, although the natural variability of the process was around ±0.15 micrometres (a fact that the operators were not much aware of). It did not help that the name of the product was '15 micron' (micrometres), so called because the product would shrink in area during several weeks after manufacture so that film produced at average thickness 14.5 would have a thickness of 15 micrometres by the time the customer used it.

The operators' main stated concern, through constant *manual* adjustments, was to produce *even* film, that is with a small range of thickness across the whole width, which they could determine by continually feeling the film as it wound onto the output roll. As Carol explained:

They don't mind what the thickness is because they are not paying for the resin. They mind what the range distribution is – not the average. . . . I think they see range as implying poor quality rolls – a large range implies an uneven roll that may be a problem for the customer to use . . . they are more interested in the appearance of the roll than how thick the film is, unlike the view of management that a too-thick film is giving the customer extra material that we don't need to.

In fact, thickness was measured (as average values and ranges) by no less than four separate checking procedures, three of which were directly carried out and recorded by the operators. Yet these record charts did not inform the team's actions; instead, the charts were at best perceived as records that were 'something for the management', about which they received little or no feedback, and at worst they were distrusted in comparison with the operators' physical engagement with the process. In fact, for many years the record charts were retained for only a few weeks and then disposed of in the bin; the current process engineer Carol had tried to retain the forms for longer, and do something with them. As Carol commented:

> In fact, they rarely use this information [on average] at all, so it seems superfluous. . . . The average is important to us, because of the overspend on materials, but it is not important to them, and they are not given information about how much things cost – which is deliberate I think.

Dealing with waste and excessive production costs had become a more urgent issue for the factory, so addressing the issue of average gauge in the film had become a priority. Carol did suggest that information was not shared by the management, especially about costs:

> Five or ten years ago we were selling rolls for a lot more than we do today, and most of the operators still think we can sell rolls at that kind of price. In their mind, we are making £20 profit on a roll, but actually it is nearer maybe £3 . . . we are just about breaking even. So the operators see the encouragement to 'do more with less' as being about the company wanting to make more profit, they don't realise how close to break-even we are.

The operators' approach to film thickness is an interesting illustration of 'craft knowledge', which tends to embrace without distinction both true and false knowledge about processes: for example, 'rules of thumb' develop reliability over time and become part of the workplace culture. But equally, false knowledge about processes had become part of folklore and was likewise persistent – for example, the Filmic operators' belief in the feel of the final roll and manual adjustment of film thickness, and their distrust of the several tools (manual-mechanical and automated-electronic) that existed to measure thickness. Also, many operators did not realise that the process had computer-controlled feedback loops that would compensate for some of the adjustments that they made.

The departmental manager corroborated the process engineer's view that more could be done to educate supervisors, and to make more use of their experience-based knowledge:

> I asked one of our process engineers if he could give some training to the guys – I feel we know how to run the line, to make the product, but we don't know the process in detail, in order to deal with problems and analyse them when they arise – to have a methodical approach to problems. For example, the basic knowledge of what is a polymer, how does it work? We don't put that in training, tell them what happens inside a machine, how temperature affects the film. To develop a culture of problem-solving we have to teach first what is the process, and after that a knowledge of analysis, SPC, and so on. That knowledge shouldn't be left only to process engineers, there is a lot of knowledge and skills in people that we could use much earlier than waiting till the Monday morning after a problem occurs at the weekend. In fact, the [previous] process engineer was very interested, and he even made a course for it, which was never delivered.
>
> (Extrusion department manager)

That course had still not been delivered at the time of our observations, the notes having been handed over to Carol. She had, however, attempted to impart this process knowledge to operators, on an informal basis, where the opportunities arose. The TEBO that we later developed was therefore designed with the possibility of it being used in a variety of learning contexts within the factory (both on and off the job) such that conversations about the work process, catalysed by symbolic artefacts, could take place more effectively.

Modelling the process and problem-solving using process data

We turn now to an example of the TmL of one experienced employee, Jim, and an episode based on his reading of historical data graphs as an element of problem-solving on the line.

Jim had no post-16 education, but had 31 years' experience of working in the factory. He tried to ensure that his shift achieved its targets and was proud of his ability to solve problems. He described himself as a 'troubleshooter' asserting: 'I like the challenge. If there is a problem I give my best shot to do whatever I have to do to make it right.' As soon as a problem was reported to him, he would look at the graphs of historical data.

We set out to try to understand how Jim used these graphs, on what kinds of mental models these were based, how these had developed, and what the implications were for thinking about (1) how Jim's TmL might be improved, and (2) how other employees might come to share Jim's understanding of the process – which led to the design of TEBOs and learning opportunities for Filmic (see below).

The episode observed concerned a problem of instability in the 'bubble' area of one extrusion line, which had persisted for several months with no identification of the cause. When Jim encountered the problem, he looked at the historical data in the computer system, as browsing the 'historics' had become his habit over quite a number of years. Thus to investigate the intermittent stability problem, Jim scrolled through the many pages of historical graphs trying to find anything unusual that had occurred at the times bubble instability had occurred. He noticed in graphs of the 'inventory' area that when the bubble was unstable, the tension in the tape at one of the 'inventories' became changeable (these machines consist of a set of rollers which can move apart to store up tape, in case there is a temporary stoppage in a later part of the extrusion process). Carol described what he did:

> Jim went through all the graphs and tried to find anything that he thought looked 'odd' – that was his expression. Because he looks at graphs often, he has learned what looks normal, what's a normal fluctuation and in his opinion when he looked at the graph of the tension in the inventory it seemed that there was an abnormal pattern of fluctuation that corresponded to the moment when we'd had the instability in the extrusion bubble.

Instead of the 'flat' wiggly lines as in Figure 2.7(a), Jim noticed what he called a 'dip', Figure 2.7(b).

Once Jim had identified that one inventory might be the site of the problem, he informed Carol, who asked the maintenance engineers what might be causing such behaviour. They did not know of a cause, but decided to open up the roller system, which had not been inspected for some 15 years, and found that the bearings inside the rollers were seized up. The resulting variable tension as the rollers moved caused the tape to be stretched unevenly, and it was this that ultimately led to the bubble's instability later in the process. Although Jim was not involved in fixing the problem, and in fact had little understanding of how the inventories worked, his involvement in solving the problem was crucial. His breakthrough was to pinpoint *where* in the process (out of potentially dozens of possible locations) the problem might be and he did this by reading the graphs.

Is this interpretation of the graphs obvious? After all, when comparing the variation in the two reconstructed graphs (Figure 2.7) it seems clear that the second tension line was very variable. There are several issues. First, the graphs were not generally regarded as useful. As Carol explained:

> No [it is not obvious], you have to specifically go and look for it, it is not normally displayed. That's why none of the other shift leaders noticed. The inventories normally sit there and work – nobody looks

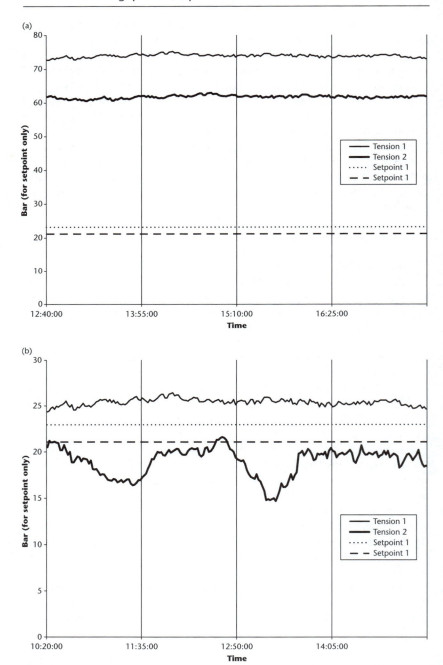

Figure 2.7 Historic data graphs of inventory tensions (our reconstructions, which remove extraneous details). (a) normal behaviour, (b) the 'odd' behaviour discovered by Jim

at the graphs for them, apart from Jim, who looks at the graphs for everything.

So the graphs first have to be recognised as worthy of attention. Second, as mentioned earlier, the graphs were hard to read given the type and complexity of the displays. Further, a variable tension such as shown in Figure 2.7(b) did not necessarily indicate a problem. To our surprise, Jim told us that such variation in the tension could happen even if there was no serious problem. When we asked him, 'When you see a graph like that [Figure 2.7(b)], what goes through your mind?' he answered, 'Well, if I've got quality rolls, I wouldn't make an alteration.' In other words, the meaning of the graphs depended on coordinating how they were read, with other information about a production problem that required some action to be taken.

A few weeks later, another episode occurred, again involving graphs. This time, Jim spotted some graphs where there was no variation, but he felt there should have been (Figure 2.8). The graphs concerned measured the speed (RPM) of a motor. Carol told us what Jim had done:

> By examining the 'revs [revolutions] per minute' historical data and seeing that it wasn't fluctuating as Jim expected but was a constant value, he determined something was wrong with it. He alerted the maintenance engineers who found the motor on the controller had been fitted to run backwards after some work done on it the previous day and so the signal it was sending for revs per minute was false. Jim doesn't know anything about motor control – he just knew that the historical data looked 'wrong'.

We found that Jim's interpretation of the straight parts as odd was far from trivial. First, there are 'set points' which do yield straight lines in

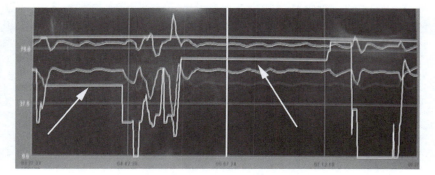

Figure 2.8 Historic data graphs of the speed of a motor. The straight parts (indicated by white arrows) in the white line are too constant. The variation in this line should look more like 'wiggles' in the other lines (the top straight line is a set point and therefore actually constant)

graphs. RPM lines on the other hand always vary slightly. Jim showed a sophisticated reading of graphs in being able to see 'wiggly' (in the previous example) or 'smooth' behaviours as not normal, and relating these to some aspects of the production process.

It was interesting to contrast Jim's reading of the graphs with Carol's. She used analytical techniques learnt as a professional engineer (for example, thinking about a process in terms of a mean value and variation around the mean) to increase her mastery with the shapes of graphs, so she was better able to spot abnormalities; and she could use the computer system to manipulate the graphs to change what she needed to see as part of investigating process problems. By contrast, Jim had succeeded in integrating the graphs into his understanding of the process through his self-imposed concern to trouble-shoot problems that occurred during his shift.

Another example of the difference between Carol and Jim's knowledge was in the language they used. It was difficult talking with Jim (but not Carol) about the graphs; we invited him to talk about the features he saw in the graphs, but whenever we tried, he would talk at length about the production process and the people who were involved whilst apparently ignoring the graphs in front of him. When we kept prompting and pointing at the graphs, he used terms such as 'normal', 'odd' and 'dips' to describe graphical features, and he was willing to make sketches of graphs that he had seen. But overall, Jim was reluctant to communicate his description of the process through the graphs. In contrast (and not surprisingly), Carol was very articulate about the graphs, using terms such as cyclic or symmetric patterns, mean and variation.

This observation underlines the importance of the 'historic' process graphs as a source of negotiation of different meanings of workplace knowledge and as a means to support articulation work about processes. Carol had already initiated this negotiation in informal ways, developing conversations around the computer control system where time allowed in-between she and the operator team dealing with process problems. Historic graphs therefore became a central part of the software simulation TEBO that we went on to develop.

There are some important similarities between Top Generics and Filmic. A computer system to model the *whole work process* existed, yet it was one with which neither operators nor technicians engaged, to the disappointment of managers. The risk, therefore, was that the numerical targets and symbolic artefacts remained merely pseudo-mathematical, so that employees were unable to connect with them, or appreciate how they related to their practice.

Box 2.4 Techno-mathematical literacies at stake

The techno-mathematical literacies at stake here are:

- understanding systematic measurement, data collection and display;
- appreciation of the complex effects of changing variables on the production system as a whole;
- being able to identify key variables and relationships in the work flow;
- reading and interpreting time series data, graphs and charts, some of which are standard and some idiosyncratic and company-specific.

Box 2.5 Symbolic artefacts for process improvement

- numerical measures of process performance: Key Performance Indicators, OEE;
- time graphs of data, including KPIs;
- computer-based process control systems;
- computer-based data systems ('events engine').

Learning opportunities for process improvement

Despite considerable support from the factories for our ethnographic work and interested reaction to our reports to each company, the co-development of learning opportunities was possible with only one of the companies discussed in this chapter, Filmic. The company agreed for the process engineer in the extrusion department, Carol, to collaborate with us on the design of TEBOs and learning activities, and to test these with production employees working on the extrusion lines.

Designing a simulation tool

The starting point for the design work was the outcome from the workplace observations of the extrusion production (see workplace observations of Filmic, above). We noted that:

1 Both operators and supervisors lacked effective mental models of the work process in general and the extrusion process in particular; this lack of transparency contributed to communication problems

such as friction with managers concerning achieving targets for film thickness.

2　The computer control system offered a ready-made, powerful resource for looking at data about all aspects of the process and through this obtaining information as to effective action. This was available in real-time, and through 'historic' data that could reveal trends and how the data looked at the time of specific incidents over several previous months. But most employees saw little relevance in the graphs – they did not communicate anything meaningful to them, not least as the visual presentation of the data was difficult for production employees to understand.

3　Using such data was evidently a great support to the problem-solving activities of several supervisors (e.g. Jim), and this was a skill that Carol wanted others to develop and that she tried to promote through informal training. However, time was short and the available tools in the computer system were not supportive.

Further guides to the design emerged from, first, our general knowledge of effective pedagogy: learning by experimenting, and using surprise situations to provoke argument (see Noss & Hoyles, 1996a) and, second, the outcomes of our ethnographic work in Filmic about the symbolic artefacts that formed part of the workplace and which would be familiar to employees (in this case the graphs of historical data), and the documentation of 'breakdowns', that is authentic episodes of production problems that could be simulated in the learning activities.

We set out to co-develop a TEBO by interaction with Carol, which would enable employees to:

- control the process for target mean and minimal variation;
- communicate about these values with other employees and with management;
- appreciate the role of invisible factors in the system.

We also wanted to address, if possible, the more general TmL identified in the case studies from all the factories in this section; see Box 2.4.

The aims of the learning opportunities were discussed in detail with Carol, and agreed to be:

1　To develop the habit of looking at historic process data graphs and to get more problem-solvers on the shop floor. It was important that more shift leaders and supervisors got a sense what to look for in historical graphs and how to solve problems using data.

2　To develop modelling thinking about the process: thinking in terms of variables [process parameters] and how they are related to each other. For example, if the temperature in a certain location goes up, what will happen to the film tension? If the speed of flow goes down, what will happen to the film thickness?

3   To use data to solve problems: exploring normal and abnormal behaviours as these appear in the historic graphs, based on actual 'breakdown' incidents such as those investigated by the supervisor, Jim.

Carol was also seeking improvements in the efficiency of the extrusion lines, and developing the knowledge and skills of the operational teams to support this.

Initial thinking was that these aims might be served by a range of software tools, but it soon became clear that what was required was a TEBO that *combined* simulation of the work process (Figure 2.5) with historic graphs output (Figure 2.6).

Box 2.6   Technology-enhanced boundary objects (TEBOs) for process improvement

Simulation of extrusion process for Filmic with historic data (see Figures 2.5, 2.6 and 2.9).

(View and use online at www.lkl.ac.uk/research/technomaths/tools/simultools.)

The TEBO simulated, in a simplified form, the start and end of the extrusion process, using approximate algebraic formulae (developed by Carol and her colleagues), and also a simple formula to model what happened in the stages between the start and the end. Random noise was added to the graphs to simulate fluctuations seen in the real data. Linking, in an explicit way, the start and end of the process was beneficial in several ways:

*   The TEBO was a reasonably simple simulation.
*   The employees' attention was focused onto the whole process: where in reality the plastic film runs for nearly 20 minutes between the end points of the process so that it is hard to appreciate inter-relationships – there is a long delay between initiating an adjustment and seeing its consequence. With the TEBO the consequences were almost immediate.
*   The TEBO moved attention away from the end of the process – where the bubble was situated and where we had noted a tendency for employees to concentrate their attention – towards the start of the process where it was usual for the process engineer Carol to do the important process adjustments.

An important design decision concerned whether the simulation should incorporate feedback loops. A truly authentic simulation would have had

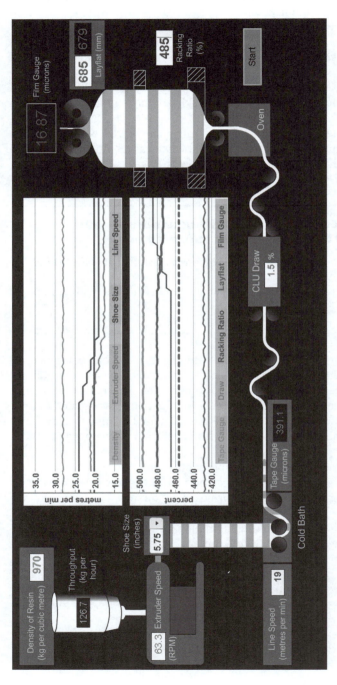

Figure 2.9 Screen shot of the process simulation TEBO (programmed in Flash). To reduce the complexity, just the start and end parts of the process are modelled, but the format of the real systems is imitated (cf. Figures 2.5 and 2.6). Numbers in the white boxes are inputs/parameters that the user can modify. The goal is to achieve stable running of the process with film gauge (thickness) at a required target. It is crucial not to make changes that 'burst the bubble' on the right (this in practice stops the production process). The graphs in the middle show historical data for 9 variables: the top set are inputs/parameters for the start of the process, the bottom set are for the end part of the process; on each graph, an appropriate scale appears when a given variable is selected.

loops, making the process largely automatic and leaving little scope for employees to experiment with the process parameters. Accordingly, it was decided not to have feedback loops, but instead to tell employees 'you are the feedback loop': i.e. when you see something going wrong, adjust it.

Through several stages of design discussion, authentic details were inserted and removed as we worked towards a simulation that Carol thought would be believable and authentic enough for the employees, but which would also be simple enough to manipulate. We made the simulation sensitive to rapid changes in parameter values, for example the flow speed of the plastic tape. This matched reality, so that if a change was made too rapidly, the process would break down and the bubble would burst.

It was interesting to see the different responses of the supervisors and process engineers to this feature. The engineers would jump the flow speed from, say, 20 to 30 metres/minute without any hesitation; if the bubble burst on-screen they could simply press 'reset' to start the process moving again. However, many operators made small changes only and were very hesitant in intervening in the process (which they also could not do in reality), increasing in increments of a metre/minute, about the maximum they would do with the real process, and they were very concerned not to burst the bubble; a real burst would be a major job for them, taking at least half an hour to fix, and potentially much longer, so they showed much sensitivity to avoiding this. This observation points up the unsurprising differences in coordinating model and reality. The engineers could live in the two different worlds, of real process and abstract simulation. To the operators however, the TEBO was fused with reality; they usually showed intense engagement with it, as if it were real, and tended to interpret its behaviour in realistic terms, and to look to the TEBO to do things which were simply not part of the simple underlying model. For the engineers, they knew it was a 'toy' that they could experiment with, without any real consequences. Nonetheless all approached interacting with the TEBO in a gamelike way – it was fun and they enjoyed testing their expertise against the model.

Examples of learning activities

The development of learning activities proceeded alongside the development of the simulation tool: our aim was for the activities and software to co-evolve. Carol showed an exceptional degree of interest in being involved in the authoring of the activities, and also took the lead in being the teacher for the learning opportunity trials.

Trials were conducted with individual employees, with Carol leading and one or two researchers observing and, where appropriate, asking questions. The trials were spread over a six-month period, largely determined by when the factory could accommodate them (restricted due to major reorganisation). The learning activities were mainly based on typical tasks of day-to-day management and minor problems of the process, which would be familiar to all the employees. There was, of course, one big difference between the familiar situation and our TEBO: in reality the control system's feedback loops would automatically correct the system for many of these types of situations and so the problems (and the means to address them) would not be visible. There was a stress also on promoting thinking about underlying constant properties – for example, density of the plastic was virtually constant within a given batch, and volume of plastic was a constant through the process, which if understood allowed one to reason about the relationship between thickness and width of extruded film. The tasks making up the activities are shown in Table 2.1.

Notice the emphasis in all these questions on testing for understanding of relationships, particularly focusing on achieving the target film thickness. The last example proved to be a surprise question – actually, the film thickness is independent of shoe size, so the answer is 'neither: it stays constant'. When we and Carol were exploring with the TEBO and saw this outcome, we assumed some error in the programming of the simulation. However, a little algebraic manipulation showed that the result was predicted by the formulae underlying the simulation, but this did not help us understand what was happening physically. The key physical insight was

Table 2.1 The learning activities tasks for Filmic

1 We have to change to a different product with the same film thickness of 15 microns but a bigger layflat [i.e. overall width of film roll] (increase from 685 to 750 mm). If we just change to a bigger layflat, will the film thickness go up or down, and why?
2 We have to change settings from layflat 750 to 950, and film thickness 15 to 19 microns. What shall we do?
3 The extruder motor is being repaired and a smaller motor is replacing it. Because it is smaller, the maximum RPM is only 60.
   (a) If we change from 80 to 60 RPM, will the film gauge go up or down, and why?
   (b) What adjustments to the settings can we make to meet the same target film thickness? Stop the process. Before you try your new settings in the tool, make a prediction of what will happen.
4 A batch of plastic resin has a slightly smaller density than usual (960 kg/m³ instead of 970 kg/m³). The feeders will make sure that the throughput, in kg/hour, is constant. Will the film thickness go up or down, and why?
5 For a particular layflat we ideally need a 5.75-inch shoe [i.e. the metal tube which is used to shape the initial thick tube of plastic], but all 5.75-inch shoes are being used on other lines. If we fit a smaller shoe, say 5.5 inch and keep everything else the same, will the film thickness go up or down?

that the same amount of 'stuff' finally arrived at the end of the line, travelling at the same speed; the width of the tape had been smaller in the middle of the process, but this was compensated later in two directions: *along* the direction of flow (which everyone is aware of) and *perpendicular* to the direction of flow (which is not usually considered).

The effort of unravelling this counter-intuitive result was a very good illustration of our articulation approach based around symbolic boundary objects, and was remarked upon by Carol, several months later when we interviewed her. She recollected her surprise on using the TEBO with operators, that they seemed unaware – as she herself had been – that the film was stretched in two dimensions. Her explanation was that the operators only ever controlled one dimension manually; the other, which they did not recognise at all, was controlled by the computer. As Carol put it: 'The things that are done by the computer system somehow become invisible.'

Outcomes for learning and practice

Impacts of learning opportunities on practice at Filmic

The reception of the learning opportunities was very positive at all levels of the company. The company proposed to adapt the learning opportunities for: induction of new operational employees; working with managers to educate them about how production teams understand the process (i.e. they do not see it as all connected up); and dissemination to other company sites for the same or similar extrusion lines.

Carol suggested several ways in which the tool would have an impact beyond its original intentions:

1   facilitating a switch between seeing lines on a graph and seeing the story they told about the work process. 'If every operator and shift leader went through the same kind of training using the tool there would be a base-line level of understanding that we risk not getting through the observational style training we currently use';
2   facilitating communication between shift leader and operator so both would have a joined-up view of the process;
3   identifying strengths and weaknesses in logical problem-solving ability and opening a window on what operators could achieve. 'I now know far more about William [a shift-leader] and the way he thinks about things than I knew before. For example, I know that I can give him a very open-ended task and he has the confidence, ability and knowledge to find a sensible solution';
4   improving communication between process engineer and operators. 'I know that . . . he's [William] happy to take a risk on certain things . . . I think this is because he "feels" the process and so "knew" that

even if he was wrong the effects wouldn't be drastic or beyond his ability to fix) and not others (e.g. risking bursting the bubble)';

5   facilitating cross-training of employees between film extrusion and the other extrusion department, as the use of the TEBO had highlighted the pitfalls and inconsistent assumptions made by the different departments.

The employees' reactions to using the TEBO tool were all very positive. They mostly showed a reluctance to burst the bubble that suggested a strong engagement with the TEBO as a simulation of reality. One operator, Bert, expressed this succinctly by stressing that the TEBO allowed him to enact situations that were not reasonable to try out in practice:

B: You can do what you like can't you? But I'm not doing anything here that I wouldn't do downstairs [with the machines]. It's very good this, I like it. It's a good training aid – for the shift leaders we've got in training now.
Carol: I agree. Because a bubble burst on here can be fixed in seconds.
B: On here, they could do the same as what happens downstairs. Like, I went from 24 to 30 [line speed], you can do that . . . But reality is not as fast as here, a lot will happen before the speed changes. . . . That was good. It will be good for training shift leaders, because there are scenarios you can't give them unless it all goes wrong – you don't want it to go wrong, but you do want it to go wrong because otherwise they won't have learnt anything to help them if such a scenario happens. So this is exactly a simulator – it's not exactly like what is down there. It will get people's heads thinking.

Reflections on the learning opportunities design process: general and specific tools

Working through all the details of the Filmic production process to achieve an understandable simulation was a surprisingly long undertaking, and the resulting simulation TEBO is strongly specific to the extrusion process as it operates at Filmic, though it will have similarities to extrusion processes in other packaging factories.

A pertinent question is, how general or specific does a simulation need to be in order to be effective with employees? The Filmic employees responded strongly to the tool, so some element of authenticity is clearly necessary, but we suspect that the fundamental requirement is about how the TEBO behaves in the interaction between output properties of the extruded film and process parameters, not the appearance or layout of the process elements on the screen.

The example of SPC tools developed for automotive companies in Chapter 3 shows that where PI techniques were operating, involving generalised process measures, it was possible and useful to develop general-purpose tools relating to those measures. The issue at Filmic was that generalised measures were not in use – it would be necessary to work with other companies to find out how to re-design the prototype tool to be more general.

Conclusions

The packaging sector provided large amounts of data about PI, and confirmed our broad hypothesis about the increasing need for techno-mathematical literacies amongst intermediate-level (production) employees. The follow-through to the development of learning opportunities was limited to just one company, though the prototypes proved very successful and are indicative of wider possibilities which we will elaborate in the chapters that follow.

A key finding across the sector was the variability of technological innovation, and, as a consequence, the role that artefacts – particularly computational artefacts – played in the production process. This, in turn, reflected a huge variation in terms of the ways that the companies viewed the knowledge – actual or potential – of their workforces, and the degree to which they were willing to invest (with us or in other ways) in upskilling the workforce. It is not, after all, a coincidence that only one firm – probably the most advanced technologically – agreed to the introduction of our learning activities: some of the other firms were simply not ready to do so, either because they had not yet appreciated the benefits that could accrue, or simply that workforce upskilling was not seen as a crucial issue.

Chapter 3

Manufacturing 2

Using statistics to improve the production process

This chapter continues the discussion of process improvement and employees' process understanding that was started in Chapter 2, dealing here with companies using methods based on statistical ideas and techniques, to support automated manufacturing, in the form known as Statistical Process Control (SPC). The companies were characterised by the manufacture of low volume, high value products, where manual sampling of products for quality control checks was an essential part of the process.[1] They comprise:

- *Classic Motors*: a mass-production, luxury car plant where the use of SPC was routine across many areas of production;
- *Sporting Motors*: a luxury, low-volume manufacturer of sports cars, where skilled manual assembly has been the norm and the use of automated processes and SPC was increasing as production volumes go beyond levels where manual assembly is feasible.

In this chapter, we also refer to some corroborative SPC-based research we conducted with Labelex, a specialist packaging manufacturer (owned by an international parent company) of self-adhesive 'label stock' that is delivered to customers to be printed for use in packaging (for example, the label on a bottle of liquid detergent). We report some outcomes insofar as they informed our understanding of the TmL at stake in coming to use SPC effectively. In both Classic Motors and Sporting Motors, we were able to undertake both phases of our research although the bulk of the work was undertaken in Classic Motors.

This chapter reviews the use of statistical techniques in both automotive companies, and the types of training in use. We summarise what we observed to be the techno-mathematical needs of the workforces. We then give an account of the design of TEBOs, and their implementation within a set of learning opportunities co-developed and piloted several times at both companies to mixed audiences of shop-floor operators, SPC co-ordinators, engineering apprentices, and manufacturing engineers, as part of existing SPC training programmes.

Process control and improvement using statistics

Many companies are making use of statistical techniques to improve production processes, often as an element of a comprehensive process improvement methodologies, such as 'Six Sigma', 'lean manufacturing', or 'lean (Six) Sigma' (Womack *et al.*, 1991; Oakland, 2003; George *et al.*, 2005; Montgomery & Woodall, 2008). Statistical techniques are generally introduced only where process improvement has been well-established and extensive work already undertaken to identify and eliminate sources of waste and inefficiency in processes, and to implement the systematic measurement and monitoring of processes, as illustrated in Chapter 2. Process control as described in this chapter takes improvement work to a next level of sophistication. Statistical techniques for process control are far from novel – they were pioneered in the 1920s in the USA by the engineer Shewhart, and developed and promoted for decades by the leading quality engineer and advocate, W. E. Deming (for example, Deming, 2000) – but their widespread use by European and US manufacturers is more recent, largely as a result of serious competition coming from highly efficient Japanese and other East Asian manufacturers, who have been using these techniques since the 1950s.

As we showed in Chapter 2, many of the elements of methodologies such as Six Sigma involve systematic thinking about reorganisation of manufacturing spaces and the movements of materials and people around the space. Our focus here is on the technique known as Statistical Process Control (SPC) – how it is used, how employees are trained in its use, the TmL needed to engage in the process and how they might be developed. SPC involves statistical ideas and techniques at its core, and some of the techniques must be used across the whole company, involving employees at all levels. This confronts companies with a key question: what does each 'layer' of the workforce need to know about the relevant statistics? How might appropriate training be put in place in such a way as to lead to more effective practices at work and also more effective communication between employee groups and with management?

The problem is often avoided by companies. Instead, there appears to be a sort of faith that going through the routines of collecting data (with the involvement of shop-floor employees), calculating charts and displaying them to employees will make production processes better – as illustrated in, for example, Hoyles and Noss (2007). This shows a neglect of a fundamental problem: that symbolic artefacts such as data and charts have to be interpreted in meaningful ways, that such symbolic artefacts have to communicate to the employees in order that they take appropriate action on the basis of the data displayed. This is unlikely to happen without appropriate engagement of employees at different levels around the symbolic artefacts, serving as boundary objects to develop shared meanings. For example, as others have noted, 'untrained users (the majority, in our experience) apply control chart procedures mechanically (often via computer software) and either interpret them incorrectly or pay no attention to them' (Alwan & Roberts, 1995: 270). A common phrase amongst SPC specialists, which was repeated to us in several places, is that when SPC charts do not connect with employees' practice they become little more than 'expensive wallpaper'.

Teaching and learning statistics is a difficult business, whether in formal education or in a workplace. As evidenced in the large body of research on school statistics (e.g. the review by Shaughnessy, 2007), most of the approaches to teaching statistics currently in use, which dwell on formal definitions as a basis for setting up techniques which are then applied to a problem in context, leave students with brittle knowledge and limited ability to engage effectively with statistical information, or to interpret it and communicate its implications. Statistics educators have been much concerned over the last 15 years with the problem of helping learners to make meaningful connections between statistical concepts and practical contexts where they should be used. There is a strong movement advocating that 'statistical literacy' is of equal importance with formal knowledge of concepts and techniques (Gal, 2002; Ben-Zvi & Garfield, 2005).

One of the major breakthroughs of modern process improvement methodologies, such as Six Sigma, is that they comprise detailed and well-tested methods for the development of appropriate knowledge amongst employees and the organisation of training, and for effective team building across different workplace communities. Six Sigma adopts a hierarchical training structure modelled on martial arts: employees are expected to achieve different 'belts' according to their expertise in 'the way' of process improvement – for example, the leaders of Six Sigma within a company should be skilled to the level of '(master) black belts', whereas intermediate-level employees in first-level management posts in different production areas are typically expected to achieve 'green belt' expertise, sufficient to participate in process improvement in their own area (directed by others, more skilled), and to act as mentors for process improvement for employees in the area.

While we do not question the motivational successes of the Six Sigma training approach (as evidenced by the considerable literature, and on the basis of our own observations of green-belt training), our research has indicated that some fundamental problems of statistical understanding remain, and there appears to be an over-reliance on formal techniques that are hard to connect with working practice.

A brief introduction to statistical process control (SPC)

The central idea of SPC is the management of *variation* in processes: some variation will always be present. For example, a machine filling one-litre bottles will always produce bottles containing slightly more or less than one litre of liquid. The goal therefore is to understand what variation can be *predictable* and hence can be 'controlled' for a process:

> A phenomenon will be said to be controlled when, through the use of past experience, we can predict, at least within limits, how the phenomenon may be expected to vary in the future. Here it is understood that prediction within limits means that we can state, at least approximately, the probability that the observed phenomenon will fall within the given limits.
>
> (Pyzdek, 1991: 101, quoting the classic definition of control by Shewhart, the inventor of SPC)

As Joiner puts it in his book on Fourth Generation Management:

> Our ability to produce rapid, sustained improvement is tied directly to our ability to understand and interpret variation. Until we know how to react to variation, any actions we take are almost as likely to make things worse, or to have no effect at all, as they are to make things better.
>
> (Joiner, 1994: 107)

In standard terminology, *common causes* are defined to be the random, and always expected, sources of variation within a system, and *special causes* are sources of variation that are not part of this background noise. The basic rule for SPC is that 'variation from common cause systems should be left to chance, but special causes of variation should be identified and eliminated' (Pyzdek, 1991: 102). When SPC is applied to a particular process, a reaction plan has to be developed, i.e. a set of rules for what the operator should do when the different signs of special causes are observed.

In a complex manufacturing operation, such as car manufacture, not all processes are subjected to SPC and it is mostly used for processes where lack of precision is a known problem and reject products expensive, or for legally regulated processes. SPC would not generally be applied to processes where the outcomes are non-functional and invisible to the end user (e.g. the lengths of wiring and tubing; but see the 'tube kink' example later where there was an unforeseen functional problem). In most companies using SPC, including Classic Motors, SPC data are collected on the shop floor and then sent to a specialist SPC person or team, where control limits and other measures are calculated and returned to the shop floor for feedback and future reference. This strict separation of the shop-floor employee from the calculations can lead to problems, as we shall describe below.

The SPC chart

Figure 3.1 shows a chart used by Classic Motors, which is typical of the manual charts that are widely used. This chart has three elements:

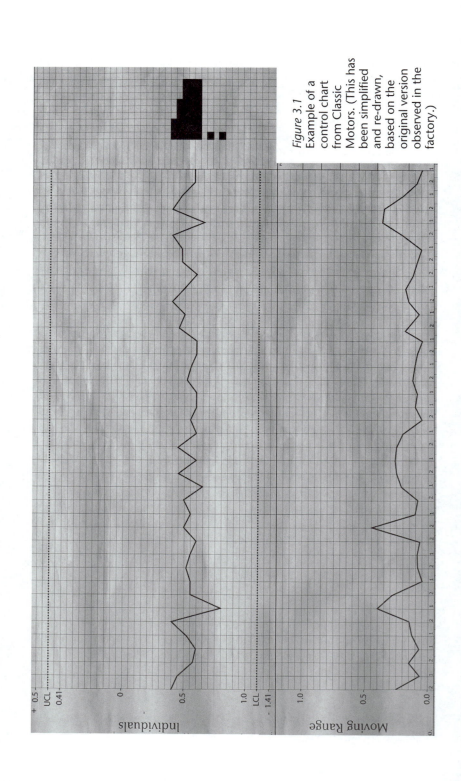

Figure 3.1
Example of a control chart from Classic Motors. (This has been simplified and re-drawn, based on the original version observed in the factory.)

- The upper left area displays the *individual run chart* of (in this case) two measurements per day; the measurements concern the 'tox strip distance', the deviation from the target in millimetres for a piece of rubber inserted around the windscreen. The nominal target is 0 mm, but a slightly low average is accepted since the process is stable and customers do not complain. The dotted lines mark the upper control limit (UCL) and lower control limit (LCL) (see below);
- The lower left area shows the *moving range chart* of measurement-to-measurement variation (absolute differences between consecutive data points);
- The right-hand side contains a *'sideways' histogram* (which is shaded in by the users), which shows the overall distribution of data points in the run chart.

For every chart a set of calculations is performed, as shown in Figure 3.2: the mean, control limits and also 'capability indices', Cp and Cpk, numerical indicators that characterise the performance of a process, used to monitor performance. All employees are supposed to read and interpret these indices.

One of the peculiarities of the way SPC charts were used in the factories we encountered was that there was an attachment to filling in the charts manually, and then – during training courses – doing the calculations of the mean and standard deviation, also manually.[2] We were told that the manual approach was preferred because it gave employees a direct engagement with the data, leading to an improved sense of ownership, and therefore a better understanding of SPC. The former claim is certainly credible. Employees were asked to annotate their control charts with 'clouds' to explain any deviations outside the control limits, or suspicious trends; this is easily possible for an operator to do with a paper chart while working, amid the noise and complexity of a manufacturing process, and keeps close reference to the actual process. The latter claim, however, is much more doubtful as we shall discuss later.

Our focus in this chapter is on the role of the whole of the control chart as a putative symbolic boundary object to monitor and communicate the functioning of workplace processes. In particular, we investigated the meanings held of the time series part (upper left), and if and how they influenced action on the shop floor. We observed in our ethnography of Classic Cars, widespread confusion between control limits and specification limits. For example, shop-floor employees often regarded control limits as imposed by management, not appreciating that they were a direct outcome (statistical calculation) of the process data collected by the employee. The problem was addressed in the training course (see below) during which employees actually performed the calculations for the upper control limit, UCLx and lower control limits, LCLx as set out in the top half of Figure 3.2.

Process average: $\bar{X} = -0.35$		Range average: $\bar{R} = -0.29$	
Upper Control Limit formula: $UCLx = \bar{X} + 3(R/d2) = 0.4$			
Lower Control Limit formula: $LCLx = \bar{X} - 3(R/d2) = -1.12$			
Range Chart Upper Control Limit formula		Range Chart Lower Control Limit formula	
$UCLr = D4 \times \bar{R} = 0.94$		$LCLr = D3 \times \bar{R} = 0$	
Pp =		Ppk =	
Cp = 1.96		Cpk = 1.50	
Period used to calculate capability		From:	To:
Sample size		Constants	
N	D2	D3	D4
–	–	–	–
2	1.13	0	3.268
3	1.69	0	2.574
4	2.06	0	2.282
5	2.33	0	2.114

Figure 3.2 The calculations that are made for each SPC chart at Classic Motors (calculations shown are for the data contained in Figure 3.1): process average, range average, upper and lower control limits, and process capability indices Cp and Cpk. The numbers at the bottom are called 'Hartley's constants' and are used for estimating standard deviations.

In practice, the confusion between control and specification limits is likely to cause problems for the interpretation of non-conforming data points: it is crucial to know whether these are outside the control limits, a source of waste and inefficiency, which will happen by chance even in stable processes; or outside the specification limits,[3] which could be dysfunctional or even illegal.

The desirable situation for a process is that the control limits should be far enough inside the specification limits so that products manufactured outside control limits are still within specification and some drift of the process mean is possible (as physical machines are always going to show some drift in this way). A rule of thumb is that the proportion of the distance between the specification limits (USL – LSL) to the distance between the control limits (UCL – LCL = 6 SD) should be at least 4 : 3. This gives the process some 'space to manoeuvre'.

Quality engineering statisticians have developed summary measures that capture such information in single numerical indicators, known as 'process capability indices' (Anis, 2008; Kotz & Johnson, 1993). The simplest index is called 'Cp':

$$C_p = \frac{USL - LSL}{6\sigma}$$

where: USL = upper specification limit
LSL = lower specification limit
σ = population standard deviation

However, Cp does not take the location of the mean into account, so a process may have very low variability, and yet be uselessly off-target (i.e. centred far from the target).[4] A second measure, Cpk, is therefore defined to take account of the position of the mean value:

$$C_p = \min(C_{pkl}, C_{pku})$$

where: $$C_{pku} = \frac{USL - \bar{X}}{3\sigma}, \quad C_{pkl} = \frac{\bar{X} - LSL}{3\sigma}$$

and USL = upper specification limit
LSL = lower specification limit
$\bar{X}$ = population mean
σ = population standard deviation

We do not expect readers to make sense of this formula unaided! It is a formal definition which does not readily convey meaning by itself, and it is hardly surprising to report the confusion experienced by employees at Classic Motors. Here, we simply mention that the SPC chart calculations, which had to be filled in by the shop-floor employees (as shown in Figure 3.2), depended exactly on these formal definitions.

Although Cpk is usually required to be at least 1.33 (that is, 4/3), Classic Motors have also used 1.5 and 1.67 at different times. One might conclude that a higher Cpk is always better than a lower one, but a Cpk can be unreasonably high. It might be the case that specification limits might have been set too wide. Also, it may not make sense to improve a process to achieve a high Cpk as the costs to reduce variation in a particular process or machine may be too high.

Neither Cp nor Cpk are particularly sophisticated numerical indicators when viewed as purely mathematical definitions – they are simply ratios of 'widths'. Yet we found the *interpretation* of these indices in terms of what the data were 'saying' to be challenging and most often they were used by shop-floor employees (and some managers) as pseudo-mathematical labels attached to control charts with little meaning in terms of the work process. Our subsequent experience in disseminating the results of our learning interventions showed that these indices were of widespread importance in workplaces and found to be complex generally across all levels of manufacturing industry.

Interpreting the meanings of an SPC chart: a case study at Labelex

This example from the project's early research illustrates some of the typical problems that are experienced by companies in the use of SPC. At Labelex, key performance indicators (KPIs, see Chapter 2) had been identified and it was standard practice for data to be collected at regular time intervals, by shop-floor employees. SPC charts were produced automatically for each KPI and these were displayed and discussed on the shop floor (the degree of automation and computerisation at Labelex was a contrast with the paper-based practice at Classic Motors and Sporting Motors).[5]

A simple example SPC chart from Labelex is shown in Figure 3.3, showing the 'historical mean', the upper and lower control limits, the customer specification and the target line just above the mean. The chart shows one point outside the lower control limit that signals a special cause. It also shows a jump around week 26 when some element of the working practice changed, and was recognised by upward adjustment of the mean and lower control limits.

In Labelex, SPC charts could be seen on the shop floor and in managers' offices. They were familiar symbolic artefacts, regarded as important and taken as the focus of discussion in regular production meetings. The data were meant to be transparent in that they were agreed measures of process

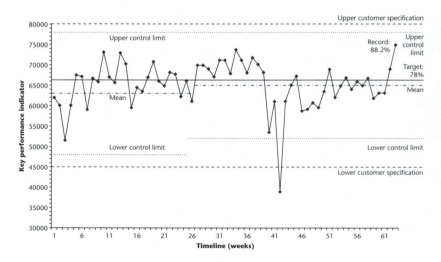

Figure 3.3 An SPC chart from Labelex

and they were input by operators in the factory – although the chart itself and the control lines on it were produced automatically by software. During our research visits we interviewed people in different areas of the factory in order to understand how the SPC chart was being differently interpreted:

Team leaders:

- saw the control chart as important to identify special causes that needed attention. The control limits provided the means to demarcate these signals. So the SPC chart was serving one role as giving 'signals for action' but the fluctuations, or common cause variation, were not discussed nor was there a sense of any need, through process improvement, to narrow the gap between the upper and lower control limits;
- interpreted the control limits as fixed and largely deterministic rather than as a property of the data set to which they were attached; for example, that the limits were determined by the possible speed of the production line. This false reasoning contributed to the belief that it was not possible to improve the process by narrowing the control limits;
- talked about actual working procedures when referring to the charts: reducing the speed of the machine, increasing oven temperature more quickly, rather than considering what the data implied for intervention. Thus the charts tended to be viewed as rather uncomplicated; just a way of displaying information which they did 'just fine';
- frequently argued that their knowledge about the conditions for each part of the process to run successfully could *not* be codified; there were just too many interacting variables to take into account in order to decide the best setting for any process.

Managers:

- displayed (as with team leaders) widespread confusion about the difference between specification limits set by the customer or by management and control limits which depended on historical data of the process;
- showed little understanding of how to move from display of information to a programme for action: 'we are not using the SPC charts properly at all . . . there is great potential here . . . most of it is for information . . . there might be some clues that really connect with runnability issues . . . '. This manager thought there might be these clues but had yet to appreciate them.

Progress with SPC work in Labelex had largely come to a halt because, it seemed, there was no push to manage the action that should follow interpretation of the data, contrasting with SPC practice in the automotive industry:

Manager: For a long while we've used them [SPC charts] as a way of presenting information so instead of looking at them in accounting terms or as you say looking at a table of numbers which is dead boring and hard to read; it's much easier to look at profit development or cost development of whatever else on a SPC. . . . What then happens is everything you look at now is on SPCs and it isn't always the best way to look at it. Especially if you are just wanting to use it to present data because people then start thinking it's just a tool to present data; it's not there to improve processes. Well they may just say it shows us how we are doing. Which is not bad but it's not really what you want because you want it to be a *catalyst for action*. [emphasis added]

Workplace observations of statistical process control[6]

In this section we report in detail the research with Classic Motors and Sporting Motors, giving a brief introduction to the business of each, the workplace practices we observed, a description of current training practices, and the TmL we located as either in use or required (or both). Both companies are UK specialist manufacturing divisions of a global automotive manufacturer. This is an important detail because SPC was part of global company practice and decisions about its use were subject to top-down impositions from the headquarters that did not always coincide with the needs of the factory or the wishes of local managers.

Our involvement with these two companies came about because of a chance meeting with a senior technical manager, a specialist statistician, at a mathematics education conference. Further conversation led to an invitation to visit a Classic Motors factory, which had implemented SPC in an extensive way and, partly through its use, had become one of the most productive factories of the global manufacturing group. All the co-development of the TEBOs and the learning opportunities was undertaken in Classic Motors (as described in the next section). Sporting Motors became involved later as a second site for further implementation and evaluation of the learning opportunities (observations of SPC in practice at Sporting Motors were only briefly made and are not reported here).

Box 3.1 Company summary: Classic Motors

Type of business: Manufacture of mass-produced luxury cars; division of a global automotive corporation.

Number of employees: About 1,000.

Profile of employees: Production line operators: no set qualifications (many operators have 25 or more years of service, some left school at age 14 [in the 1970s]); process and manufacturing engineers are graduates; the SPC department consisted of a time-served trainer, and graduate engineers.

Current use of process improvement methods: Statistical Process Control for regular monitoring of selected 'quality-critical' processes; process improvement teams in different production areas work on specific improvement projects.

Current training in process improvement: SPC course, and the SPC department acts as mentors/advisers to process improvement teams.

Participation in the TmL research: Ethnographic observations of manufacturing and training activities; co-development of learning opportunities; company adoption of tools and activities for further development.

Box 3.2   Company summary: Sporting Motors

Type of business: Manufacture of luxury sports cars; division of a global automotive corporation with headquarters in the USA; has been a low-volume, mostly hand-built production process but automation and use of process improvement methods is increasing as production volume is increasing.

Current use of process improvement methods: Six Sigma, Statistical Process Control, process improvement project teams working on particularly problematic processes.

Current training in process improvement: Six Sigma 'belt' training (training courses developed by parent company).

Participation in the TmL research: Ethnographic observations of training activities (and very brief look at areas of production); co-development of learning opportunities; dissemination and promotion of TmL TEBOs.

Observations of SPC in practice in Classic Motors

Classic Motors were generous in allowing us to speak to senior managers and SPC specialists/trainers in the SPC Department, to visit all the main production areas and have the use of SPC explained to us by the production employees themselves. They prided themselves on the quality of their cars, and were more than willing to work with us if there was any possibility it would help them improve their practice. The company implemented SPC across all of its UK plants in the late 1990s. Huge efforts were invested in training employees at all levels in how to fill in control charts and how to respond to anomalies. All production processes were videotaped and analysed so as to standardise them and reaction plans were formulated.

Some plants had been more successful in implementing process improvement techniques than others. The particular plant where we researched was the most successful user of SPC, where it had become part of the work culture, to the extent that operators with little formal education were generally familiar with SPC, and its symbolic artefacts such as control charts. Many employees we interviewed had been trained in SPC and knew the standard 'mantras': for example, that variation should always be reduced, though not at any cost. Perhaps more importantly, employees seemed to know what SPC meant in practice in terms of collecting data and recording on the charts, potential causes of outliers or patterns in the data.

Yet our impression from the interviews was that employees tended to have fragmented knowledge of what the statistical concepts meant in terms of the actual production process in which they worked. For example, we saw some tendency to use Cpk simply as a target (e.g. Cpk = 1.33) – as a pseudo-mathematical label with little meaning in terms of performance in relation to specification. Improving a process can mean both raising the Cpk of an under-performing process through examining its engineering basis, or questioning when a process has a high Cpk. This might mean for example that the specification limits had been set too wide to be effective. It was reported that component supplier companies had a tendency to quote 'inflated' values of the capability indices for their products, in the belief that Classic Motors would thereby be impressed by the product quality. Dealing with the questionable claims of such suppliers for an area of production was typically the job of a first-level manager or 'SPC co-ordinator' with limited background in the rather complex mathematical ideas at stake. We illustrate such a case later and the role our TEBO turned out to perform (see 'Dan's problem solving' in this chapter).

Kevin, a shop-floor employee in Classic Motors

We report here our observations of how a typical shop-floor employee used SPC in his practice. Kevin was an operator with no formal education after the age of 16, who was responsible for checking the airtightness of cars:

> If the car is too airtight you will get a problem with the windows misting up all the time; also the doors will not shut. You need to lose some air otherwise the door is just so airtight you would have to run at it and give it a good push.

To check if the airtightness was within specification, Kevin pumped air into the car and read off the pressure this produces. Mostly the measurements were fine, but occasionally they were out of specification. Kevin had learned the statistically based rules for trends and patterns, although he did not know how they originated. He also understood that there were situations where SPC data might fail to detect a problem:

> My main failure at the moment is on estate cars on the left hand rear wheel arch. . . . In two of the cases the car was not out of spec but I was going round doing my checks to make sure there were no unusual leak paths and we found that they had missed some sealing. So although the car was in spec I raised an AP [Assigned Person – as soon as Kevin 'raised an AP' he had done his job, and the problem was not his responsibility any more] and still got all the investigations done because there was an unusual leak path.

From our interview, we were convinced that Kevin knew his area of the process very well: he knew what to look for, what might cause a problem, what implications it may have, and what to do about it. He was acutely sensitive to reading the physical signs of problems: for example, 'as soon as I turn the gauge on it kicks in normally at around 60 to 70 Pascal. If it kicks in at around 30 I know full well that we have got a big leak somewhere'.

However, when statistical issues were involved he felt less comfortable. For example, when interpreting the control limits he and his colleagues received from central office:

> What [the office] actually said to us is that it should have been 120 [weight per] cm squared +/− 3 sigma. It is very, very complicated because they gave us a lot of specs [actually, these were control limits] to work on and it did not mean a lot to anybody in this company. We asked the questions to all the different people and no one could give us a definite, here's what you work off, this this this.

We were curious to what extent the SPC chart made sense to Kevin. When asked if the sideways histogram (to the right in Figure 3.1) helped him, he said:

K: It does and it doesn't because it just gives us an idea of where we are working. I mean that [histogram] is just little boxes to colour in for me. [he laughs]

Res.: Well, seriously, what could it tell you?

K: It tells you whereabout you are working. If you are running high or running low, but I concentrate on this [time series to the left] more because this tells me more than that [histogram]. That [histogram] will just give us an idea. Obviously you are supposed to get the peak in the middle behind the average line but that will tell us if we are running on average. I can look at the chart but to look at the histogram, I mean the obvious reason is that it will tell us if we are running just above the average or just below the average. . . . Really that should be in a nice spike right in the middle, right down the average line [he is probably describing the theoretical bell shape with the mode near the target line].

We concluded that Kevin had a functional understanding of the core statistical concepts in relation to the mechanisms underlying the work process: he appreciated average in relation to a target, variation in that it should be within certain limits, and distribution in that it should be roughly bell-shaped. However, he kept calling control limits 'spec limits', a phenomenon we had commonly observed at Classic Motors and elsewhere (see the Labelex example above, and see Hoyles *et al.*, 2007). The SPC trainers told us that this lack of understanding sometimes caused problems in communication between different groups in the company: the key point – and one which they sought to address in their training – was that control limits emerged from the distribution of data, whereas specification limits were externally determined by the overall design of the car, and how the build sequence needed to work on the assembly line.

SPC training in Classic Motors

The SPC training course in Classic Motors lasted for one day (it had been two days, in the intensive implementation phase of SPC during the 1990s), and took place whenever a sufficient number of people had expressed an interest for it. We found this a little surprising, as we had anticipated that management would specify when the courses would be run and who should attend. The participants were diverse, ranging from production-line operators to professional engineers working as production managers or specialist problem-solvers in different areas of production.

Peter was the trainer for this course. He had worked more than 25 years on the production lines, before being appointed to work in the SPC department. His reaction to this move and the importance of the career opportunities offered to him are captured in the following interview extract.

P: I left school at 18 with O-levels and A-levels and went to Classic Motors at 21, I've been there now for 34 years, 25 of which were spent on the line as an operator. Generally speaking you can describe the jobs on the line as putting six screws in six holes, it's very very repetitive, they're all variations on a theme. In 1999 when the factory was reorganised, I was offered the opportunity to join the SPC Department and it was a pivotal point in my life, it gave me an interest, it took me away from being a drone if you like . . . to someone whose opinion could be heard.

Res: So beforehand your opinion – even though you knew a lot your opinion was not really heard or listened to?

P: It has changed quite dramatically since 1999 but in those days you were quite robotic and your opinions did not count. . . .

Peter was passionate about how moving to the SPC department had 'given [him] a voice' where his opinions were heard and valued. He now had responsibility for managing the use of SPC around the factory, calculating process information from charts collected from the shop floor, particularly the Cp and Cpk values, and giving feedback about this information to employees. Peter had become a skilled and effective trainer, and his long experience on the lines gave him a rapport with operators, and an appreciation of the workplace, which the abstract professional skills of an engineer could not match. As we shall explain, even though Peter's knowledge of SPC concepts revealed fragmentation and was sometimes statistically incorrect, he was able to communicate the practical meanings of the symbolic artefacts very effectively.

Observations of the SPC training course

The course contained many theoretical ideas about process improvement methods and SPC, which as far as possible were put into context through a simple physical 'process simulation', the Coin Exercise that involved a hypothetical manufacturing problem for the Government Mint of coins that were stamped out with sides too rough and had to be buffed smooth. The 'buffing machine' in fact took the form of a traditional board game, 'shove ha'penny', in which coins are pushed along the board to stop at a specified grid space. The specification for the machine was to achieve a target of nine 'buffs' (i.e. to stop in the 'nine' grid-space) with an allowed range of $+/-$ two 'buffs'.

This exercise was repeated several times, with trainees divided into teams, and SPC charts were filled in with data, and process information manually calculated (see Figure 3.4). The first run involved setting up a 'buffing table' (just a piece of heavy paper rolled out on a table with a scale of equally-spaced lines marked on it), and firing a £1 coin along the table by shoving it by hand – the aim being for the coin to stop in the space marked 9 on the table (meaning 'nine buffs' of the coin). Of course, the hand shove is very variable, as became evident when the data for 20 'shoves' were plotted and Cp and Cpk values were calculated to be around 0.2 to 0.5, compared with the company norm of 1.33. For the second run, the teams analysed the causes of variation in the buffing process, mainly individual skill and variability of shove strength. They then devised a mechanical coin launcher using various clamps and rulers. The results for Cp and Cpk for this mechanised process were much improved, around 0.9 to 1.0, though still some way from the company norm.

It was not expected that the operators would be fluent in SPC calculations. Rather, the intention was that they would develop an awareness of what the SPC concepts were about, what calculations are routinely done for them by the SPC department, and how these data derived from, and gave important messages, for practice. As Peter remarked:

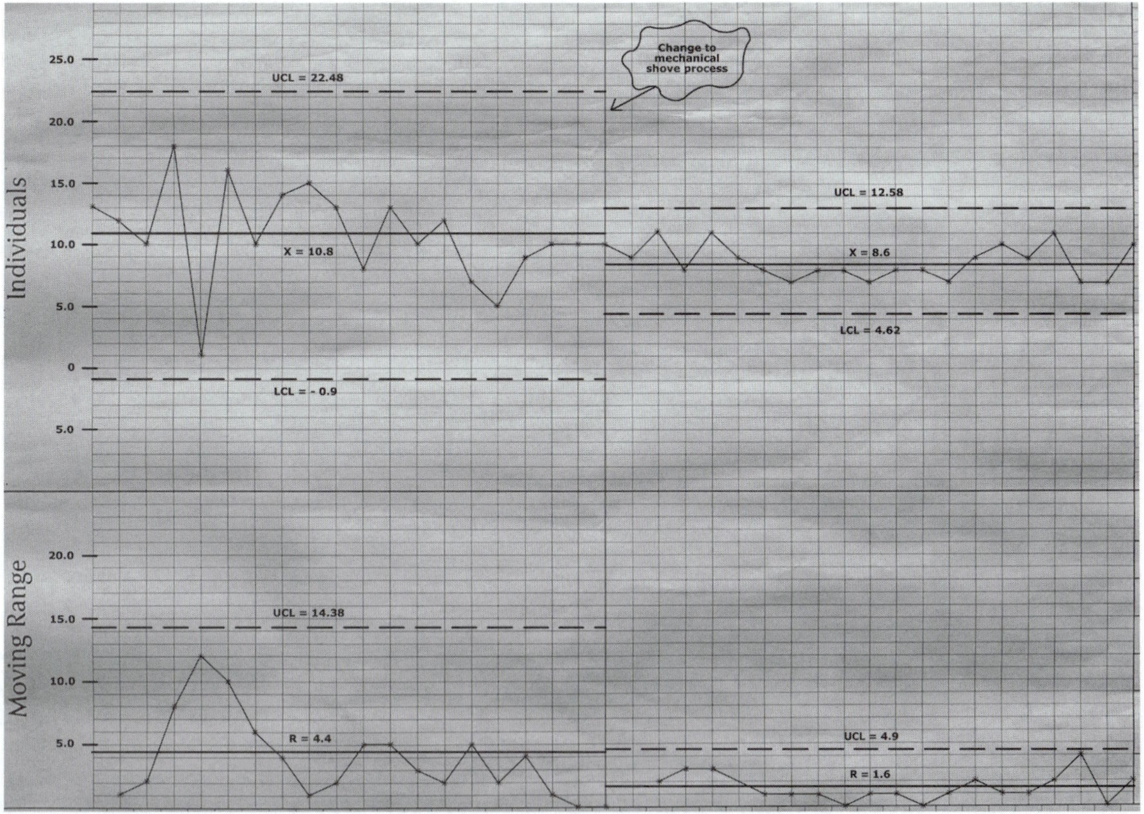

Figure 3.4
An SPC chart filled in by trainees for two rounds of the coin exercise. The second half of the chart, where the process performance became significantly improved (narrower control limits), stems from the second round in which a mechanical launcher using a clamped ruler was employed. (This is a simplified and re-drawn version of the actual chart used by the trainees.)

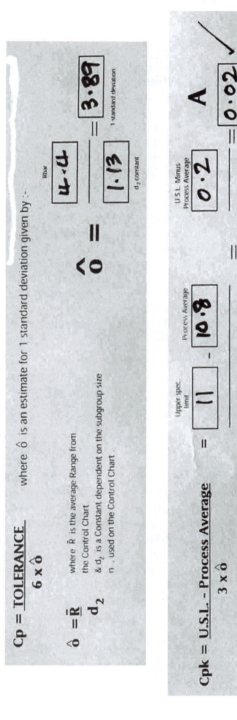

$$Cp = \frac{TOLERANCE}{6 \times \hat{\sigma}}$$ where $\hat{\sigma}$ is an estimate for 1 standard deviation given by :-

$$\hat{\sigma} = \frac{\bar{R}}{d_2}$$ where $\bar{R}$ is the average Range from the Control Chart

& d_2 is a Constant dependent on the subgroup size n, used on the Control Chart.

$$\hat{\sigma} = \frac{\overline{4 \cdot 4}}{1 \cdot 13} = \boxed{3 \cdot 89}$$

Rbar / d_2 constant / 1 standard deviation

$$Cpk = \frac{U.S.L. - Process\ Average}{3 \times \hat{\sigma}}$$

$$= \frac{\boxed{11} - \boxed{10 \cdot 8}}{3 \times \boxed{3 \cdot 89}} = \frac{\boxed{0 \cdot 2}}{\boxed{11 \cdot 67}} = \boxed{0 \cdot 02} \quad A \checkmark$$

Upper spec. limit / Process Average / 1 standard deviation

U.S.L. Minus Process Average / 3x1 standard deviation / Cpku

Figure 3.5 Two parts of the SPC calculation template filled in by trainees for the first run of the coin exercise (data points 1 to 20). (The $\hat{\sigma}$ symbol is supposed to be a sigma, σ, standing for standard deviation.)

The first point is that we want to encourage line teams to better understand how their processes change over time, to understand the variation that is inherent within any process. We want to promote the use of
line-based problem-solving teams who will actively reduce variation
within those processes using data rather than opinion, I think that's a
vital point. In the past the guy with the loudest voice or the biggest
manager, he knew the answer . . . this is the problem and this is the way
we'll fix it. SPC takes that away and it's now data driven. Show me the
data – a man without data is just some bloke with an opinion.

Peter used a metaphor of car parking, to introduce Cp and Cpk in a very
skilled way, guiding participants to think of the target value as a particular
location in the car park, and the specification limit being the width of a
parking space. What seemed to be missing was any attempt to link these
meanings to the algebraic formulae on the control chart – crucial, we think,
to the development of TmL. Peter knew that shop-floor employees found
the algebra hard, even totally inaccessible. His motivation was to show that
Cp and Cpk had a scientific, systematic basis. It might be that he wanted to
use the algebraic symbols as a badge of authority provided by mathematics;
but it is also the case that in the absence of any other way of representing
these ideas (such as a computer simulation) it is hard to see any alternative
to algebra! Finding an alternative to algebra became an important element
in our TEBO design.

Evaluations of the SPC course

Based on our observations of the training, the interviews with operators,
and the results of an evaluation questionnaire we distributed to the training
participants, we summarise our evaluation of the SPC course as follows:

1   The most successful part of the course was the plotting of the points
    on the control chart and seeing the effects of process improvement on
    the Cpk value of the process. What was not so apparent was what the
    operators understood by the calculations they performed: for example,
    to obtain the upper and lower control limits.
2   Performing calculations of control limits and capability indices involved
    arithmetic and even algebra, with which most participants were not
    fluent or even familiar. For example, some did not know that they had
    to divide two numbers in boxes if there was a horizontal line between
    them, or how to do calculations in the right order (e.g. the need to
    multiply before subtracting), or how to subtract a negative number from
    another number. Additionally, as Figure 3.5 shows, formal symbolism
    was employed and the meaning of 'Hartley's constants' (in this case 'd2',
    to estimate the standard deviation) was not explained, even though
    every control chart specified their use.

3   Cp and Cpk were ranked by participants as the most difficult concepts addressed in the course. The participants nonetheless judged them important: they needed to know about them because these measures were part of work practice in many areas of the factory.

4   We were struck by Peter's desire to give some meaning to the conceptual origins of Cp and Cpk, contrasted with the inaccessibility of the algebraic formulae. Peter's knowledge of statistics and statistical software was limited, and we infer that he could see no other way of representing the statistical ideas involved.

5   All the manual calculations required time and attention, and distracted participants from the main ideas of what SPC was attempting to achieve. For example, the ideas of distribution and the standard deviation provide a way of predicting how many products will be produced within a certain distance of the mean value – hence the choice of $+/-$ three standard deviations as the location of the control limits, as the probability of a product measurement being outside these limits is 'very small' (0.3%).

In short, our main observation of the SPC course was that the SPC charts, and the Cp and Cpk indices, despite having great importance in practice, were largely failing in their intended role as symbolic boundary objects conveying more abstract meanings. The training course was well-liked by employees, having a good pedagogical style (practical group exercises, opportunities for discussion of personal ideas) and a very good trainer. All the participants displayed a willingness to try and engage with the charts and capability indices.

SPC training in Sporting Motors

The training at Sporting Motors was observed much later than at Classic Motors, after our TEBOs and learning opportunities had been provisionally designed. The training at Sporting Motors had a similar teaching style to the course at Classic Motors (many practical group work exercises), but the content and format was different: Sporting Motors had implemented a Six Sigma programme of PI. The course we observed was 'green belt' training lasting five days, based on training materials originating from the headquarters of the parent company. Every trainee had a thick binder of many hundreds of pages, and the trainers used a standard set of PowerPoint slides numbering in hundreds; each hour of the course was itemised in terms of the number of slides that had to be 'got through'. Thus the pace of the course was very fast, and we saw a number of interesting and important discussions opening up amongst the participants, which the trainers had to curtail prematurely because there was no time to continue.

Patrick was the trainer on the course. As with Peter, we noted a similar passion resulting from the process improvement-related career opportunities from which Patrick had benefited:

I started at Classic Motors in 1998 and I spent two years on the shop floor. This involved working on the station, two and a half minutes cycle time, and I was just doing up bolts, one car would come, I'd do up the bolt, the next car would come, I'd do it up, next car would come I'd do it up. This was working ten-hour shifts, on night shift, all my friends were going out enjoying themselves while I was working what I call a very repetitive job and I felt I was getting institutionalised and I was quite worried at the time that this job was going to turn me mad. . . .

Patrick had enrolled for SPC training and over a period of years developed himself to achieve 'master black belt', the highest skill level. We asked him what SPC had meant to him in terms of his own development and thinking about the work process:

It has given me a focus . . . it really has changed my life . . . I could have been still working on the track. I enjoy the combination of the mathematics and working on the shop floor with the shop-floor people, the engineering teams and working with these cross-functional teams from different backgrounds. I really do relish the opportunity – I really enjoy my job. It also has allowed me to travel, to learn off really well educated statistical people . . . and so many opportunities in my life and a great sense of satisfaction that I cannot see I could get elsewhere.

Compared with Classic Motors, the content of this training course was more conceptually focused, and this seemed to be expected by the participants (perhaps a result of there being formal definitions of competence in the Six Sigma programme); moreover statistical software (Minitab) was demonstrated to show, for example, Cp and Cpk calculations from a set of process data. Many participants wanted to know the *how* and *why* of these numerical indicators, and asked very perceptive questions. From the discussion, it was clear that at times participants and trainers alike were confused. A few of the participants were high-level managers (e.g. a car designer/manager) and they contributed answers and ideas to the general discussion, as well as helping people in group-based activities.

Negotiating the skills gaps

The problems of understanding capability indices that we have reported typify the problems of SPC and were generally agreed to be issues in the companies in which we worked. Shop-floor employees were knowledgeable and well-trained in following SPC procedures, and skilled in how their processes worked and the problems that occur. In Classic Motors, the shift leaders were used to SPC charts, and having Cp/Cpk values on their notice boards; but to most operators and shift leaders these seemed to be rather alien things that were often ignored. In addition, at best, Cp and Cpk were understood by many employees (certainly, the majority of those that we met directly) as 'pseudo-mathematics': as labels for 'good' or 'bad' processes which do or not meet required targets (such as Cpk=1.33) without meaningful connection to their basis in the manufacturing process. Yet the company wanted the indices to be meaningful as prompts for appropriate action, and the investment in training was intended to help employees to do this.

Similar problems occurred with the SPC charts. There was frequent confusion of control limits and specification limits – control limits were perceived as being defined by managers or customers, not as the direct properties of the process data which shop-floor employees collected. It was crucial but hard for many employees to distinguish between common-cause and special-cause variation. As in other companies, we heard many complaints from engineers and managers that operators and shift leaders often 'chase ghosts' or tamper with the process by adjusting it when one data point is higher or lower than most other points. According to SPC, random variation will result in such 'peaks or troughs', and if the process is stable the overall settings should not be changed. At Classic Motors, managers revealed to us that they knew of some machines fitted with dummy control panels which operators were allowed to alter but which in fact did nothing!

Box 3.3 summarises the techno-mathematical literacies which we identified as important for Classic Motors and Sporting Motors, and Box 3.4 lists the symbolic boundary objects that we identified as having a crucial role in the workplace, and thus candidates for development in the form of technology-enhanced boundary objects.

Box 3.3 Techno-mathematical literacies at stake

- understanding systematic measurement, data collection and display;
- appreciation of the complex effects of changing variables on the production system as a whole;
- being able to identify key variables and relationships in the work flow;
- reading and interpreting time series data, graphs and charts;
- understanding distributions of process data, their mean and variation (spread);
- distinguishing mean from target and specification from control limits;
- knowing about the relation between data and measures, and between process and model;
- understanding and reducing variation, and appreciating the basis of process capability indices and how they are calculated.

> **Box 3.4   Symbolic artefacts for SPC**
>
> - SPC Control chart; and, in training, 'buffing machine' (Shove Ha'penny) simulation;
> - Process capability indices, Cp and Cpk.

Learning opportunities for statistical process control[7]

In all companies that we observed, there was limited access to appropriate statistical tools to explore data expressed in the form of time series charts, and for making graphical representations of the capability indices: no access in the case of production-line operators. Sporting Motors used Minitab, which is a very sophisticated piece of software, inaccessible without considerable knowledge. Elsewhere, we have seen Excel with some bolt-on statistical macros, which was just about usable by the engineers who knew what they were doing, but useless for others. The capability indices were clearly poorly understood by employees despite their importance for process improvement. They were key numerical indicators for communication between employees and managers, in ways that other SPC concepts were not. As we have seen, production employees had to monitor the Cpks of the processes with which they were involved. If their Cpk was too low, they would be asked by managers what was wrong with their part of the production process. As Peter the trainer told us, semi-jokingly: 'you can be beaten up for a low Cpk!'

For us as educators, it was striking to compare this situation with the huge amount of effort that has been put into statistics education to produce more accessible and more meaningful software for learners – for example, the systems TinkerPlots (Konold & Miller, 2005) and Fathom (Finzer *et al.*, 2005). We did in fact do some early prototype work with the TinkerPlots software (described in Hoyles *et al.*, 2007) and received positive feedback from employees and managers in workplaces. In the end, though, for statistical process control we decided to use the Flash language to create web-based TEBOs.

This section gives an account of design and piloting of TEBOs and a set of associated learning opportunities that we devised in collaboration with Classic Motors, and tried out as a modification of part of the company's existing SPC training. The learning opportunities were then adapted for use in the green-belt training at Sporting Motors. At the heart of the activities were three TEBOs, two to explore capability indices, the *Cp and Cpk tools* and the third, the *Shove Ha'penny tool*, to simulate the generation of a control chart and to calculate the capability indices automatically for different data sets.

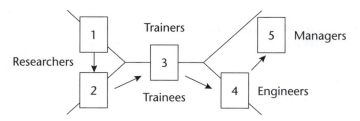

Figure 3.6 Trajectory of the TEBOs at the boundaries between different communities

We will illustrate the trajectory of TEBO design (Figure 3.6) from our intensive interaction with the trainers (box 1), with early versions of the tools shared between us, to the tools used during training courses, first by ourselves (2) and then by trainers without our involvement (3). Next, we show how the tool helped an employee to communicate with a supplier (4), and finally, we summarise the further independent life of the TEBOs in other factories (5). The lines represent boundaries between different communities and the boxes the TEBOs being used at those boundaries.

Our aim was to co-design learning opportunities that incorporated our TEBOs into the existing training of Classic Motors. Our activities were allocated roughly two hours, fitting into the training sequence after the several exercises with the physical coin buffing game, and the trainer's usual introduction to the capability indices.

TEBOs 1 and 2: the Cp and Cpk tools

The main challenge we set ourselves for the tools was to design a representation of the capability indices that would be more comprehensible than the formal algebraic symbols used in the training course. What was needed was a *representation of the relevant relationships* between mean, variation, target and control/specification limits, and one that was both visible and manipulable. It should make the algebra come alive, be more transparent and thus more effective in supporting users to obtain a sense of what the indices actually represent in terms of both work-process and mathematical points of view. A key idea drawn from observation of the training was the importance of the 'fitting' metaphor, which the trainers used frequently and illustrated through diagrams of normal curves (representations of 'the process') that fitted or not within specification limits, and asking 'How many times does the process fit within the spec limits?'

In trying to make the mathematical relationships of Cp and Cpk easier to communicate, one key design decision was to identify and then make visible the key aspects, which employees could manipulate and change the

---

Box 3.5   Technology-enhanced boundary objects (TEBOs) for statistical process control

TEBO 1: Cp tool
TEBO 2: Cpk tool
TEBO 3: Shove Ha'penny tool

(View online at: www.lkl.ac.uk/research/technomaths/tools/spctools)

---

things that matter. In the case of Cp, this meant being able to represent and manipulate the tolerance '(USL – LSL)' and '6 times SD', the numerator and denominator of the formula (see earlier). We decided to implement this with two linear bars (see Figure 3.7), in place of the widths used in the company's own diagrams for normal curves. Thus the interpretation of the ratio in the formula for Cp became directly translated into 'how many times does the SD bar fit into the tolerances bar?' Note that both mean and control limits can be moved in order to change the SD bar and where the curve fits inside the specification limits. In addition, the algebra can be hidden or revealed, along with the calculation of the Cp value.

The Cpk tool was slightly more complicated, since instead of tolerance there was a need to consider two bars: one for distance of the upper specification limit above the mean '(USL – mean)' and the other for the distance of the mean above the lower specification limit, '(mean – LSL)'. A similar representation of bars to represent the formula was adopted, so the meaning of Cpk became: how many times does the '3 SD' bar fit into whichever bar is the smaller out of (USL – mean) and (mean – LSL). See Figure 3.8.

The Cpk tool follows the same design as the Cp tool; it is more complicated only in that the calculation of Cpk requires the calculation and comparison of two numbers, the Cpk upper and lower. In fact, it is not *necessary* to calculate both numbers, as we learnt from the SPC trainers (see below).

In both tools, the meanings of the ratio of the bars were supported by the visual display of the normal curve and its position in relation to the control and specification limits. Another key point about the representation was that it deflected attention from numbers as such, towards the meaning of the numbers as ratios that related the process distribution to the specification limits. This effect was strengthened in the final version of the tools, where we put a button to hide or reveal the numbers involved.

The learning opportunities using the Cp and Cpk tools also focused on visual estimation of the Cp or Cpk values. Trainees were asked to work in pairs so they could challenge each other to estimate correctly, and ask

Moving the discs alters the mean and variation of the process, while the blue squares change the position of the specification limits.

What is C_p?

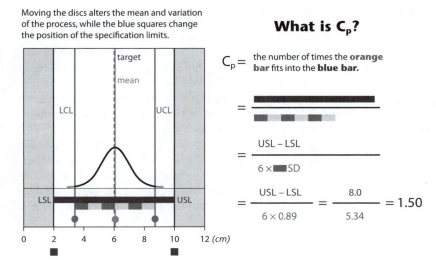

$$C_p = \frac{\text{the number of times the \textbf{orange}}}{\text{\textbf{bar} fits into the \textbf{blue bar.}}}$$

$$= \frac{\text{USL} - \text{LSL}}{6 \times \text{SD}}$$

$$= \frac{\text{USL} - \text{LSL}}{6 \times 0.89} = \frac{8.0}{5.34} = 1.50$$

Figure 3.7 The Cp tool. Note use of a visual bar representation. In this case, Cp = 1.5 as the bottom (orange) bar fits 1.5 times in the top (blue) bar

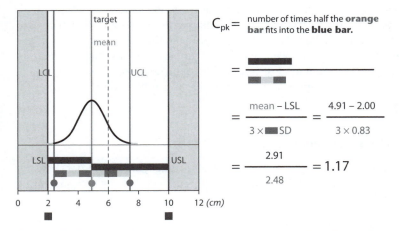

$$C_{pk} = \frac{\text{number of times half the \textbf{orange}}}{\text{\textbf{bar} fits into the \textbf{blue bar.}}}$$

$$= \frac{\text{mean} - \text{LSL}}{3 \times \text{SD}} = \frac{4.91 - 2.00}{3 \times 0.83}$$

$$= \frac{2.91}{2.48} = 1.17$$

Figure 3.8 Detail view of the graph and bar representations in the Cpk tool (TEBO 2), with numerical values shown (a control button, not shown, turns on or off the display of numerical values)

challenging questions: e.g., what is the meaning of Cpk=0, or Cpk negative? In the trials, we found ample evidence that trainers and trainees could effectively use the ratio of bar lengths in place of symbolic formulae to estimate Cp and Cpk, and from this use were able to appropriate the 'fitting' metaphor.

TEBO 3: The Shove Ha'penny simulation

The third TEBO tool that we co-designed was a version of the coin buffing, or Shove Ha'penny, simulation (Figure 3.9). We set out to make a tool that would satisfy the trainers' requirements. The overall goal was to make an interactive tool that would give trainees a sense of what it means to optimise a process; the tool allows to generate a set of process data, display it in a control chart, calculate capability measures, and to do this many times under different conditions under user control.

The Flash tool was a close copy of the form of the paper SPC chart used in the factory (with individual run chart, moving range, and sideways histogram). Our first idea for a source of variation that needed to be 'optimised' was that we would use 'operator' as one of the input variables with different process settings for three different operators. Participants would then find the best operator by exploring with the simulations and examining the control limits and process measures. The trainers questioned this design, as one of their core messages during training was that all work processes should be operator-independent – so we had to think again. After some negotiation with the trainers we settled on 'ruler material' with three different settings – plastic, wood and metal – which we designed to lead to different variation in the data. We conjectured that metal would lead to least variability in coin distance, ahead of wood, and then plastic. This source of variation reflected the physical game in which a ruler was used as a launching device. The other control was the launch strength of the ruler (the 'release distance'), which had to be varied so that the mean of the process data went as close as possible to the target of nine 'buffs'. Again, this reflected the steps in optimisation that were followed for the physical game.

Reflections on the designs of the TEBOs

These reflections sample the highlights of the engagement of operators and trainers with the TEBOs, focusing on their enhanced role in communicating meanings across boundaries.

Opening windows on different interpretations of Cpk

During the co-design of the tools, significant differences were revealed between our own understanding of Cpk (from a mathematical perspective) and that of the experienced trainers (Peter and Sean). The reader may recall that the mathematical definition of Cpk is the minimum of the lower and upper numbers (Cpkl and Cpku). For this reason we made two columns in the Cpk tool – one for each of these two indices, Cpkl and Cpku. We expected users to estimate both values and take the minimum, thus

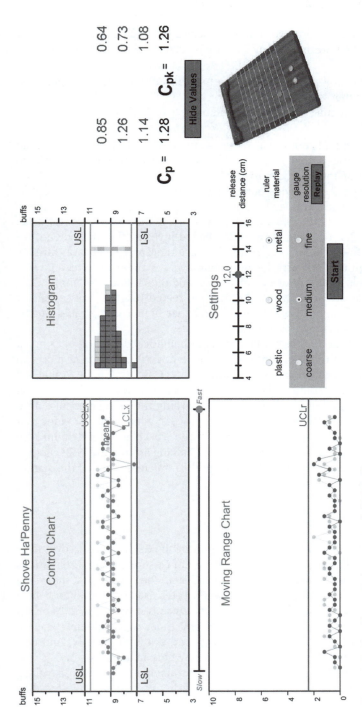

Figure 3.9 The Shove Ha'penny tool (TEBO 3)

following the definition. We found ourselves so conditioned to follow the formula that we were taken by surprise by Peter and Sean's reaction:

S: All we ever talk about is the closest specification [lower or upper].
P: The side that is most at risk!
S: We never actually say 'the minimum of'.

They were right, of course, since they would only ever be interested in the side of the process that was 'at risk' of violating a specification limit, so would focus on that side, choosing it by using the sense of the context. Sean therefore suggested 'greying out' the side of the calculation (Cpkl or Cpku) that was irrelevant. This led to some discussion amongst the research team. Some of us argued that we should not take away the opportunity for users to discover that only the at-risk side needed investigation. In the end, we decided to follow Sean's suggestion because the Cpk concept was already hard enough to work with for most employees without introducing what might be seen as an irrelevant calculation and then taking a minimum. We decided that attention would be better directed to other messages: for example that 'higher Cpk is better', and that higher Cpk should not be achieved by widening the specification limits.

The discrepancy between the formal mathematical definition of Cpk and the trainers' approach of ignoring the 'side not at risk' hints at a crucial point. When defining a precise measure such as Cpk, it has to be formalised into a statistically sound definition, taking on a form that is different from how it is interpreted in practice. When learning the mathematical definition, learners have to undergo a reverse process: what is the core idea that was formalised here? What meanings in the workplace world should we attribute to this mathematical statement? Talking around the TEBO helped us coordinate these two views and adapt the implementation of the mathematical definition accordingly.

Helping trainers to reflect on their TmL

The next episode shows Peter and Sean using the Cpk tool to discover facts that surprised them. They predicted values of Cpk for certain distributions and found that they were incorrect. In addition, they discovered that some of their rules of thumb just did not work. Peter used rules of thumb such as: 'if Cpk = 0.8 then 80% of what we produce is in spec and 20% out of spec'. His reasoning puzzled us for a long time: it only seems true for processes that are uniformly distributed (rather than normally) and that are centred on the target value, and it only would make sense for $0 < Cpk < 1$. While working with the Cpk tool, the trainers made new discoveries. They were playing with the Cpk tool when the researcher suggested they predict:

Res.: How about making a Cpk of negative 0.5?

P: It needs to be *all* outside specification and a little bit more. Minus 0.5 means that what you are building is outside spec [he seems to be using his rule of thumb].

Res.: What does the minus sign mean?

P: The minus. Nothing that you build is within specification. . . .

Then Peter decided to test his prediction with the TEBO (see Figure 3.10):

P: If you just press 'show' it should tell us. . . . Hang on a minute. Hang on! . . . We are getting confused on this one.

Peter realised that the reasoning based on his rule of thumb did not lead to the right results, so he needed to rethink his understanding of Cpk. He and Sean next tried to make a curve with Cpk = 0 (see Figure 3.10). According to the rule of thumb everything should be 'out of spec', but they discovered a problem with this assumption too:

P: Come on, try that [shifting the tool handles such that Cpk = 0]. So half of it is within specification and half outside. It is me that is confused.

Peter thus discovered another fact, 'Cpk = 0 means half in spec', which contradicted his rule of thumb. He told us, 'I have never thought of 0 until that came up'.

At this point, we thought that he had concluded that his rule of thumb did not work. We were inclined to claim that the TEBO had done some work as a mediating tool for communicating about Cpk and engaging with the statistical ideas behind it. But we were premature in our judgement. In

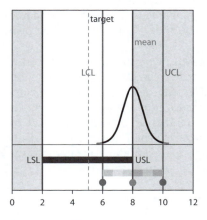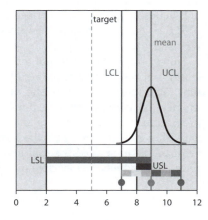

Figure 3.10 The 'confusing' cases of Cpk: (a) Cpk = 0, (b) Cpk = –0.5

fact when explaining the Shove Ha'penny game five months later, during the second pilot training course, Peter both used the same rule of thumb that was underlying his interpretation of Cpk = 0 and also repeatedly mentioned how confusing he found the case of Cpk = 0.

We became intrigued by how such contradictory information could co-exist for Peter. We therefore sent him an email to push him on this point. He responded:

> Whoops – a slip of the tongue, in order for everything to be out of spec the Cpk needs to be at least Cpk = –1. My gu-estimates should refer to Cp values and in the examples quoted [Cp=0.17, 0.02 & 0.4], and very roughly speaking, (at best) 83%, 98% and 60% will be out of spec. I know that strictly speaking this isn't so – it doesn't take the tails of the distribution into consideration. It also only works for values less than 1, in that even if the process was perfectly centred the spread would be greater than the tolerance, values equal to or greater than 1 merely indicate the potential for the 'spread' to fit within tolerance.

We should not underestimate that coordination of fragments of knowledge is non-trivial and takes time and repeated engagement. In the end, we concluded that within the training, Peter tried to give participants a sense of how bad a process could be with certain Cpk values, and by being pessimistic about his percentages of items produced out of spec he was staying on the safe side. More generally, we observe that Peter's rules of thumb drew on his rich experience of being on the production line, and however partial, provided thoughtful advice for an operator on the line. The fragmented model reflected the fact that operators were not expected to have a broader and coherent appreciation of the SPC concepts, and were not supported to develop it. The flaw showed up, for example, in the case of Dan described later, where operators appointed to the newly created role of SPC coordinator, found themselves to be under-skilled and, in their own words, 'struggling to cope'.

This example indicates that working with the symbolic artefacts of the workplace and designing them to be interactive in our TEBOs, was important for trainers, operators and ourselves and did indeed facilitate communication between these groups. It is also interesting to note that the programmer of the TEBO, a first-rate mathematician, also learned by exploring with the tool after he had coded it. The interaction and visual feedback as he moved the tool about gave – even him – meaning to the formulae, and new perspective on what Cpk actually meant:

> [Y]ou know you have got close to a useful tool when you as a programmer have an aha moment. – for the Cpk tool it is interesting to ask yourself when does the Cpk tool go negative. I know the maths,

I know the code – I know a lot about it because I have just spent months on it, but I didn't realise when Cpk went negative – and by playing with the tool that I coded I realised, oh well when the mean goes outside the spec limits the Cpk goes negative. I could have worked that out through the algebra but I kind of got that aha moment from the tool that I built!

Outcomes for learning and practice

The TEBOs and learning opportunities were used directly by us in three training courses at Classic Motors and Sporting Motors. All were extremely successful in terms of the engagement with ideas that we saw happening, and the positive responses of the participants. Participants typically spoke about the visual and interactive nature of the TEBOs, compared with manual work with algebra, for example:

[T]he tools help you to play and understand what effects process change has on Cp and Cpk values. I would use these again to clarify my understanding. I have done green belt training, but the difference between the two can be difficult to remember.

Almost all of the participants asked for the website address of the TEBOs so they could revisit them in their own time (and some did, as we learned later). The trainer, Sean, confirmed the importance of the visual representation in the Cp and Cpk TEBOs:

[P]ersonally I have got a pattern in mind: I see pictures, other people see numbers. Putting this thing in front of me was a world apart from throwing up a formula . . . and that is the sort of response we have had from our people.

Sean also talked about the interactivity and visual effects of the Shove Ha'penny tool:

we show them how the data forms itself on the chart. The tool is very very good for that as it enables them to see the dots forming and the histogram forming . . . we encourage the teams to play with the different dimensions of it . . . and then they start to get a feel for how the different variables affect what they are actually seeing as the data is plotted.

The most significant learning outcomes that we wish to describe are those where there was identifiable impact on practice, as we now show in several episodes derived from the company in the months following the trials of the TEBOs and learning opportunities. We further report on outcomes as the tools began to be used independently from us in company practice, and also how they surprisingly developed into a 'global phenomenon' as their use spread across the world.

The impact of the TEBOs

We now describe the impact of the work undertaken in the different contexts, within and beyond the companies with which we worked.

Impact on operator training in Classic Motors

We spoke to Peter on several occasions in a 12-month period after our training collaborations, about whether his approach to training had changed. One example he gave us, revealed that he was now critical of his use of analogies:

> [P]rior as to using [the tools], we tried to explain the difficult concept with a car in a garage. We compared the spread of the process with the size of the car and the tolerance with the size of the garage. Obviously, the first reaction you get is that you can't park half the car in the garage because you hit the wall, so that was quickly changed to a parking space. So you can now straddle the white lines. Cp is relatively easy. My car has the same potential to fit in the car parking space as the manager director's. In reality, he parks outside the office, and I park half a mile away. So the Cpk has a concept [he means: there is a reason for Cpk]. It is no longer where it needs to be. But again it was extremely difficult to put across.

He explained that the visual dynamic tools made it easier to explain Cpk:

> One of the hardest things we have to get across is what the Cpk means – once you're familiar it becomes trivial, but to translate that to someone who doesn't know is really difficult, the tool enables you to show in a dynamic way – if I move this then this moves. It's like creating a cartoon from a load of slides. When the operators chart data they are taking little snapshots in time and your tool brings it all together like a cartoon, animating it.
>
> The tool makes it very, very visual. And the guys themselves can play with the distribution, and they can move it as they will, and they can see, hopefully, that the Cp value does not change.

Looking at the wider impact on training across other sites in the same company, one very experienced quality engineer (QE, head of 250 engineers) told us one year after the pilot training that our intervention had achieved lasting impact on the company's training courses.

QE: The tool itself can be replicated by Excel or by Minitab or any other statistical package in terms of representing the data, but what it does do is, it made us question how we deliver the training in terms of process capability.

Res.: Did you? You questioned it?

QE: Yes, because if someone is offering a different perspective of how it was being done, is there a better way? Then you should take note of that, and analyse on how it's changed, because it's changed certain behaviours within training sessions.

The engineer stressed the tools' usefulness to explore 'what-if scenarios'. He noted that this contrasted with their usual training where there was a right or wrong answer and little discussion as to how they came to any decision. When we asked him if the tool allowed a change in pedagogical approach making use of 'what-ifs', he responded:

Yes, it is all about checking the understanding, which you couldn't do in a scenario where you get twenty answers; how many people achieved the correct answer? And then you have to diagnose why they either miscalculated, and why, worryingly, some people have the correct numerical answer, but won't know why, and there is no point in sending them back into the workplace if they don't know that reasoning behind it.

Extending impact to other communities in Classic Motors

Peter told us not only would he use the tools in his training but he would also encourage others to use them. First he mentioned managers – implicitly suggesting that they too were not comfortable with some of these ideas: 'I have sent it to managers, so the managers can use the tools as well'.

This same issue was suggested by QE. He described how 'eyes glazed over' when different communities were faced with the Cp and Cpk algebraic formulae, including senior managers and even more importantly, the finance people who had to approve funding requests:

In terms of the senior management, one would hope that they have an in-depth understanding of variability and design methods. It is not always the case, and there might be a reluctance to admit that. And therefore using the tool, I would ask the same what-if questions or at least describe the scenario and in an abstract form say 'the consequence of this action is', rather than putting up a page and a half of standard deviation calculations and mean calculations. You say that describes the population, if we do this the consequence will be X and the estimated cost effect will be Y, in the abstract form. And that led to a better dialogue. . . . what we were able to do with the tool was to convert it from the formula to the graphic in terms of 'where are these processes?'

(QE, Classic Motors)

He also mentioned another use, which was to negotiate critical indicators across boundaries; for example, with suppliers about the capability of their parts: 'And I am also trying to promote it on the supplier base because after all the aim is not that just we build parts to Cpk values but also our suppliers give us parts that are fit for purpose.'

The following episode involving Dan suggests some of the issues that arise in dealing with suppliers.

Impact on an operator's problem-solving in practice

We were not able to follow our training participants directly back to the assembly lines, in order to assess the effect of our learning opportunities on practice. Nevertheless, we tried to assess the impact of our work by following up with email and telephone interviews. The following incident is indicative. In a post-course email interview, one of the participants of the first training pilot, Dan, wrote to us that he had bookmarked our website immediately after the course and had used the TEBO tools many times since then. Dan was a former operator employee promoted to a role of SPC coordinator within one manufacturing area; his lack of formal education meant that he had to draw heavily on his practical experience and it was very interesting to see how he put together ideas to reach a solution to a problem that he faced.

When we asked Dan what exactly made the tools so invaluable, he responded that 'the dynamic interaction made the Cpk tangible as opposed to the algebraic formulae being a bunch of numbers until they were calculated'. In the following, we show how Dan made use of the tools when solving an actual production problem.

The problem at stake was that in some estate cars too little water was coming out of the rear washer jet. After investigation, it was found that the rubber tubes running from the water reservoir in the engine compartment via the roof to the washer jet had a kink in them, which prevented water going through the tube. The faulty tubes had a large overhang and pushing this into the roof body during assembly caused the kinking. In line with the process improvement approach, Dan started measuring the tubes he got from the supplier and noted a range from −4 mm up to 50 mm overhang, whereas 10 mm was the target (−4 means that the tube is 4 mm too short). The assumption was that with a large overhang if 'you push it back on itself, it'll make a big arc', but what nobody had realised, until Dan actually started measuring, was that with a range of smaller overhang 'it just kinks' and 'then restricts the water coming from the washer jet'.

Once he had collected his data, he tried to map them mentally to the curve in the Cp tool. He told us: 'I look at your tool, put my numbers against yours, and drag them sideways, and just watch the waves spread into a little ripple, and then, you know, it's miles out of spec.'

Dan had little problem in mentally transforming the shape of the distribution from his own values to the ones in the tool (between 0 and 12 cm); for example, he just interpreted the 0 to 5 cm scale displayed in the TEBO tool as standing for 50 mm overhang. Apparently he used the tool as a model of what processes should look like. So when looking at our tools he also realised that 'we did not have a tolerance'.

Interv.: Has using the Cpk tool made you realise the spread of the process?
Dan: Oh god yes, not half. They [supplier] just said 'our tube is 2.8m long', what's that got to with 10 mil [millimetres] hanging off the back. That was of no consequence to them.

The tube supplier only cared that it supplied 2.8-metre tube lengths, plus *some* overhang, but had no understanding of what was the *acceptable range* of overhang for the tube to function correctly. Classic Motors had apparently only asked for 10 mm overhang and had not given the supplier any specification limits. This had resulted in too wide a range of tube lengths, a particular sub-range of which led to kinking tubes.

What followed was a data-informed discussion between the car manufacturer and the supplier of the tubes. The advantage of collecting data was that this discussion was based on facts, not opinions. In Dan's words:

[Before] I would simply have said, 'I think they are too long' . . . now it's a fact. The fact that all these tubes are these lengths and they're causing a problem is not because I think they are a bit longer than they should be, it's the fact of the measurement, and a rubber tube of a certain diameter bent at a certain angle will kink at, I dunno, 80 degrees. And it's gonna kink every time, it's a mathematical fact. So we knew it had to be under a certain length not to kink, we had all the information.

We cannot claim too much from a single episode. Nevertheless, Dan had incorporated our Cp tool into his tool kit for solving problems, and he had used it in a non-standard way. He re-contextualised the tool in a new situation, in which Cp (and Cpk) should not have been helpful as there were no specification limits. We conjecture that he realised the problem of specification limits because he tried to map his data onto the Cp tool. Thus, although the tool was designed for understanding Cp and Cpk, it here mediated his thinking for a different purpose.

Extending the functionality of the tools

Designing software, especially in situations where there is co-design across the boundaries of expertise and practice, is often a setting which affords both sides of the boundary a *window* (Noss & Hoyles, 1996a) onto each other's perspective. In this episode, we illustrate this point.

One of the features users repeatedly requested, was that *local* data should be used as the basis for the TEBOs. It was quite complex to unravel what different users meant by this. Most basically, this seemed to be a request to be able to set the scales of the Cp and Cpk tools, for example, to the numbers users were dealing with in their own process data:

> Would it be possible to enable the web tools to accept different numbers – it would be quite a powerful tool if we could input our own tolerances and spread numbers? Then it could give an instant representation of real processes – we could then demonstrate to shop floor teams exactly how their processes are performing in relation to customer expectations (specifications).
>
> (Peter, Classic Motors)

Classic Motors in fact proposed to appoint one of its new graduate employees to re-program the tools to allow for this.

Another interpretation of this request was that it stemmed from a dissatisfaction with existing statistical software tools (e.g. Excel and Minitab), which were deemed over-complex for most employees involved with SPC and, more fundamentally, lacked the possibility to directly manipulate the distribution rather than changing it through modifying the numerical input data.[8]

A final interpretation is offered by the case of Dan above, for whom the tools' visual representation had become a form of mental model that could apply to the sets of actual data that he needed to analyse for his work.

Global dissemination

Patrick, the master black belt and trainer from Sporting Motors, developed an instant and enduring enthusiasm for the Cp and Cpk TEBOs; he is still an enthusiast to this day, having moved on to an international career as a full-time Six Sigma consultant and trainer.

Patrick has demonstrated the TEBOs at several international conferences of SPC specialists, generating a significant global interest that we had hardly expected. For example, he told us about one international Six Sigma conference as follows:

> I presented the Cp, Cpk and shove ha'penny tool for around 15 minutes within a one-hour presentation. I also spent five minutes discussing

how we had worked with your team to use your academic experience to improve learning within the workplace and how you had conducted research to try and alleviate the need to use complex calculations whilst training shop floor workers with difficult subjects.

After I demonstrated the tool, a couple of people commented on how impressed they were with the tool. But, I was surprised that it did not receive more reaction.

However, at the end of my presentation, one of the delegates asked if I could write the web address on the flip chart to allow them to access the tools. When I turned round after writing on the flip chart, there were approximately 20 people crowding around me saying how impressed they were with the tool! So, yet again, wherever I present the tool it *always* receives an extremely positive response!

Visitors to the TEBO website (typically a few new ones each month) have originated from the USA, Canada, Sweden, Germany, Turkey, and elsewhere. In online feedback, visitor comments confirm the impression gained at Classic Motors and Sporting Motors that the capability indices are little-understood concepts, and that the representation of the tools offers a novel way of thinking, which is relevant primarily to shop floor employees, but also to engineers and managers.

Conclusions

The research reported in this chapter for the automotive sector represents the most complete trajectory of development that we were able to achieve in the whole project, starting from ethnographic observations and identification of skills gaps, through to the co-design of learning opportunities and TEBOs, through to the learning opportunities being independently developed by companies, and disseminated widely across the worldwide automotive sector, being recognised as addressing a learning need that is widely experienced.

This is a strong justification of our key claims that there are urgent and serious skills gaps we characterise as TmL, and that carefully designed software can be effective in changing both workplace training and workplace practice to deal with these skills gaps. A significant role that is commonly claimed for technology-enhanced learning, though less often convincingly demonstrated, is to break apparently intractable problems in cultures of learning. The work described here on the SPC TEBO tools is an example of such cultural change: the several tools that we developed, modest in themselves, have stimulated major changes in two companies in the way people think about SPC and how it can be learnt. Moreover, they have attracted international attention amongst process improvement specialists in the automotive industry; this was not planned by us. The transformative potential of TEBOs was a design focus throughout our research. As this chapter has illustrated, the crux of the research is iterative design of the TEBOs in collaboration between programmer, practitioners and researchers – offering the companies concerned an answer to a real question – even if implicit: to what extent is it reasonable to develop mathematical understandings of complex notions like capability indices, in ways that are not reliant solely on traditional mathematical knowledge and techniques (such as algebra), and which connect with actual practice?

Chapter 4

Financial services 1
Pensions and investments

We now turn to our research in financial services, beginning in this chapter with two companies dealing in pensions and investments, and in the next, a mortgage company. The major characteristics of this sector, and the differences in relation to manufacturing industry are: (1) the *virtual* nature of the products (mathematical abstractions, rather than physical artefacts), and (2) the *existence of the customer* as a private individual – actually, millions of individuals – which means that companies operate enormous systems to manage product sales, and customer service systems to support the needs of existing customers. As in the manufacturing sectors, we placed our focus of investigation on intermediate-level employees working within these two service systems.

An idea that we will stress in this chapter and the next is the growing place of symbolic articulation work in the work of service employees (see Chapter 1; Hampson & Junor, 2005): that is, the need for the employee to operate at the interface between the company and the customer, and to deal with increasing amounts of technically expressed information, that form part of symbolic artefacts, such as numerical tables and graphs.

When we started writing this chapter, the 'credit crunch' of 2008 had yet to happen. We wrote a draft opening of this chapter, which argued that communication within and between financial institutions, their managers and their customers was paramount, and that one key ingredient of what needed to be communicated was an appropriate view of the mathematical elements of the artefacts being traded, some appreciation of the models at stake. The evidence of the credit crunch shows that our conclusion has to a large extent been proved correct, as the crisis at least partly arose from a failure of managers to understand the mathematics of their business, and of the mathematically expert product designers and risk managers to communicate it (see, for example, Hand, 2009). Our concerns in this book are with the day-to-day work of retail financial services and ordinary customers, not the exotic, multi-billion business of investment banking, but the argument remains pertinent nonetheless.

In the pensions/investment sub-sector that is the focus of this chapter, the two companies in which we conducted our ethnographies were each among the top ten of UK life companies, dealing in pensions, insurance and related investment funds, each with more than a million policyholders. They were:

- *Lifetime Pensions Limited (LPL)*: involving employees from three 'back office' areas of the company – correspondence-based customer services for pensions, and telephone-based enquiry teams for two types of investments;
- *National Mutual Pensions (NMP)*: involving two administrative support offices for pensions sales, one located in London, handling many high-value pension plans for clients working in financial services; and one located in southern England, handling a more typical mix of clients.

In the financial services sector we also developed a productive dialogue with the Financial Services Skills Council (FSSC), which helped us understand the nature of work in the sector, the mathematical skill requirements, and provided the introduction to work with NMP. Research started with LPL in the second year of the project, and was then extended to NMP (and to the mortgage company, which we report in Chapter 5) around six months to a year later, on the basis of an initial complete design and trial cycle of both phases of the research in LPL.

The techno-mathematics of pensions and the work of customer services

The changing business of private pension plans

To understand the TmL involved in customer services work, we first need to present some background details about the pensions business in the UK. We will be concerned specifically with *private pension plans*. This type of pension is basically a form of long-term investment (30 or more years) that comes with a 'wrapper' of tax advantages: (1) the investment is not subject to tax at any point (provided it is used to fund living in retirement, and not more than a prescribed amount, 25%, is converted into cash); and (2) contributions to the investment, up to a certain maximum per annum, enjoy full tax relief.

This kind of pension is distinct from the 'salary-defined pension' that is available to government and public sector employees, and in some large companies, which guarantees an amount of income in retirement based on the employees' salary and the number of years of service with the organisation. The private pension plan does not guarantee anything: everything depends on the long-term performance of the investment funds in which money is placed. At the point of retirement, the major part of the accumulated investment must be used to buy an *annuity*, which guarantees an income every month until death.

Private pension plans and annuities are both complicated. In recent years there have been serious problems due to the difficulty of obtaining reliable, impartial expert advice, coupled with the poor performance and high management charges of many investment funds recommended for pensions. This has led to widespread distrust of the companies providing pensions among the UK public. Pensions companies, including the two that we researched, have therefore been making considerable efforts to improve their relationships with customers as part of their drive to attract business.

In UK financial services, intermediaries known as *financial advisers* play an important role in selling products and giving advice to customers. The term *adviser* has a technical and legal meaning in that an adviser has to be qualified and licensed to operate, based on obtaining a specified level of qualification in the area of financial services in which they operate (insurance, mortgages, pensions, etc.). Some advisers work for financial services companies, but in the case of pensions, the adviser is nearly always an *independent* financial adviser (IFA), who should select a pension plan most appropriate to the customer's requirements, and is paid either by a direct fee from the customer, or by a commission paid by the pensions company. The use of commissions has been identified as a difficult area of practice, as IFAs might be tempted to select companies and products with good commission rates, although they might not be optimal for the customer. Indeed, pensions companies typically operate complex incentive schemes with various enhanced commissions in order to attract IFA 'business'.[1] The IFA, and not the pension company, is responsible for applying for and setting up a new pension plan and communicating to the customer the details of the pension or investment; we observed that many customers had a poor appreciation of what should be the responsibility of the IFA or the company.

As well as 'adviser', the term 'advice' also has a precise legal meaning for financial services – it means making a recommendation to a customer to take a specific action in terms of buying a product, or changing a product (for example, cashing-in an investment, or transferring money to a product offered by a different company). In the everyday sense, advice has a broader meaning that also includes providing information that is relevant to the customer's interests, and companies do need to do this. In our observations reported in the next section, we found the idea of advice to be problematic, since customer service employees were generally not adequately qualified, and it was not their role to give advice. They were taught specific strategies and forms of words so as to *avoid advising* while still providing 'non-advice', factual statements of information helpful to the customer (in the case of services for existing customers), or as part of the overall sales/marketing strategy to attract new customers (see Chapter 5 on mortgage sales).

Changes in the customer experience and the articulation work of employees

Along with all pension companies, our two companies had been changing radically to offer their customers a different kind of service, a better 'customer experience', where more information about pensions and investments was on offer and customers could telephone the company for a quick response to their questions. Previously, companies tended to offer limited communication with customers, based on a slow exchange of written correspondence.

In analysing how the work of the customer service employees had changed in the light of enhanced customer focus, we noticed how symbolic articulation work had become more central, since employees had a more demanding role in negotiating between the informational needs of the customer and the IT-based information systems that held the customer and product information, systems whose outputs were symbolic and whose meanings needed to be interpreted. As companies increasingly recognised, the shift from correspondence-based to telephone-based working called for a certain quick-wittedness and good verbal skills, in order to be able to explain products in a language that the customer could grasp. For these reasons, recent graduates and part-time university student workers were sought-after employees (and this also fitted with the evening and weekend work schedules of call centres). What was less apparent to companies, and a key question for our initial workplace investigations, was the role of technical knowledge in these interactions.

From analysis of our ethnographic data, it became clear that customers were frequently suspicious of what companies were doing with their money, demanding more data and more information, which led to pressures on employees. We give just one example here.

A type of With Profits investment offered by Lifetime Pensions (see explanation of With Profits below) had experienced a period of declining investment values, which resulted in many difficult telephone enquiries during which customers demanded explanations as to why the surrender value of their investment was less than anticipated:

> An angry telephone exchange: Telephone call from policy holder [PH], a woman and her partner, both angry ('we are recording this conversation!'). PH wanted to surrender a With Profits bond that was over five years old (so no early surrender penalties applied). A 'Market Value Adjustment' of 8% [i.e. reduction in value of the money paid back] was to be charged. PH claimed they knew nothing about this, and was going to complain to the IFA who sold it to them: 'it is adding insult to injury' since the bond has performed badly, 'we would have been better to put our money in a banana republic!' The current value was £16,212. The original investment was about £15,000, and PH was expecting to receive about £19,000 as a 'five-year investment'.[2] PH also

objected to the fact that the surrender value changed from day to day [yet this was how it was calculated]. In the end, PH reiterated that he was going to complain to the IFA for compensation for being sold this investment. The employee said to the researcher: he had to be careful in cases like this not to offer advice . . . 'there are a lot of sad cases – a lot of old people badly advised by IFAs to buy certain investments which have not performed well and have high charges'.

(Field notes from LPL)

Our overarching finding from the workplace observations was that despite the changing customer focus, the status of service employees' *technical knowledge* to understand and explain the financial products with which they dealt had changed rather little, although there was typically concern about employees' general communication skills. We found that the articulation work they tried to do was often compromised by limited TmL; indeed, their roles in relation to the IT systems had generally been set up *not* to require such literacies, nor to be able to 'interpret' the screen output in any detail. This had not changed significantly. Responses about technical details were largely based on pre-written scripts, and customer queries that went beyond the scripted information were often handed on to technical departments in the company. There appeared to have been an intentional system design on the part of managers and financial-mathematical experts, such that the mathematical models and relationships used for the calculations within the IT system had been left invisible to its routine users. This is not so surprising given the shortage of mathematical skills in the UK labour market, and the wage premium employers would have to pay to obtain them. The question we posed was how could employees perform the technical/symbolic articulation work necessary for engaging with customers, and how could we develop a way to address this through training?

Some service employees certainly felt they could do more if they received appropriate training, a shift that would save the time and money needed to call in technical experts. Thus we were cutting with the grain: several employees reported dissatisfaction in that for them, they could not see where calculations came from, resonating with our wish to replace black boxes with at least a partial model of the mathematical structures of the IT system. The question we needed to explore through our workplace observations and the training already on offer was which parts of the structures could be opened up, and how?

Opening up the mathematics was, however, a delicate matter – far more so than in the case of process improvement in manufacturing, where a more equal relationship amongst different employees was an explicit and much-desired goal. At least some of the financial managers' reluctance to give employees more knowledge was to do with the thorny issue of advice: the more information some customers would be given (the 'difficult' ones, as in the telephone call quoted above), the more they would want to know, and this would become both unmanageable and dangerous in the context of a telephone conversation. Thus, though it might appear cynical, some managers took the view that customers' experience would be better closed down than opened up.

The techno-mathematics of pensions

In two of the workplace observations in the next section, the central symbolic object that was supposed to communicate information about a pension was the *pension projection*. The projection appeared in two forms, either as an annual 'pension statement' sent to an existing customer, or as a notional pension that formed part of a sales quotation provided to a potential customer. The mathematical model for the projection was the same, although one form involved actual money, and the other hypothetical money. It was interesting to observe that existing customers tended to have expectations about projected values for their pension that had no basis in reality – for example if the actual pension value did not grow according to the projected figures from one year to the next.

Both pension statements and quotations are regulated documents with strict rules for the calculations used and the form of wording prescribed by the national regulator. Figure 4.1 shows a typical form of pension quotation.

Anticipated plan start date: 19 January 2006

Male, born 19 January 1951   Chosen retirement date: 19 January
2016, at age 65

Plan term: 10 years

Transfer payment: £74,550

Total monthly payment: £150

What your pension fund might be at age 65:

	5%	7%	9%
If our investments grow each year at			
your pension fund would be	£134,000	£159,000	£190,000

	2.7%	4.7%	6.7%
If interest rates when you retire are			
you'll get either a pension each year of	£7,830	£11,300	£16,100
or a tax-free cash sum of	£33,500	£39,900	£47,500
plus a smaller pension each year of	£5,870	£8,540	£12,100

Figure 4.1 A pension quotation (based on the type used by National Mutual Pensions)

Figure 4.1 shows that the pension will start with £74,550 transferred from a previous pension plan, and £150 will be paid in each month, for ten years. The calculation of the annual pension amount is based on assuming an effective bank interest rate (5, 7 or 9%) minus 2.3% (which has complex origins to do with historical performance of long-term government bonds). Then the value of the annuity is, say, 2.7% of the final fund value. However, there is a second stage of the calculation: people do not live forever, so pensions are not paid out forever, hence the 2.7% number is multiplied by a life expectancy factor that is derived from the complex mortality models that pensions companies have constructed over many decades for their millions of policy holders.

The models underlying the pension projection

Underlying the pension projections are two calculation models. The first is the growth of the policy holders' investment by compound interest: at rates of 5, 7 or 9% per annum, like a cash savings account.[3] Our ethnography revealed several types of confusion over this. Why were the values of 5, 7, and 9% used, when UK bank interest rates had been around 5% for many years? We heard policy holders ask 'why didn't my pension grow by 7% last year?' – a confusion between model and reality that we found service employees could often only answer by quoting from standard scripts. Neither was it easy for customers to think about a long-term investment (that is, 30 years or more) when nearly all other investments with which they might be involved were for considerably shorter periods of time. Finally, as we shall see, there was the need to appreciate what was meant by a percentage growth rate and how it would impact on the pension; all too frequently, this was read as a pseudo-mathematical label, without any rationale for its derivation or any coherence between the calculation of the different percentage values.

The second calculation model in the statement/quotation concerns the *conversion of the pension fund into an annuity*, a calculation that determines what is received as the monthly payment after retirement. This model is complex, and life expectancy factors are highly confidential, since the key to the annuity business is maximising the pension offered to a customer whilst building in profits for the company by getting the life expectancy calculations correct.

With Profits investment funds

In order to present our workplace observations, we need to explain one more detail, which is the investment fund type known as With Profits. The peculiarity of the With Profits fund is that it is *smoothed* as a kind of rolling average. It grows every year, by an 'annual bonus' percentage decided by the pensions company, that is given even if the actual value of the

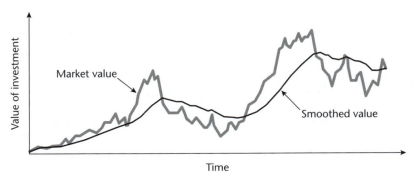

Figure 4.2 Smoothing of investment return in a With Profits fund

investment fund has fallen. Conversely, when the investment fund grows well, the bonus given is less than the actual growth, in order to pay back for the badly performing years. See Figure 4.2.

As we shall describe in the next section, the interesting point is what happens if the investor asks to cash in a With Profits investment after a period of negative performance and before the investment grows again. Then the company reserves the right to take back a proportion of the bonuses paid, through a *market value reduction* penalty. We initially developed a TEBO around this issue, which seemed a promising topic as the mathematics involved is rich, and (at the time of the research) the market value reduction was a frequent subject of concern for customer service. Having piloted the TEBO, we realised that we were too ambitious and the mathematics too complicated – at least for the time we could allocate.

Workplace observations in pensions and investments

We report in this section on our observations in Lifetime Pensions Limited and National Mutual Pensions, covering different company departments, and (where found) current training practices.

Lifetime Pensions: pensions customer enquiries[4]

We began our case study work at Lifetime Pensions (see Box 4.1) by talking to a national training manager at the company headquarters, who suggested that our interest in intermediate-level jobs and employees would be best served by investigating the *back office* departments of the company. The 'front office' is the direct point of contact with the customer, traditionally a physical office, though now mainly via call centres. The back office is where the administration of existing policyholder business takes place.

Box 4.1   Company summary: Lifetime Pensions Limited

Type of business: Pensions, investments and insurance (not observed).

Location: Several offices across the UK. Research was done in back office departments at (1) the headquarters office; (2) a large administrative office in a university town; and (3) a retail investments administrative office in a regional city.

Number of employees: Thousands for the whole company across UK; directly studied for the research: 25 in pensions enquiry team, 27 in bonds call centre, 60 in retail investments call centre.

Profile of employees: GCSE mathematics with a good grade is expected (and maths tests for job applicants); A-level maths fairly common (10 to 20% of employees); increasing numbers of graduates in call centres ('that is quite depressing – why go and get a degree in order to get an entry-level job' – trainer comment); one office had large numbers of university students working part-time evening and weekend shifts, who effectively provided the company with higher levels of articulation skills than could typically be expected for such jobs at the salary levels offered.

Employee skills development, including technical training: Induction training is given; employees are expected to pass external, UK-standard qualifications for the business area they work in (during two to three years of employment – company pays all fees for this); only the retail investments office had training specifically targeting mathematical skills (because the qualifications had explicit mathematical content).

Participation in the TmL research: Ethnographic observations of customer service work; co-development of TEBOs and learning opportunities and two separate trials.

The pension statement: a symbolic artefact and its role as a boundary object

Our case-study observations covered back office departments that included but were not restricted to pensions. However, it was quickly evident that much back office activity, though complex (e.g. closing and paying-out matured life insurance policies) involved rather little personal com-munication with policyholders. In other cases, the back office work was fragmented into discrete tasks that required limited appreciation of the whole life cycle of products. Thus in such back office areas there was little need for TmL, so we turned our attention to pensions, and the work of one back office Enquiry Team (ET).

The work of the ET involved interactions with customers, and with other company departments; see Figure 4.3 for a partial illustration of these

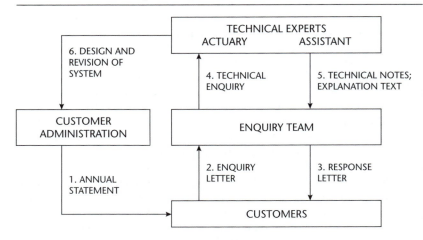

Figure 4.3 'Interactions' involving the pensions Enquiry Team at Lifetime
Pensions. Interactions 2 and 3 were increasingly telephone-based
to improve the engagement with the customer

interactions. It was articulation work of this kind, coordinating and expli-
cating across diverse boundaries, that made TmL a key issue for these
employees. The high-skill technical/IT departments and product development departments (which employed the actuaries who were the central
source of expertise about pensions) were generally remote and inaccessible
to the back office team – a source of difficulty, and of the failure of some
of the symbolic artefacts, such as the pension statement, to serve as boundary objects and communicate information as intended.

The ET handled most enquiries by post (around 80%), although there
was a move to do much more by telephone. Telephone work demanded
that each individual be able to communicate clearly and knowledgeably. It
was not possible to rely on the distributed knowledge among the team, as
was the case in the shared production of response letters. The ET handled
a range of pension queries, which often involved the annual pension
statement (which took a form similar to Figure 4.1), sent out to all pension
plan holders. The ET dealt directly with about 80% of queries received; the
remainder had to be passed on to technical experts, principally an actuary
who (unusually, it seems) had been appointed to work in a supporting role
in the back office. This actuary was much liked by all the back office team
for his approachability and willingness to take time to explain technical
details of pensions; this contrasted with the actuarial department as a
whole that was perceived as remote and unwilling to help. The actuary was
further supported by an assistant who was a mathematics graduate.

Prior to the shift to telephone responses, the basis of the work of the ET
had been the production of response letters, which comprised pieces of
explanatory text, many of which were standardised. In general, the ET knew

how to match the appropriate text with a customer enquiry. Those they could not match were handed on to the actuary or his assistant to produce new text for the ET to insert into letters to policyholders. These explanatory texts were a mixture of answers to the specific situation of the policyholder, and general descriptions of how pension plans work with illustrative examples. A typical hand-on query would involve questions about management charges, sometimes accompanied by the policyholder's own set of calculations that were at variance with the company's. The ET saw such queries as the most problematic, since to answer them required an appreciation of the inputs and constraints of the mathematical models arising from individual customer characteristics. We also found that the actuary regarded his carefully crafted explanatory texts as not only for the policyholder, but also as a means for the ET to learn about the underlying mathematical models. He told us that he was constantly disappointed that this rarely happened, commenting that he saw the 'same' query coming to him over and over again. His meaning of 'the same' was that there was a common underlying general situation – the same relationships merely with changes in the specific values. Yet employees in the ET could not perceive the similarities. Our observations of the ET supported this: even if ET members did understand a particular text, they did not see it as an example of a more general category, so the actuary's explanations were not generalised. Fundamentally, the major issue was the limited appreciation of any *general* structure that underpinned the models, which became central in the design of our TEBO and the learning opportunities conducted in Lifetime Pensions.

Observations on training

We found surprisingly little trace of company-based training for the ET. There was mentor-based induction training, where new employees would be supported by experienced colleagues as they started work, but little, if any, off-the-job training courses on offer, despite evidence that it would be appreciated.

> Manager comment: 'There is a central training team doing generic things, introduction to pensions, introduction to investments. We don't often use them, because they are not often available . . . . There is a compulsory central induction course, which only runs when there are enough people to take it, so it could be three or four months after the new person starts . . . in reality we hardly use central training. I have complained to the HQ training manager about that, and he is working on it. They are always saying they are under-staffed, or they need a minimum of eight participants for a course.

The company expected all employees to become qualified in the basic levels of the UK national 'pensions administration' certificates within a few years of joining the company, and funded them to do this. Our surprise in reviewing the content of these qualifications was that, even at the highest level (tier 5) the course text consisted of hundreds of technical details (definitions and regulations) with only a few mathematical formulae and calculations that would have afforded some coherence to the volume of details.

Lifetime Pensions: With Profits investments telephone-based enquiries

We visited a call centre at LPL after the area manager expressed interest in her employees becoming involved in the learning opportunities trial that we had been invited to devise for the pensions ET. The call centre dealt with various types of bonds, i.e. lump-sum investments, rather than continuously paid investments, such as pensions. There were several manual calculations with which agents had to deal:

> Standard things are automated, like surrender values, but not queries like 'what if I took this?', 'how much can I take without penalty?', 'if I take another £100 what does that leave me on a monthly withdrawal basis?'. There are scenarios which customers ring up about which the agent has got to sound confident on the phone, otherwise that is going to generate more phone calls or letters. . . . If the customer says 'if I take a withdrawal of . . . and then do . . . ' then it starts to get more complicated, and some people can't do it and so they have to call up someone in the team who can do it. We do have a big mix of people in the team, from school-leavers to graduates, so there are different levels of maths knowledge. Some people can do it and some can't, and I worry about them doing it wrong over the phone – I just don't know how much this goes wrong, because we only sample ten calls per month [for each agent] and each person is taking 60 calls per day.
>
> (Call centre manager)

The most challenging queries at the time of our observations (autumn 2005) concerned With Profits bonds. The company had sold a large volume of these bonds, starting in 1999. Customers nearly always treated them as 'five-year investments' – based on the advice apparently given by IFAs and agencies (building societies and banks). Lifetime Pensions, however, described With Profits bonds as long-term investments, more than ten years. They were only five-year investments in the sense that a significant surrender penalty was applied if the bond was cashed within the five years. Thus in 2004 and 2005, many policyholders were calling up for a valuation of their investment, looking to cash it in. Unfortunately, the various economic and political events around 2001–2 ('dot com' bust, 9/11 terrorism) meant that a bond purchased in 2000–2001 would be liable to a large *market value reduction*, MVR, in 2005, and IFAs certainly had not been keen to emphasise the existence of such a penalty at the time of purchase.

> The agents may quote from policy terms and conditions, if people are not aware of those, and we can send customers the With Profits Guide. But some people just don't get it – they say 'the stock market collapse of 2001 is so long ago, it must have recovered by now' and so we have to explain that the With Profits fund has still not recovered. We do get a lot of calls about MVR [market value reduction]. The agents have a table of MVR percentages, based on year/quarter of issue and invest-ment type. The percentages are set by the actuarial experts. We're not part of that.
>
> (Call centre manager)

Given that our observations indicated that investors – and even employ-ees – had limited understanding of the MVR, we developed a learning opportunity and associated TEBO to open up the ideas of MVR penalties, which we elaborate in the next section (under the heading TEBO 3).

Lifetime Pensions: retail investments telephone-based enquiries

The administrative office of the retail investments division of Lifetime Pensions operated quite independently of the parent company. It was a young organisation, established around ten years previously, and appeared to have a different culture from the other offices we visited. Company-based training seemed to be more active, and included mathematical train-ing as part of induction, offered on a voluntary basis.

We observed work in the call centre, talking to one of the most experi-enced employees, and listening to phone calls. Compared with the previous observations, there was rather little non-routine activity that would chal-lenge agents in the need to explain and articulate. We were told this was due in part to the nature of the products – whereas for pensions there was a definite model (projection of fund values) that could be queried, in invest-ments the base of most products was the stock market (UK, or other markets, or other types of equities). The customer expectation was therefore that there was no rational basis or model for understanding any increase or decrease in fund values. There was also a general issue of keeping control of 'advice' versus 'non-advice' (information) in a telephone dialogue:

Researcher: Do you get issues when customers think their fund is worth something different from what you say, or they don't follow how charges have been applied?

Agent: I would not have a problem with those. Say, a fund was worth £3000, a 1% charge was applied, which is £30. Or for finding a value, it's the number of units held times the bid price. We don't go much beyond that, over the phone. We're not trained to be advisers here. If more complicated questions come up, it's tricky to deal with those without seeming to give advice, which customers may act upon.

The main focus of interest for us at this site was the training organised for staff as this had not been seen at other LPL sites. The director of training felt that new employees adapted well to the day-to-day work, supported by putting some mathematics into the induction training as an optional course. His major concerns were the challenges faced by employees studying for the national qualification (IAQ, Investment Administration Qualification), which included many calculations, with some mathematical complexity. The area where the trainer felt we could best contribute was helping employees 'warm up' to the IAQ level 1 training. Two key issues which we exploited later in TEBOs were compound interest and present value. The trainer said that (lower-qualified) employees usually became highly functional in the practice, around specific procedures for calculating, but without going into 'why things work', that was needed in IAQ.

There is a period of six months between induction and being entered onto the IAQ programme. In that time they will hopefully develop maths skills, based on answering customer enquiries. So the problem is that they may have mastered the calculations for different products, but when they get to the IAQ with its generic approach to the topics, they can't marry the two together. They don't understand that answering the customer query is the same calculation, such as averaging an index. Then we have to start teaching them again.

We see here the same issue as in pensions enquiries: IAQ often came as a shock to employees, since it required moving to a level of conceptual generality, but with an added problem as it had limited links to what could be effective in practice. Indeed, we found that employees who had successfully passed two or three levels of IAQ, had retained little knowledge about the mathematical contents of the IAQ, and they said that such calculations were rarely encountered in routine practice. IAQ level 1 included topics such as compound interest, interest rates (including Annual Equivalent Rate – AER), bond yields, and the effects of taxation on interest and yields.

The learning opportunities that we developed for this site paid attention to each of these topics, but with an emphasis on interest rates and compound interest (for which we had already developed learning opportunities whilst working with other sites), and connecting these calculations to practice by incorporating discussion around authentic symbolic artefacts transformed into TEBOs (TEBOs 1–4). We also developed two further TEBOs (TEBO 5 and TEBO 6), specifically to enable exploration of compound interest and present value by allowing the manipulation of the key variables, suppressing detail and relying on visual interactions. As with other companies/sites, we undertook the first pilots of learning opportunities expecting to be able to return for further, more extensive trials with an expanded range of topics. This turned out not to be possible as (yet again) there was a major reorganisation of the business. Later, we report our findings from the pilot and our reflections on the design of the TEBOs.

National Mutual Pensions (NMP): pension sales support

Our research with NMP took place on two sites, both offices where small teams of Sales Support staff provided an administrative role for Sales Consultants, who spend most of their time on the road visiting networks of IFA offices. One office was in London, and was atypical in that it dealt with a large number of high-income clients (City workers) with high-value pension plans. We were told that the City-based IFAs tended to be much sharper and more demanding than the average.

The London office employed eight sales support staff, producing about 700 quotations per week for new business – 65% pensions, 25% life products (ISAs, investment bonds), 10% protection products (insurance). The office handled about 1,200 phone calls per week from IFAs. Some of these calls were 'post-sales' and so strictly should have been dealt with by another office, however the idea was to build relationships with each IFA, so handling these calls had become part of providing an enhanced service.

Box 4.2   Company summary: National Mutual Pensions

Type of business: Pensions, investments and insurance (not observed).

Location: Many offices across the UK. Research was done at two pensions sales administration offices, one in London and one in Southern England.

Number of employees: Thousands across the UK. Each sales administration office had about ten sales support staff, working for a similar number of Sales Consultants.

Profile of employees: GCSE mathematics with a good grade is expected, and maths test for job applicants; A-level maths fairly common (10 to 20% of employees), some 'Arts' degrees. Financial services qualifications would far outweigh academic qualifications in appointing new staff.

Employee skills development, including technical training: Induction training is given; employees are expected to pass external, UK-standard qualifications for the pensions business, during two to three years of employment (company pays all fees for this, but will not fund study for the higher qualification levels which allow someone to operate as an independent financial adviser).

Participation in the TmL research: Ethnographic observations of customer service work; co-development of learning opportunities and two separate trials.

The London manager, Patrick, had been working in the office for 15 years. Numbers of staff had fallen from 60 previously to 25 at the time of our observations in 2006. Patrick said that arithmetical skills used to be essential, at least in terms of manually extracting values from tables: before 1995 there were many manual calculations using formulae, e.g. interest rate tables. Now, 'people punch numbers, without knowing why things happen'. We were not able to discover to what extent employees used to know 'why things happen' before computers rendered manual skills unnecessary, though Patrick felt there was a difference.

In dealing with pensions quotations, the key information was fed back to the office from a sales consultant working with IFAs in the field. The office staff then produced a full quotation, including the projection for value of the investment at retirement (such as Figure 4.1 above) and sent it with supporting documentation to the IFA. If the client signed up for the pension, the office served as a point of contact for tracking the process of the pension set-up.

Our findings concerning the degree of employee understanding of the pension quotation were similar to those from Lifetime Pensions: most employees could describe in words what the quotation involved, but the numbers appeared to be pseudo-mathematical, labels and fragments with little effective knowledge of the mathematical relationships underlying them. Patrick agreed: he was concerned that this superficial reading of the symbols meant that employees were passive in their interaction with customers. He wanted his staff to be actively 'helping the sale' by promoting the positive benefits of the National Mutual pension plan, compared with competitor offerings that IFAs would also be assessing for each client. For example, National Mutual, unlike its competitors, offered a reduction in annual management charge for larger funds invested, *a large fund reduction*. The problem was that in the computer-generated quotation this reduction was simply applied automatically and was consequently invisible – to sales employees and to customers. There was no way to 'see' the change that the reduction had made to the long-term value of the pension. In the TEBO and learning opportunities therefore, we devised a 'discussion activity' with Patrick's help, which asked employees to study the effect of large fund reduction using a spreadsheet model, and to find a way of explaining it to an IFA in a convincing way (see next section, TEBO 2).

Summary

Observations across the two companies and their different sites pointed to a consistent set of issues that are summarised in Boxes 4.3 and 4.4. Despite a recognition, by both managers and employees, that knowing more about the mathematical calculations performed by the IT systems should lead to better performance by service employees in articulating information for customers, there was a general pattern of 'maths avoidance' running through working practices and training. We therefore set out to develop learning opportunities for employees that would open up some of the models in the IT systems, and allow them to engage with parts of the model where lack of visibility had impaired articulation. The major issues identified in our case studies were: pension projections, large fund reduction in annual management charges (at NMP), smoothing and MVR for With Profits funds, compound interest and present valuing.

Box 4.3   Techno-mathematical literacies at stake

- reading and interpreting financial statements (e.g. pension statements/quotations);
- growth (interest rates, compound interest) and 'present value' of money (including frequency of interest payments, management charges applied to financial products);
- developing personal models – generalising from individual cases based on similar mathematical structure.

Box 4.4   Symbolic artefacts for pensions and investments

- pension statement/quotation based on projection by compound interest;
- large fund reduction (at National Mutual Pensions);
- With Profits funds and smoothing, market value reduction penalty;
- compound interest and present value for investment products.

Pensions and investments: TEBOs and learning opportunities

The findings from our observations in pensions and investments indicated that understanding of the mathematical models involved in financial products was limited and not expected for service employees; this was evident even for the most basic mathematical models, e.g. compound interest. Employees usually knew where a compound interest calculation was used, some could state what compound interest involved (it pays 'interest on interest'), yet very few were able to make a calculation, estimate a result, or recognise the elements of the relevant mathematical formula. Crucially, many could not distinguish between the fact that compound interest was a calculation whose outcome they could estimate or calculate quite simply with a calculator, while other calculations, particularly for annuities purchased using pension funds, involved complex models that were not easily calculated or approximated. All the numbers in the pension projection were equally perceived as invisibly performed by the IT system. The pension projection was therefore identified in the workplace observations as a crucial, but not very effective, symbolic boundary object.

This led us to design TEBOs and learning opportunities around this artefact and the ideas of compound interest and projection that we judged could be understood by customer service teams. Our aim was to address the problem in terms of literacy: how could the projections be read to make sense? What were the crucial variables? What was invisible and needed to be highlighted? What were the 'landmark values' for compound interest calculations? How could some awareness of these relationships assist in the difficult articulation work that was increasingly demanded?

We carried out four cycles of design and trialling of the TEBOs, in the following sequence:

1   Lifetime Pensions, Southern England office;
2   National Mutual Pensions, London office;
3   National Mutual Pensions, Southern England office;
4   Lifetime Pensions retail investments, national administration office.

In the following, we will not give details of these cycles, but rather describe the major TEBOs developed and how they were used within different learning opportunities.

We do stress the methodological importance of iterative cycles of development. A major evolution through the cycles in financial services was our growing realisation of the need to maximise dialogue, between employees, and between us and the employees. The first cycle of learning opportunities were over-full of activities, driven by a desire on our part to address as many authentic problems based on practice as possible. Yet it was quickly evident that dialogue around activities was essential for employees to reflect their experiences back into practice and to begin to develop a language to express themselves. The Lifetime Pensions actuary, who advised us extensively on the design of the learning opportunities, put it like this:

> Telling the customer, 'I've used a spreadsheet and the answer is correct', doesn't go far enough. It is the explanation which tests you. Because, does the customer understand? What you've done so far [i.e. the first development cycle] seems to be beginning the enabling of our staff about where the numbers come from. The next step is maybe, 'now explain it to the customer'.
>
> (Interview with actuary, Lifetime Pensions)

Following feedback, with each cycle, we reduced the number of activities, and introduced *discussion activities*, whose aim was to invite employees to articulate and explain their new knowledge triggered by problems drawn from customer interactions we had collected in our ethnography. The development of the TEBOs involved a similar process of trial and refinement, so that they effectively coordinated our pedagogical approach and the development of the relevant TmL.

Box 4.5   Technology-enhanced boundary objects (TEBOs) for pensions and investments

TEBO 1: Spreadsheet models of pension projections

TEBO 2: Spreadsheet model of Large Fund Reduction

TEBO 3: Spreadsheet model of smoothing of With Profits fund and market value reduction

TEBO 4: Spreadsheet model of investing for a future value

TEBO 5: Visual tool for compound interest

TEBO 6: Visual tool for 'present value' of an amount required in the future

---

Preparatory activities

In all four cycles, we started with two preparatory activities not concerned with actual financial products. Our intention was to familiarise participants with some of the mathematical machinery (such as percentages) and the spreadsheet tools needed to interact with the TEBOs. We also aimed to introduce the dialogue-based style of the sessions, substantively different from some employees' idea of training courses. In each cycle, we also aimed to make space for discussion in order for us to learn from the participants and to try to connect better with their goals.

New York Shopping Trip

The first preparatory activity was based on the hypothetical context of British tourists on a shopping trip in New York:

> Geoff and Susan book themselves a bargain long-weekend break in New York City. Going into shops, they find it a bit confusing that all prices are given without 'sales tax' added, and then a sales tax of 8% is added when they pay at the till.
>
> In one electronics shop, they find a special offer of all digital cameras with 15% discount. They decide to buy a camera which has an original

(pre-discount) price of $250. At the till, the shop assistant takes 15% discount from the original price and then adds the sales tax.

Geoff is not happy with this and complains to the manager: he thinks the assistant should add the sales tax first, and then take off 15%, because that way he will get a bigger discount.

Who is right – Geoff or the assistant – and why?

In fact, there is *no difference* in the final price of the camera by one order of calculation or the other: the mathematical structure of percentages is that multiplication is commutative, a formal way of saying that the order does not matter. Out of about 30 employees/managers across the four cycles (as well as many more educators, mathematicians, scientists, etc. at seminars and conferences where we discussed this research), only a handful suggested initially that the price would be 'about the same' and there was a general feeling that there must be a difference between the two calculations. One reason that employees might not have realised the structure, is that when using electronic calculators, as they mainly did, one actually presses '+ 8 %' so that it appears to involve addition/subtraction. The act of devising percentage formulas in a spreadsheet forces attention on the mathematical structure of the '+ 8 %' key presses, and so on.

This activity worked surprisingly well as it provoked a range of responses and opened some windows on the mathematical issues at stake:

- *How contexts frame thinking.* From a mathematical perspective, the context is irrelevant and the question requires: a) the expression of the percentage changes as multiplicative (not obvious); and b) recognition of the commutativity of multiplication – specifically that 0.85×1.08 is equal to 1.08×0.85. By contrast, employees took the context seriously and in several cases insisted that only one way would be *legally* correct, an interpretation that simply had not occurred to us in designing this activity: 'The 8% tax has to be on the price paid, so the customer is not right'. Whilst there is no difference in the price paid by the customer, employees were concerned that the *amount of tax paid to the government would be different.*
- *Equivalence of numerical outcome was not convincing as an argument for equivalent structure.* This was equally surprising to us. When one employee checked the two options with a calculator, he said that 'the numbers come out the same', and accused us of 'cooking the books' by choosing particular numbers that gave this same result. This conveniently motivated a follow-on step that we used in all the cycles: to model the situation in a spreadsheet so that how the situation worked with other numbers (and developing formulae) could be explored.

In summary, the activity served as a useful starter, in order to consider the relationship between calculations and contexts, and appreciate calculations as outputs to a model. The activity also served as an example of how we thought we had fully understood the problem context and knew what the employees needed to learn; in fact, the employees knew something that we needed to learn.

My Rich Aunt

The second preparatory activity aimed mainly to introduce participants to the use of formulae and calculations in Excel. We amended a well-known introductory spreadsheet activity (from the 'SMILE' curriculum materials[5]), 'My Rich Aunt', as follows:

> My aunt is very rich. I am her only living relative. She invites me round to afternoon tea and informs me that in her will, she is leaving all her wealth to the local cats' home. However she is willing to give me an annual allowance until her death. She is currently 70 years old. I can choose one of the following options:
>
> - £1 this year, £2 next year, £4 the following year, doubling each year;
> - £100 this year, £200 next year, £300 the following year, and £100 more each year;
> - I may take £6,000 now to invest for myself but only access after ten years, or my aunt will invest the money for me and give me £10,000 in ten years' time.[6]

The three options are represented graphically in Figure 4.4.

We found that nobody predicted the explosive exponential growth of the doubling option, which is not apparent in the early years compared with

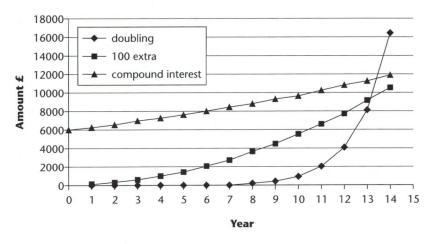

Figure 4.4 A graph of the growth of the three options of 'My Rich Aunt' for 14 years

the other options. Our experience with My Rich Aunt was that, except for two employees who criticised its unreality (i.e. the aunt could not be rich enough to offer the first option), the activity was very engaging and successful in opening windows on the mathematical issues at stake. First, it evoked genuine surprise: 'I would never have thought [in Option 1] that the money would have been more after the twenty years than the other ones. So I just found that really interesting.' Second, participants reported they had learned new functionalities of Excel as a modelling tool, needed later for exploring the actual financial products with which they were familiar. We found that although all the participants were regular users of Excel at work, few realised that formulae could be entered, and models constructed – at work, all usage was simply entering numbers in pre-written templates, thus rendering the models essentially invisible.

Following the preparatory activities, participants explored issues arising in finance with our TEBOs.

TEBO 1: spreadsheet models for pension projections

Our first TEBO was a reconstruction of the pension projection (Figure 4.1), using a spreadsheet. The task involved creating formulae for interest amounts and fund values for all the years up to retirement; a given template spreadsheet laid out all the columns and rows required. Through the dragging down of formulae in the spreadsheet, the participants could calculate growth by compound interest without the need to use the standard mathematical formula (which would be, for example, £14,223 $\times$ $(1 + 5/100)^{16}$ to find the value of a fund after 16 years with 5% annual interest – see Figure 4.5). We judged that introducing formulae with powers would be off-putting. However, this structure of repeated multiplication is implicit in the drag-down relationship in the spreadsheet, and the repeated application of the same dragging operation (for the 5, 7, 9% interest rates) emphasised the presence of the *same* formula underlying the calculations. We knew from earlier interviews that such knowledge was lacking.

> We don't know [about the calculations in the system]. We've been asking for a long time for things like this . . . we [would] like to know how a benefit system projects the figures, what is the calculation behind that, we probably wouldn't understand it if we were just given the calculation, but for someone to explain properly how they come to these figures, how it has been input onto the system. . . . The [statements] project forward maybe 40 years' time to an estimated fund value. Obviously that's projected forward at a growth rate but the actual calculation I haven't a clue how it is done. . . . Some [actuaries] are still very reluctant to give any information to you – they just say, 'the customer doesn't need to know this' – but I can't tell a customer that, they won't accept it. It would make our jobs a lot easier if even a

	A	B	C	D
4				
5				
6	Year	Value	Interest earned	Interest rate
7	0	14,223.00	711.15	5.00
8	1	14,934.15	=B8 × /D8/100	5.00
9	2	=B8+C8	784.04	5.00
10	3	16,464.90	823.25	5.00
11	4	17,288.15	864.41	5.00
12	5	18,152.55	907.63	5.00
13	6	19,060.18	953.01	5.00
14	7	20,013.19	1,000.66	5.00
15	8	21.013.85	1,050.69	5.00
16	9	22,064.54	1,103.23	5.00
17	10	23,167.77	1,158.39	5.00
18	11	24,326.16	1,216.31	5.00
19	12	25,542.46	1,277.12	5.00
20	13	26,819.59	1,340.98	5.00
21	14	28,160.57	1,408.03	5.00
22	15	29,568.60	1,478.43	5.00
23	16	31,047.03	1,552.35	5.00
24	**Annuity**	838.27		
25				
26	**Lump sum**	7,761.76		
27	**Annuity**	628.70		

Figure 4.5 Extract from an Excel spreadsheet for simplified pension projections (TEBO 1), for the case of 5% annual interest growth. Cells C8 and B9 show the two formulae in use, which simply repeat in every row (calculate interest for year, and add to the total for next year)

few experienced members of the team knew how these in-depth calculations were done.

(Lifetime Pensions, Enquiry team)

Our concern in the time available within the pilot training was to establish connections to the workplace context, and show the calculations behind the numbers without recourse to standard algebra. Thus we did not worry about leaving participants with only the alternative symbolism of the spreadsheet. The major TmL here was developing an appreciation of the existence of relationships that are built into the IT system, rather than their explicit (algebraic) representation.

We started with the simplest case of a 'closed' fund without any new contributions. Employees then progressively explored more complex layers in the models underlying the pension statement by building in more details, such as regular annual or monthly payments into the pension fund and management charges which the company deducted from the fund. We did not attempt to model the exact calculation of the annuity, as it was beyond a simple treatment; we used the approximate version of *(final fund value)* × *(the percentage used for projection minus 2.3%)*, which is $(5 - 2.3) = 2.7\%$, the case shown in the actual pension projection of Figure 4.1.

Employees were impressed, and so were we, that the spreadsheet models were able to calculate to within a few pounds of the actual pension fund values as generated by the company IT systems – our TEBO proved to be quite authentic!

Through these activities, the participants were progressively able:

- to make visible and work with the different parameters and models in the pension statement, e.g. lengths of time, management charges as well as interest rates;
- to differentiate between relationships and values that were *real* constraints in the models from those that were conventional or hypothetical;
- to appreciate that the way the fund value accumulates through compound interest was the result of a *fixed* relationship, while the interest rates used were both conventional (specified by the national financial regulator) and hypothetical.

The level of engagement with the activities around this TEBO was very high, and participants evidently began to appreciate elements of the mathematical models underlying pensions calculations and to distinguish the different elements and layers of the model that were accessible to them from those that were not (such as the annuity calculation). One employee commented:

It's not just magic . . . to me projections were just – someone gave you the figures over there and how they arrived at them was just magic! Now I can see what it is, it makes sense.

TEBO 2: spreadsheet model of large fund reduction

TEBO 2 used a spreadsheet model of the same form as TEBO 1, but added what was an invisible feature of the NMP pension plan, the Large Fund Reduction of management charges. We asked the employees to calculate the effect of the LFR using the TEBO, and then, in discussion, to construct an argument to convince an IFA of the benefits of NMP's pension plan. The charge reductions were:

Total fund value LFR each year

£10,000–20,000   0.05%
£20,000–50,000   0.10%
£50,000 and over 0.20%

These do not seem large differences, yet the accumulating effect of compound interest leads over time to surprisingly significant effects. The activity is given in Figure 4.6.

This calculation required simply to use TEBO 2, first to calculate the fund growth over 42 years at, say, 7% annual interest, and with the monthly payments increasing each year by an inflation factor (NMP used 4% as a notional figure for this), and a management charge of 1% per annum. This charge could be applied by reducing the annual interest growth to 6%, although this is an approximation and is not quite the same as the exact calculation of deducting 1% from the value of the fund each year. Then, the effect of LFR is determined by progressively adjusting the interest rate upward to 6.05%, 6.10% and 6.2% as the fund value grows. The net effect for this imaginary client, who quickly reaches the threshold of £50,000, was an increase in final fund value of nearly 5%, a significant advantage.

An IFA calls to the office with a query about a quotation that has been prepared for his client, Mr Smith. The IFA is comparing quotations from several different companies and he does not understand what is the actual financial benefit to his client of the Large Fund Reduction.
Here are Mr Smith's details:

- Current age: 23
- Planned retirement date: 65
- Approximate annual salary: £90,000
- Proposed monthly payment: £1000, index-linked

What could you say or show to the IFA to illustrate how the LFR will work for Mr Smith, and the amounts of money involved?

Figure 4.6 Activity on the large fund reduction (TEBO 2)

This activity worked very well in engaging the employees and encouraging them to think about 'selling the product' – the manager's primary aim. In a follow-up interview several weeks after the training pilot, the manager and employees told us that several instances had arisen where 'selling the incentive' to the IFA had happened. The manager reported to us that his staff had developed the ability to explain the LFR, something which had not existed before:

> I had an IFA who phoned and said that he had a client who wanted to know how much he would have to put into an ISA over 23 years at 7% growth to get £189,000 back at the end of 23 years. What would the monthly payments be? The IFA was asking for a quote. I almost felt like saying, well me doing a quote I can tell you now on an Excel spreadsheet, but because the ISA was a 1% contract it is very easy to work out how much you would need per month, 7% growth with a 1% charge to hit a certain amount. . . . I don't think I would have had that conversation prior to the training that we did with you.
>
> (Employee interview, National Mutual Pensions)

TEBO 3: smoothing of With Profits funds and market value reduction

For TEBO 3, we set up a spreadsheet that showed historical data for the FTSE100 index[7] contrasted with growth curves for 'smoothed investments' bought at different times (see Figure 4.7). The smooth curve on the left (the lowest in Figure 4.7 referring to an investment in April 1984) could be controlled by a slider to vary the annual growth rate, and then compared to the FTSE100 index growth. We asked the employees to look at the different investments shown, made at different times, and to estimate where an MVR would be applied and its approximate size.

Whilst this TEBO did reveal underlying ideas about 'where MVR came from', we found that there was not much for employees *to do* with the TEBO, and making the model more realistic and open for exploration rapidly became too sophisticated; for example, actual funds have variable annual growth rates, variable management charges depending on how they were sold, etc. Thus after trying it out once, in spite of having much interesting detail, and being a direct response to an observed need for employees to be able to explain more, we decided not to develop it further.

TEBO 4: investing for a future value

TEBO 4 represented a further step towards using the spreadsheet models of pension projections, this time to explore *projecting backwards*, i.e. the opposite of compounding. This phenomenon was illustrated in the following question:

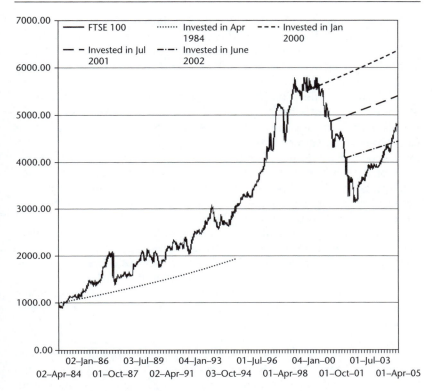

Figure 4.7 TEBO 3: spreadsheet with interactive graph to model With Profits smoothing and the MVR. The lines on the right show cases of investments where (from left to right) maximum, medium and zero MVR would be applied: the line of small dashes shows an investment made in Jan 2000 (at the peak of market values), and with a smoothed growth of 2.5% per year. In April 2005, it is evident that the gap between the current 'value' of the investment and the current market value (FTSE index) is of the order of 22%, hence an MVR of about this amount would be applied; for the investment bought in July 2001, the gap is of order 11%, and for June 2002, the gap is negative, hence no MVR is applied

Assume I want a certain annuity, say £24,000 per year, at the age of 65, what yearly premium should I pay starting now, given that my current age is 20, or 25, or 30, or 35?

From the prior perspective of the employees, we observed that *this seemed like a totally different question to making a projection* and indeed, in terms of writing down a formula, it is a more difficult question to answer mathematically. However, we wanted to stress the structure in common with the previous calculations. We did so by introducing an *approximate* backwards calculation. Thus we utilised the same spreadsheet model and emphasised the existence of the same mathematical relationships as TEBOs 1 and 2, by trying iteratively with different yearly premiums to arrive at the required annuity.

This pedagogic decision illustrates our general design concern: not to attempt to bring into the foreground all that may be considered essential from a mathematical point of view (the exact formula for the backwards calculation is not difficult to state, but it requires a substantial mathematical diversion). Rather, we decided to let the software tool black-box some of the mathematical details, thus leaving some layers of the model deliberately hidden, while opening others for investigation. It was a co-design decision among managers and research team as to which layers were opened and which were left closed.

The backward approximation activity led to an interesting discovery of Patrick's personal techno-mathematical knowledge. Patrick was the department manager with considerable experience in the business. He had developed his own general and precise strategy for hitting future fund targets, by manipulating the inputs and outputs of his company's pension projection system. Given a target value for a fund (T), he would guess a monthly premium (Mg) and calculate the resulting final fund value (Vg) in the system; then the required monthly premium, M, is given by $T / Vg \times Mg$. Although he was not able to express any of his strategy in conventional mathematical terms as algebra, he nevertheless had a good appreciation for how it worked which he could explain by engaging with the backward-calculation spreadsheet, TEBO 4:

> What I'm doing is, if we had done this figure [Mg] and it [Vg] had been exactly half of what we needed [T], then it would be obvious just to double the payment. So all I've done is that – divide what we wanted by what we had and use that as a factor to apply to the contribution . . . so basically just pro-rata'd it up.[8]

Patrick made use of a powerful heuristic: 'use simple numbers to see what happens'.[9] He also appreciated the range of applicability of his technique; he knew that if the initial fund value was not zero, then it was necessary to separate the calculation into two parts: use compounding to calculate the growth of the initial fund, and then use a target value for the monthly premiums, which is the difference between the total target and the final compounded value of the initial fund.

TEBO 5: visual tool for compound interest

During our development cycles and from our ethnography, we noted a need for a different type of TEBO for working with ideas of compound interest. We found a common and overriding problem with understanding the effects of compounding interest over different periods: for example, what would be the equivalent rate for a monthly compounding to give the same growth as an annual compounding of, say, 5%? We first noted this problem in working with the pension projection spreadsheet, when we asked participants to switch from annually compounded growth of the pension to the more realistic case of monthly compounded growth. We expected that they would be able to make the change approximately by dividing 5% by 12, even if they could not calculate the exact equivalent. However, we found that most employees in our sample did not recognise any relationship between the two rates. Others did indeed assume that the simple division or multiplication (annual rate = 12 times monthly rate, or monthly rate = annual rate / 12) gave the *precise* answer.[10]

We tried various ways to explore the relationships between different compounding periods using a spreadsheet, but we found this did not lend itself to clarifying the relationships. We noticed that the sheer volume of numbers in columns and rows of spreadsheets, often hindered the development of a global picture of a situation. Additionally, the intricacies of entering formulae often led to obscure syntactic errors that were very hard to trace. Moreover, it was not easy to think visually in a spreadsheet as the numbers themselves were the main interface. Of course, it would have been possible to program buttons, slider controls and graphical windows in a spreadsheet to hide the numbers, but this required a level of sophistication that the employees did not have. Moreover we wanted to stress in using the spreadsheet the direct engagement with the numbers and their relationships expressed as formulae, so that additional, hidden programming would be a source of confusion.

This led us towards developing another kind of TEBO for financial mathematics in the form of a simpler, visual tool with a manipulative interface, which aimed to focus attention on one key financial-mathematical concept – in this case, compound interest.

In TEBO 5, the learner can manipulate the major three parameters in calculating compound interest, namely: starting value, interest rate per period, and number of periods. The TEBO then calculates the final value, using the standard algebraic formula:

$$Final\ value = (starting\ value) \times (1 + (interest\ rate\ \%\ per\ period) /100)^{(number\ of\ periods)}$$

We used the TEBO to explore the mathematical relationships of the formula: for example, if the starting value was doubled, what happens to the final value? If the interest rate was doubled, what happens to the final value?

Employees had no confident prior answers to such questions, yet they are important 'rules of thumb' – if a customer wishes to double his/her

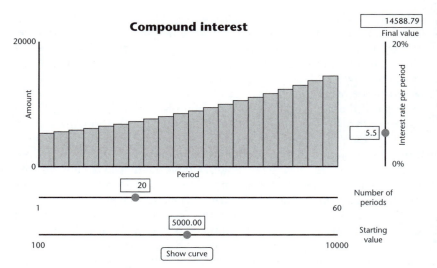

Figure 4.8 TEBO 5: a 'visual calculator' to model compound interest. The parameters can be changed by typing numbers into the boxes, or by dragging the sliders.

initial investment in an interest-based product, it needs no calculation to know that the final value of the investment will be doubled also. Another rule initially mentioned by the Lifetime Pensions actuary was the '70/*i*' doubling time, i.e. the time required to double an initial investment is approximately 70 divided by the interest rate *i* expressed as a percentage (so the doubling time for 5% growth is approximately 14 years). The actuary said that he used this rule frequently as a mental aid whilst in conversations or presentations where a calculator or pen-and-paper was not accessible.

This kind of 'landmarking' is more than knowing some special cases: on the contrary, knowing key pieces of the puzzle gives form to any formal or quasi-formal rules that may be implicit, and helps to give a sense of, for example, the directionality of the relations, the local maxima and minima and approximate shape of the function(s).

TEBO 6: visual tool to calculate the present value of an amount required in the future

We designed a second visual tool, TEBO 6, a calculator for the 'reverse' of compound interest, the *present value*: If you know the final value of a compounded growth after N periods of time, and you know the interest rate per period, what is the starting value?

In Figure 4.9, the vertical decreasing bars show the current value of money required to grow (by compound interest) to the value of £200 after

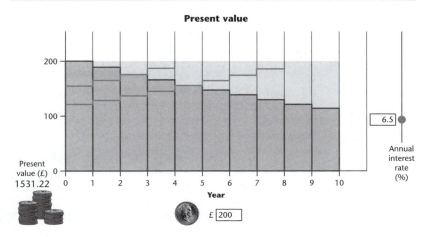

Figure 4.9 TEBO 6: visual calculator for present value.

1, 2, . . ., 10 years. For example, if you want £200 in five years' time, you simply read off the height of the appropriate bar (approximately £160). If you require an income of £200 every year for four years, say, the value of the amount required to be invested *now* is the sum of the first four bars (the higher stepped line going up shows this growth, the lower for eight years).

Present value calculations occur often in financial mathematics, and Lifetime Pensions employees had to be familiar with two cases: the valuation of a bond, and the calculation of an IFA's commission payment if he/she wished to take it as a single payment up front rather than as a sequence of monthly or annual payments. The TEBO fitted with contextual examples of both of these calculations.

We had limited opportunity to test TEBO 6, as it was only designed towards the end of our iterative development cycles. However, there was some evidence to suggest that the visual and manipulative software tools offered an effective means for exploring financial models, and served a complementary role to the spreadsheet TEBOs. We saw employees cross-checking and comparing calculations between the two types of software as they worked on contextual discussion activities simulating customer questions.

Outcomes for learning and practice

Impacts on practice

In terms of impact, our findings were convergent for the different companies and sites, although we were only able to conduct one follow-up visit to each site, one to two months after the TEBO activities had concluded. In these visits, we tried to assess employees' learning in terms of effects on their daily practice. First, there was some evidence that employees found a higher degree of confidence and agency in terms of knowing *how* the artefacts they used actually worked, rather than their superficial form, and this impacted on their articulation work with customers:

> What I see as nice about this project is that it ties in with making the sales support teams more proactive with IFAs. Some of that is about being more confident about the products they work with, which means understanding some of the basic maths behind them.
>
> (Sales support trainer, National Mutual)

> I don't do calculations [in practice], but I understand more, and explaining to the clients. For example, the interest rates on our investments – the activity you had in the session. That's a usual query. Customers say, 'you quoted 7.5% a year, but I'm not getting a quarter [of that, every three months], it gets adjusted'. Before, we used to either get in contact with the finance department [i.e. hand the customer on to get an explanation], or we had a text to speak that we did not understand. It makes you more creative. . . . I don't have to put them on hold, saying 'can I come back to you, because I don't know'.
>
> (Employee interview, Lifetime Pensions)

The most commonly reported effect was in the use of Excel. For example, two team managers reported an immediate change in their using spreadsheets to gather and analyse performance data for their team; one manager said that he had experienced a new understanding of percentages, something he previously disliked, through working in the spreadsheet. Another employee reported:

> I would just say that it feels like I [now] have an extra tool in the toolkit. . . . That little bit of knowledge on Excel, that little bit of formula-type knowledge and a renewed emphasis on mathematics that really had been forgotten for the best part of 15 to 20 years.
>
> (Employee interview, National Mutual Pensions)

This finding is important for understanding the development of TmL. Evidence suggested that we were right in judging that Excel could be employed as an accessible mathematical tool to help employees develop a generalised understanding of relevant financial models underlying the artefacts in use. All the employees had Excel running on their desk computers as part of the standard software set-up. Putting Excel to use was not straightforward, as the regulated practices of financial services did not easily allow employees to make their own innovations in work practice, such as introducing their own tools (any tool used has to be robust enough and thoroughly tested to be compliant with regulations). Nevertheless, as we pointed out above, many of the employees met their first Excel formula with us, despite using implicit formulae all the time in their normal work.

What made a financial TEBO work?

We asked ourselves why reconstructing pension projections turned out to be so successful, and what were the implications of this for our design principles? (see Box 1.1). Part of the answer is, as we have pointed out, the pension statement is the major form of communication between a company and its pensions customers. It was therefore a symbolic artefact that could serve as a boundary object. Service and sales employees needed to deal with it in dozens of cases every day, and explain its output to customers. This is, however, only a partial answer. We had other examples of authentic objects that we unpacked with participants, such as calculations for MVR penalties on investments (TEBO 3), which were not as successful. Conversely, we also saw how far-from-authentic preparatory learning activities set in contexts irrelevant to the workplace – 'New York Shopping Trip' and 'My Rich Aunt' – were successful in generating discussion and mathematical insight.

In retrospect, it seems that one important feature of the pension statement was that we found a way to *layer* the pedagogical approach to match the progressive complexities in the mathematical model of the artefact: first exploring the simplest model for the financial product object (just growth by compound interest), then adding the effects of management charges, then investigating the effects when premiums are paid each month into the pension fund, then the effect of index-linking of payments to compensate for inflation, and so on. The increasing contextual complexity mapped well to the increase in mathematical complexity. In other examples, such as TEBO 3, such a smooth pedagogical process was not accomplished, or perhaps was not possible, despite their mathematical richness and authenticity in practice.

When the TEBOs worked, rather than attempting to bring *all* the mathematical details of the model into the foreground, we let the software tool mediate the mathematics – so the spreadsheet in many situations kept the algebraic formalism encoded within its structure in such a way that the learner could see quite clearly what the formalism was achieving

A further factor concerns the extent to which the TEBO itself affords an illumination of *both* the context and the mathematics involved. We have seen, for example, that the spreadsheet was not an ideal means for gaining an overall picture of the variables and relationships, in which cases rather simpler (visual) tools proved – in some, but not all respects – to be more accessible.[11]

Relating learning opportunities to training

A significant aspect of the co-design process with companies was to understand how our learning opportunities might come to fit into the training and learning cultures of each company. Participants generally recognised that the approach we adopted was effective; yet this was in tension with the current learning culture of some workplaces. In Lifetime Pensions for example, training focused on mentoring and 'buddy learning' with new employees sitting in front of computer screens and learning about specific system functions and procedures. The idea of taking a group of employees away from the workplace for several hours for off-the-job discussion seemed to be regarded as a luxury that needed significant justification. Attitudes to training were different in sites with call centres, where off-the-job training was common and training approaches typically involved much dialogue and sharing of ideas.

Other tensions also became obvious between our pedagogic approach that emphasised exploration and discussion, and the approach adopted by the company trainers. One company training manager at Lifetime Pensions strongly advocated e-learning, in the standard sense of self-study packages that can be accessed flexibly at personal computer terminals. He argued this on grounds of costs and efficiency of employee time, but also because weakness in mathematics was a sensitive issue for an employee, who might therefore wish to address it privately rather than engage in a public dialogue as we had done.

Conclusions

The research reported in this chapter for the financial services sector indicates positive results for the impact of the learning opportunities in the trials. However, unlike the case of the automotive industry in Chapter 3, we were not able to achieve the follow-through into the learning opportunities being independently developed by companies, and disseminate more widely across the sector. In both the companies involved, reorganisations of their service departments happened during the periods of our trials, and this worked against us being able to develop continuing relationships. One sales area trainer at National Mutual reported five major reorganisations of the sales business within two years; he commented, 'you get used to not knowing what is going to happen or where your next job will be'. A further barrier to more widespread implementation in financial services is its highly regulated practices, which do not easily allow employees to make their own innovations or question common practice.

The dominant theme of the work with financial services was the importance of employees coming to appreciate the models underlying financial products. As we have seen, some attempts at developing TEBOs and associated activities were more successful than others. Nevertheless, the widespread perception of key numerical values, such as interest rate, simply as pseudo-mathematical labels was a critical idea that was challenged by the design and deployment of our TEBOs.

We have presented illustrative evidence that after engaging with our activities, customer service employees were more able to appreciate that the numbers did have some rationale, and they were beginning to develop mental models of the products and use them to interpret outputs and respond to customer queries. This impact was evidenced in three main ways: as an enhanced ability to appreciate mathematical abstractions situated in the TEBOs' deployment; a more effective way of articulating the relevant TmL to customers; and an expanded role of service staff in thinking and acting as more autonomous agents able to respond more directly to the problems and technical queries of customers and other employees.

Chapter 5

Financial services 2

Mortgages

This chapter continues the review of our research in financial services workplaces, looking at a mortgage company, Current Mortgage Ltd (CML), which specialised in just one mortgage product, a 'current account mortgage' (CAM). The CAM was a complex product and it was not a simple matter for a prospective customer to understand how s/he might benefit, since there were many factors to quantify and compare with other possible types of mortgage. So it was not an easy sales task to make the case for the CAM. The company therefore became interested in the notion of techno-mathematical literacies and how our approach to improving TmL could impact on their sales practice. At the time of our work in this company (2005–2006), the UK mortgage market was booming and frenetic, with thousands of different mortgage products on offer. Whilst the credit crunch of 2008 has had a huge impact on the mortgage business, we are confident that our findings remain relevant; indeed, as we already noted in Chapter 4, it was the widespread lack of understanding of the mathematics underlying financial products that was a key factor in the financial crisis.

We describe in this chapter what the current sales practice of Current Mortgage was, the existence of gaps in TmL amongst sales agents, and the TEBOs and learning activities that we co-developed with company trainers to address these gaps. In this chapter, we raise two new issues for TmL, in comparison with Chapter 4. The first is that the employees involved were dedicated sales agents rather customer service agents, and the need to sell created tensions about not giving 'advice' to customers yet still promoting the sale of the CAM. The second emphasis concerns the meanings and interpretations of *graphical artefacts*. Due to the complexity of the CAM, Current Mortgage introduced graphs and diagrams in leaflets and publicity to support explanations of the product, in contrast to the standard practice amongst financial services companies (such as those reported in Chapter 4) that did not favour using graphical information as it was more likely to lead to misunderstandings between customers and companies.

The techno-mathematics of the current account mortgage

What is a mortgage?

A mortgage is a loan taken out in order to buy property, and the loan is secured against the property; that is, if the customer is unable to repay the mortgage, then the company has the right to enforce the sale of the property to recover its money. The risks inherent in this arrangement (that the market sale value of the property is not guaranteed to match or exceed the current debt value) mean that the *loan-to-value ratio (LTV)* is crucial: that is the ratio of the amount of money in the debt to the market (or realisable) value of the property. The LTV influences whether a mortgage will be offered to an applicant and the interest rate applied – a high LTV is a greater risk to the company and this is compensated by charging a higher interest rate. This is important, since it was a point of complexity in the calculation of mortgage interest rates that was not appreciated by many customers.

The UK market was very complex at the time of our research, not least because of the frequency of 're-mortgaging', where customers kept a discounted mortgage for the short-term discount period (two or three years), then moved to a new discounted-rate mortgage with another provider. Each time customers moved, they had to pay entry and exit fees, which had to be costed against the cheaper monthly repayments, and compared with maintaining a 'standard' rate mortgage over an extended period of time. Re-mortgaging was one of the complexities of the mortgage market. Others relate to the different mortgage deals on offer, as summarised below.

The current account mortgage (CAM)

The CAM product was introduced to the UK in 1997. The basic idea of the CAM is that the mortgage loan is combined with a savings account and a current account (i.e. a bank account for daily transactions) into one 'bank account'. Any savings or incomes (salaries will be the major regular incomes) put into the account have a *positive* value, which is offset against the *negative* mortgage debt, so that interest is paid only on the difference between the outstanding debt and the amount of savings in the account. For example, if on a certain day the mortgage debt stands at £95,000, or in terms of a single account '–£95,000', and a positive saving is added to the account of £5,000, then the mortgage interest is payable that day on the combined amount, –£90,000.[1] Thus, customers with considerable savings, even for a temporary period, can significantly reduce the overall cost of their mortgage.

The CAM operates essentially as a very large overdraft, that is, a loan facility attached to a bank account. While this is a helpful way to think about the CAM in isolation it cannot be used to make comparisons with a conventional mortgage where different parameters are at work. Moreover it is the conventional mortgage that characterises the discourse of mortgage advertisements, with an overriding concern for low interest rates – even though low interest rate is only one variable that needs to be taken into account.

As the company readily acknowledged, the CAM was not suitable for *all* prospective mortgage customers. The cost of all the flexibilities allowed by the CAM (and consequent risks to the provider) meant that the interest rate was high, at least 1.5% above the national base rate. This made the CAM more expensive than the best repayment mortgage deals around, *unless* the flexible features could all be exploited, in which case there were significant benefits.

> There are three reasons [why the CAM is hard to understand]. The first is paradoxically that the [CAM] is the simplest thing for your finances. You don't need savings, loan, mortgage, you just need one account. However, explaining it to people is quite hard – where are my savings gone? Well, they are in there. But all I can see is a debt. The second reason is that it is not cheap. If you are managing to a budget each month it is not the most economical thing to do, you can get a cheaper fixed rate mortgage and change it again in two years' time. If you are living hand-to-mouth it is not particularly advantageous. And the third reason is, it is almost a sort of emotional difficulty around – all my eggs are in one basket, which is irrational but it is there. You know, when I go to an ATM and the balance of my account doesn't say '+1,000', it says 'minus 93,000'.
>
> (Senior finance manager, interview)

So sales needed to be customised to the individual needs of several target groups, and the distinctive features appropriately articulated by sales personnel. These four features were:

1. Overpayment and underpayment

The CAM has no required monthly payment, unlike a repayment mortgage – although there is a guideline amount to pay based on the standard equalised monthly payment. Underpayment is allowed provided that payback remains broadly on target; hence CAMs are good for people who have irregular incomes and find fixed monthly payments difficult; e.g. self-employed people, who often struggle to be accepted for standard mortgages. Additionally, overpayment beyond the guideline amount is also possible without charge or limitation as is usually the case for repayment mortgages. This means that it is possible to save up in order to pay less later, or make a quick pay-off of the whole mortgage without penalty. This latter case is used as one of the major selling points of the CAM.

2. Negative money

The use of 'negative money' leads to unfamiliar and even counter-intuitive ideas. For example, making a mortgage payment corresponds not to the usual case of actively paying money out to somewhere else, but to the inaction of leaving money in the CAM. All that is taken out of the account is the interest payable on the balance, calculated daily and deducted once per month.

3. Saving interest rather than earning interest

In the CAM, savings have the effect of 'avoiding interest' on a loan rather than earning interest on savings as they normally do. This had an important advantage for tax purposes, as savings in the UK are almost always subject to government tax. Thus 'interest avoided' was at the mortgage interest rate, say 6.5% at the time of the observations, but a 6.5% savings account was not easy to find, and tax at 20% (standard rate) or 40% (higher rate) would have to be paid on the savings interest, reducing the effective interest rate to 5.2 or 3.9%. Higher-rate taxpayers had most to gain from this and were therefore one of the key target groups for CAM sales.

4. Consolidating debt

Another key target group for CAM sales comprised people who had large outstanding debts on, say, credit cards or other high-interest loans. We were surprised to learn that high-interest debts of greater than £10,000 were common amongst prospective CAM customers, involving paying interest at annual rates of 15 to 20%. The benefits of consolidating such debts into a mortgage seemed to us rather clear, as one only needs to compare 20% with 6.5% to sense what can be saved. However, we learnt that this direct comparison of interest rates was far from obvious for customers and even for many employees.

Workplace observations in mortgage sales and customer service

Current Mortgage made direct sales through telephone and internet, with no physical premises for customers to visit. Fifty per cent of new customers had direct contact with the company via telephone or internet, while an intermediary sales department generated an equal amount of new business through dealing with IFAs selling the CAM on a commission basis (see Chapter 4 for a discussion of IFAs in the UK).

Our observations of the company initially ranged across all departments. Eventually we focused on the sales departments, and particularly telephone sales, where we saw the strongest evidence for the necessity of articulation work around technical details of computer output offered by the mortgage

---

Box 5.1   Company summary: Current Mortgage Limited

Type of business: Current account mortgage product; company was wholly owned by a major UK banking and financial services corporation.

Number of employees: 1,200 in total, about 50 in telephone sales.

Profile of employees: For sales work, GCSE mathematics with a good grade was expected, and maths tests were required for job applicants; A-level maths was fairly common, and also non-numerate degree qualifications. This was a university town with a large pool of student/graduate workers. Also it was a base for several large financial services companies, creating a pool of experienced workers.

Employee skills development, including technical training: Induction training for sales work (direct sales and intermediary sales departments) followed by mentored practice on the telephone; special training for different versions of the CAM product and reorganisation of sales functions (which was becoming more frequent).

Participation in the TmL research: Ethnographic observations of sales and customer service work; co-development of learning opportunities, and one trial with telephone-based sales employees.

---

illustration tool (see later, Figure 5.2) and a clear need for TmL amongst intermediate-level employees. The company agreed that this was the case, and allowed us to develop and try out with telephone sales employees and their trainers some prototype TEBOs and associated learning opportunities. These are discussed in the following section.

Telephone direct sales

As was the case in pensions companies (Chapter 4), we observed that articulations between sales or customer service departments, and customers nearly always took place around symbolic artefacts, documents, or IT systems operated by the employee and usually invisible to the customer. For the CAM, the company web site also offered a 'mortgage illustration calculator' with similar functionality to the sales employees' computer system; however at the time of the research observations (summer 2005), the majority of prospective customers using the telephone did not appear to be familiar with the website.

Mortgage illustration tool: the repayment graph

The major symbolic artefact designed to facilitate communication between customer and sales agent (the intended boundary object) was the *mortgage*

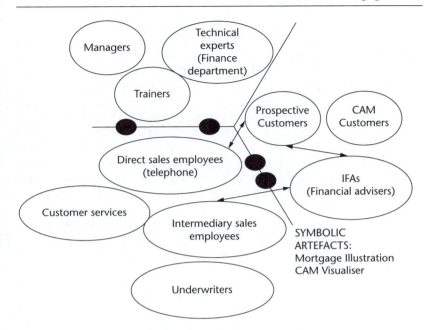

Figure 5.1 Interactions (double arrows) across communities in Current Mortgage Limited. The focus of research was on direct sales employees' engagement with prospective customers, and to a lesser extent intermediary sales engagement with IFAs. The black ovals refer to boundary objects sitting in the middle between different communities.

illustration tool. This tool required the customer (or the sales agent on his/her behalf) to input personal and financial details, as well as data on the property for which the customer was seeking a mortgage, e.g. amount to be borrowed, value of property. If some basic lending criteria were satisfied (e.g., there was no history of failure to repay a mortgage or other mortgage debt), the sales agent entered into a computer-assisted dialogue with the potential customer for 20 to 30 minutes, or sometimes more – the company ethos was to take time to establish a rapport with callers and to make the case for a product that was hard to sell (the standard sales target per employee was 12 full applications per month). During this interchange the customer would be offered different CAM options including assessing the effect of:

*   regular monthly overpayments;
*   lump sum payments put into the CAM on a regular (e.g. work bonuses) or irregular basis (e.g. inheritances);
*   lump sum withdrawals (increasing the debt);
*   other debts consolidated with the mortgage (particularly credit cards).

The dialogue led to the generation by the mortgage illustration tool of one or more printed illustrations of how the customer might use the CAM. Each illustration output a graph and numerical table (see Figure 5.2), showing the repayment curve for a CAM where £20,000 of savings have been offset over the whole lifetime of the mortgage, against the repayment curve of a 'standard' repayment mortgage for comparative purposes, along with values indicating the money that would be saved by taking out the CAM option. (This is an overly simplistic case as most users of a CAM make quite variable repayments, overpaying and underpaying with respect to the 'standard' guideline amount as their financial circumstances change, nor is it likely that £20,000 of savings would sit constantly inside the CAM for such a long period of time; nonetheless this gives an idea of the significant effects of offsetting.)

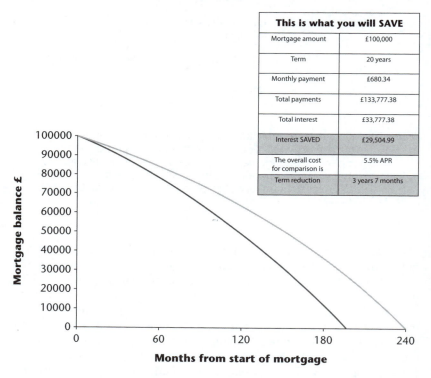

This is what you will SAVE	
Mortgage amount	£100,000
Term	20 years
Monthly payment	£680.34
Total payments	£133,777.38
Total interest	£33,777.38
Interest SAVED	£29,504.99
The overall cost for comparison is	5.5% APR
Term reduction	3 years 7 months

Months from start of mortgage

Figure 5.2 Repayment graph and savings information as generated by the mortgage illustration tool. Shows a standard repayment mortgage of £100,000 borrowed over 20 years (240 months, grey line), compared with offsetting savings of £20,000 for the life of a CAM mortgage (black line). By saving on interest (more than £29,000 over the whole term), capital can be repaid more quickly, saving in the case shown 3 years and 7 months on the 'standard' mortgage term, assuming that the same monthly payment is made regularly

The illustration was not a formal offer of a mortgage – that happened in the next stage of the application process. Illustrations were sent by post and not described in detail during the phone call. Instead, the agent would just summarise the illustration in one sentence as follows:

> Mr Smith, on the basis of the information you have given me, with a current account mortgage you could pay off your borrowing three years and seven months early, and save yourself £29,504.99 in interest. Is that all right for you?

We found it was not clear what the caller was supposed to make of the apparent saving of nearly £30,000. Obviously the intention was to convey that the CAM was a good thing. However, the company told us that these conversations often suffered from the *'too good to be true' factor*: the caller *just did not believe the number quoted*, and – perhaps more important still – *nor in general did the sales employee!* If any caller queried the savings, most employees were unable to make a convincing explanation. The employee generally could do nothing more than simply read from a screen that gave specific information in response to specific data – with no hint of how the system arrived at its calculation, why *that* calculation was the key, or how the specific case might vary with variation in input data. The illustration tool combined all contributing factors into one 'saving' and one graph. More subtle features that were invisible were, for example, the connection between the graph's shape and the amounts repaid each month and how the contributions to capital repayment or interest payment on the debt varied over the lifetime of the mortgage.

The challenge for the company in telephone sales was, therefore, within the space of a brief sales dialogue:

- to help a prospective customer to understand how s/he might benefit by taking out a CAM, in comparison with a repayment mortgage;
- to identify callers whose circumstances were such that they would not benefit from a CAM.[2]

Typical and atypical customers

As suggested by the main features of the CAM outlined earlier, there are several typical customer 'types' judged by sales agents as relatively easy to deal with: an example would be a person with very large credit card debts. The illustration software had been refined over time to match these types, and well-established 'scripts' existed that guided agents how to explain the CAM in appropriate ways and deal with common queries. The minority of prospective customers who asked unusual questions, or who did not wish to follow through the standard long script for illustrations, were likely to find the sales agent 'floundering' – to use the expression of one of the training managers – and unable to answer the customer's question beyond vague generalities.

At the time of our research, the sales climate was changing. Whereas Current Mortgage started out as the dominant provider in a niche CAM market, many competitors had appeared, so that it was no longer possible simply to focus on typical types of customer and non-typical callers needed to be more actively recruited.

The mortgage illustration tool as a potential boundary object: a case of persuasive graphics

In listening-in to telephone sales, we were struck by how prospective customers were sent multiple illustrations corresponding to the different scenarios of use of the CAM, which had been discussed with the sales agent. The graphs and tables were pseudo-mathematical: we observed no attempt made by the company, for its customers or its employees, to highlight the key variables and relationships in the model and how particular values and inter-relationships of these variables resulted in this financial outcome. Moreover, although illustrations were cases of a general model, this was not evident in any of the interactions we observed, even though we could see that the interaction of several variable factors might be important to the prospective customer.

A standard mathematical approach to making these interactions evident in the graph would be to use families of curves for a range of values of one or more of the variables. In fact a presentation with variables and relationships would in our view be a more transparent description of the situation as well as offering some tools for prediction and explanation. Putting oneself in the position of a customer, one with some mathematical literacy, it seemed logical to want to know the answer to questions like 'What is the effect on repayment for every £1,000 lump sum added?', rather than an 'illustration' based on a single lump sum of £1,000.

On reflection, we wondered if we had once more oversimplified the situation: we saw the appearance of graphs and numbers, as in Figure 5.2, as an attempt at explaining the benefits of the CAM by the company for the prospective customer. The company's view however, seemed to be that the main drive for selling the CAM was to present it as a 'lifestyle' product using psychological techniques of telephone-based sales (i.e. targeting people with certain patterns of working and living). Thus the mortgage illustrations became 'persuasive graphics' to emphasise potential savings or product flexibility, whose underlying details were *not* important for the sales dialogue.

There was nothing in principle wrong in the company using mathematical objects in this pseudo-mathematical way. But the need to engage with atypical customers required, in our view, something different: sales agents needed to be able to communicate features of the mortgage *relevant to the particular customer*. This required TmL in the form, for example, of being able to work through a network of mathematical reasoning steps to link a customer characteristic to a feature of the product. Indeed, the manager of Telephone Sales had hinted at this in an early interview: 'The key problem is to coordinate listening [to a customer on the phone], doing [quick computations] and talking [explaining], and not slavishly following the order of [the input] boxes on the [computer] screen.'

We did observe this kind of ability in the work of two very experienced sales employees, yet their approach was deliberately non-mathematical. Rather than talking about the CAM's technical details, they always sought to guide conversations towards discussion about lifestyles, empathising with customers about families, pets and so on, and often pointing out that they too were holders of the CAM.

Probing 'graphical thinking' about the mortgage illustration

The outstanding balance graph within the mortgage illustration intrigued us for several reasons. We appreciated from observations of sales employees at work that such graphs were used as persuasive graphics, to illustrate the possibility of early pay-off and the resulting savings, rather than to communicate mathematically expressed information. As such, the graph was widely used in CAM information booklets and the website, as well as in the illustration tool. We wanted to check if its meaning was as self-evident as it was assumed to be, even just as a persuasive picture. As mathematics educators, we were highly aware of the extensive research which shows that graphs do *not* speak for themselves – the reader of the graph needs to have a sufficient understanding of the context and the conventions and relationships within graphs to understand the message to be conveyed. We also wanted to find out more about employees' thinking about the graphs and the underlying mathematical model, as this would be important for developing TEBOs based on the mortgage illustration.

We therefore decided to use workplace interviews as an opportunity to discuss graphical representations with employees. To stimulate the interview discussion, we created a graphic in a spreadsheet, see Figure 5.3, which combined repayment graphs for three different interest rates. The rates were not labelled or mentioned, but were in fact X: 0, Y: 5, and Z: 10%.

We showed the graphs to about ten employees in different departments and asked them what might be the factors underlying the shape of the graphs, that might explain why the slopes were different. Only people in the Finance Department (i.e. the small number of technical graduates who managed the technical operation of the CAM) could give anything like an adequate explanation or even make any connection at all between the shape of the different graphs and the interest rates.

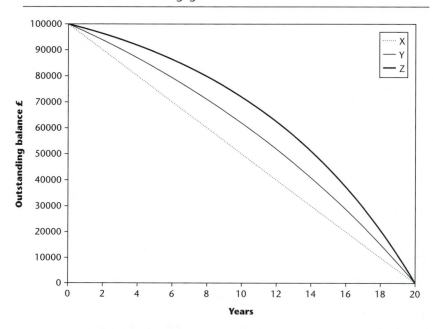

Figure 5.3 Outstanding balance graphs for different interest rates, same loan amount and same mortgage term in all three cases (X: 0%, Y: 5%, Z: 10% interest per year)

The best explanation came from an experienced underwriter who, from a confused start (he first said that since all three curves had a 20-year term then the total paid by the customer would be the same), managed to piece together a reasonable argument about the three graphs. His strategies were interesting as he used the company illustration tool in an exploratory way to help him solve the problem. First he tried to generate graphs that matched the graphs in our spreadsheet picture – this did not work, but appeared to help him think about the situation. He was then able to look critically at the shape of the graphs, at which point he immediately knew that a straight line was 'wrong' – it was not possible. He was not, though, able to connect this conclusion to a 0% interest rate.

These discussions suggested the importance of making visible the *connections* between key variables, such as interest rate, and the graphical appearance of the repayments curve, and ultimately between the balance–time relationship and the total interest saving, which was the headline savings number most often used to impress the prospective customer. This kind of understanding would, we believed, help agents to have a better appreciation of how the different aspects of the CAM fitted together as a basis for explanations that were tuned to each customer need.

Highlights from observations in other parts of the company

Induction training for sales

Observations of training involved extensive interviews with several trainers, and sitting in for one day of a one-week induction training course for new sales employees, both telephone sales and intermediary sales. In the early years of the company, recruitment policy for telephone-based work deliberately targeted graduates, who typically had a higher level of mathematical understanding and 'common sense' reasoning. The new company recognised at that time that such skills were necessary to deal with the complexities of selling the CAM. In a focus group meeting, trainers generally agreed with the findings from our ethnographies; i.e. that employees who had well-developed TmL could achieve better sales performance. The rationale was that enhancing TmL generated confidence in doing mental calculations whilst speaking, listening and typing information into the system, and facilitated employees in integrating technical information into their articulations with prospective customers.

As time passed, the company felt that it had learned how to train employees successfully, and the recruitment strategy switched towards lower-qualified, 'less expensive' people. The main characteristics of the observed training approach were:

- There was an expectation that employees would be *numerate* and this was tested in aspects of a product knowledge test that all new employees had to pass.
- *Mathematics was avoided* in both initial training and continuing development of employees, because it was argued it would frighten and alienate most trainee sales agents. Simple calculations of mortgage multipliers and loan-to-value ratios were dealt with in the training. For example, calculating the maximum loan possible as the larger of 2.75 times a joint total income, or 3.75 times the income of one applicant plus 1.0 times the income of the other was included, and not done by the computer system. Agents needed to work them out using a calculator, generating tensions around issues of mathematical calculation. For example, we noticed that among the 'Top 10' skills listed on a wall chart in the training room, mathematical or computational skills were not mentioned. We asked why, and were told that 'mathematics is a difficult topic' that made some trainees (and trainers?) nervous.
- *Role-play scenarios* were used as exercises to test participants' progress. These involved the trainer posing as a certain type of prospective customer, entering into a sales conversation with one of the participants which subsequently was discussed by all participants. All the scenarios involved tricky details in order to test the ability to bring out

the required information from the caller. What was noticeable here (more so than observing the sales area, where people were experienced and tended to automate what they were doing) was the importance of organising a customer's key information quickly to build up an image of what he or she was seeking. The trainees who immediately started to input information into the system often lost the overview of this image. This suggested that not everything could be outsourced to the system: sales employees still had to process all the different types of information – including the numerical – and make judgements based on them.

We were particularly struck by the role-play scenarios as learning exercises and made use of that format in the learning opportunities that we later co-developed with the CML trainers.

Customer services, problem management and retention

We carried out observations and interviews in a range of service departments dealing with existing customers. The extent of employees' understanding of the CAM was broadly similar to that we identified in the sales departments. However, for service work, the engagement with customers rarely involved a requirement for explanation of technical details.

The most striking observation of these areas was the number of customers who, even after several years of being a CAM customer, showed serious misunderstandings about the CAM, or a lack of knowledge of the options available. This was most evident in two departmental teams:

- *Problem Management*, which dealt with customers who were not maintaining the scheduled repayments of their debt;
- *Retention*, which dealt with customers who had requested to transfer their mortgage to another provider, so staff were seeking to negotiate with them to stay with CML. A typical case was when an IFA was trying to 'poach' a customer away from Current Mortgage by offering a low interest rate product elsewhere (for which the IFA would likely earn a fee from the other provider).

A common issue of confusion we identified, that was not explicit in the mortgage illustration tool, was *not understanding that the interest rate charged depended on the loan-to-value ratio*. This meant that it was worth having a re-valuation of the property even though it cost £75, because after several years the value was likely to have risen. This meant that the LTV would be at a lower level, with a lower interest rate that could translate to saving at least £20 to £30 per month in interest. This finding was not surprising in that the LTV was mostly invisible and not explained – something we sought to address subsequently.

The Retention observations confirmed our thinking that there was potential in developing tools so that employees, and possibly customers as well, could see how the CAM worked over time, and how it compared with the immediate and direct cheapness of a discounted mortgage. Even more than in the Sales areas, Retention team members needed to be able to appreciate customers' and IFAs' perspectives on mortgages, in particular the total costs and benefits over the long term, considering the various fees (start-up fee, early repayment penalties, etc.) that were payable with conventional low-rate mortgages, compared with the low fees but higher interest rates of a CAM.

Summary

As we had observed in other financial services companies (see Chapter 4) and had expected to observe for Current Mortgage Limited, the overall picture of technical knowledge of the CAM was of a fragmented knowledge base among the employees, an invisibility of the technical details within IT systems, and an assumption that intermediate-level employees would not be willing or able to engage with such details. We reckoned that, in a workforce of more than 1,200 people, perhaps a handful of employees (in the Finance Department, the most technically qualified) had a comprehensive picture of how the CAM business operated as a whole, in terms of how wholesale money was sourced to be lent on to individual customers, how the interest rates charged related to the different levels of risk associated with each mortgage, and how the different features of the CAM were inter-related. When prospective customers approached Current Mortgage for information about the CAM, they found it complex and very different from other mortgages. There were confusions about how it worked, how it was represented, and how information flowed between customers, company and intermediaries (IFAs), and was rarely facilitated by the use of symbolic artefacts, particularly the mortgage illustration with its graphics that were supposed to serve as boundary objects.

Clearly, issues were involved other than the mathematical, and often the lifestyle argument was paramount. There were psychological factors too. For example, some prospective customers had both a large credit card debt and, at the same time, relatively large amounts of money untouched in savings accounts. One employee termed this the 'nest-egg psychology': the person *likes* to have the feeling of having money always available even thought it is costing a lot in interest. It was evident to us, however, that the only convincing rationale for the distinctiveness of the CAM was essentially mathematical, and that this had to co-exist alongside the 'soft' description: without the mathematical perspective, everything depended on the bond of trust established between buyer and seller in a phone conversation.

Following our observations, we prepared a summary report for the company of our workplace observations and discussed this with the company in several meetings. One of the sales trainers undertook an informal survey of sales managers based on the main findings of our report. His findings exactly confirmed the areas of weakness in current practice that we had identified as follows:

- Most people didn't understand much of the maths that underpins the illustration. The biggest area is the effect of underpaying and over-paying taken in the long-term. Staff cited that they were trained to speak about the effect of (say) overpaying, and understood it in broad terms, but could not explain the detail if pressed. Typically, they rely on the totals the screens give them and cannot make a 'common sense' judgement as to whether the figures are realistic, correct or how to bring them to life. Many people we spoke to thought the illustration was not correct.
- Making the figures meaningful is a *real* struggle – there are just too many of them and they read from the screen without understanding them. If these areas were understood, the communication would be considerably easier.
- Comparisons with other companies' deals (e.g. fixed-rate or discounted repayment mortgage) are down to statements they are trained to recite, rather than a true understanding (in figures relating to the customer).
- They are trained to cover the illustration in one way – like a script – and if the customer wants the illustration to cover a strange scenario, they make a guess and hope the paperwork or internet explains it to the customer.

We took these key points along with our findings from observations and interviews as the focus for the development of TEBOs and learning opportunities, as we describe in the next section.

Current account mortgages: TEBO and learning opportunities

The main issue was to foster engagement with the mathematical models underlying the CAM, that would involve *generalising from particular cases* and recognising an illustration as an instance of a larger family of cases.

Our general aim (as in other companies, in Chapter 4) was to reconstruct the symbolic artefacts with which the employees were familiar (particularly in this case, the mortgage illustration) and open them up using mathe-matical software so they could become the focus of a discussion between employees, and between employees and ourselves – that is, to become TEBOs, for communication, shared understanding and articulation work.

We summarise the main issues addressed:

- the invisibility of variables and connections between variables in the symbolic artefacts;
- the balance–time relationship and the total interest saving;
- the peculiarities of the CAM, e.g. saving rather than earning interest and the nest-egg psychology;
- the problem of dealing with special cases rather than general relationships.

We therefore identified the TmL at stake listed in Box 5.2.

Box 5.2   Techno-mathematical literacies at stake

Complex modelling: Recognising one case as an instance of a family of cases – that is developing some appreciation of the underlying model that defines a product; coordinating and evaluating the effects of different variables in a complex model, matching this to customer needs and communicating mathematical-financial features of the product to customers.

Modelling with IT: Having an overall model of what the IT system 'needs' from customers, and the confidence to use the IT models flexibly in order to perform calculations and to facilitate calculations.

Graphical thinking and communication: Understanding the structure and key components of graphs, and what they represent; understanding graphs as a means of communication and the effects of changing parameters while keeping the underlying model unchanged.

'Mathematics of money': Understanding debt and saving in terms of compound interest, and how various parameters impact on returns and payments; appreciating the meaning of, and relationships between, interest rates and the period/frequency of adding interest to savings, or charging interest on a debt.

Box 5.3   Technology-enhanced boundary objects (TEBOs) for mortgages

TEBO 1: Building a model of credit card loan for comparison with the CAM.

TEBO 2: The mortgage illustration tool and the graphs produced as illustrations.

TEBO 3: The CAM Visualiser for day-to-day transactions and their long-term consequences.

Our trial sessions covered nine hours spread over two days, with a volunteer group of seven sales employees, whose work experience in telephone-based sales ranged from a few months up to three years. One of the company's senior sales trainers helped us in the development of the learning opportunities, and took leadership of the trial sessions.

The learning opportunities we devised for CML made use of spreadsheets as the tool for modelling the financial-mathematical situations. Spreadsheets were in widespread use within the company, although we found that few employees had used a spreadsheet as more than a data record, or as a calculator with hidden formulae (which, it turned out, many did not know existed) programmed by someone else (a similar situation to that reported from the pensions field in Chapter 4). Thus we assumed only a minimal knowledge of the software.

Our activities fell into five parts:

1   Preparatory activities about money not directly related to Current Mortgage's business, which served to get participants adjusted to the style of learning (which combined whole-group discussion with working in smaller groups on spreadsheet-based activities): these included New York Shopping Trip and My Rich Aunt – described in Chapter 4.

2   Activities dealing with financial products that were *elements* of the CAM product: credit cards, savings accounts and repayment mortgages (TEBO 1).

3   Activities around TEBO 2: a simplified spreadsheet model of the CAM, which was used to explore different scenarios such as overpayment of the mortgage, offsetting with savings, borrowing extra money part way through the mortgage term, etc.

4   Activities around TEBO 3: a spreadsheet model of the CAM that dealt with day-to-day transactions and their long-term effects.

5   Two role-play activities, in which we challenged the participants to make use of the knowledge and techniques gained during the earlier activities, and the TEBOs developed. They were asked to interpret a customer situation quantitatively, make a model of it, and use the model to explain CAM features in appropriate language to the customer in a simulated telephone call (members of the research team taking on the roles of the two customers).

TEBO 1: building a model of credit card loan for comparison with the CAM

We used spreadsheets to build models for credit card debts, cash savings accounts and the standard repayment mortgage. For brevity, we only describe the credit card model here.

Models of credit cards

We began by presenting a simplified model of how credit card debt works, with the intention of showing how the same model could be used to calculate what happens if credit card debt is consolidated with the CAM. A difficult point of explanation for employees was that the IT system did not show the credit card debt isolated within the CAM, simply lumping everything together so that the direct savings on the debt, because of the lower interest rate of the CAM, could not be seen. We therefore made this point the focus for one of the articulation work scenarios around TEBO 1.

We thought it was important to show that a credit card was in essence a loan with interest (ignoring special features of the credit card to do with interest-free periods on purchases, variable repayments, etc.), just like a mortgage. The main differences on which we focused were:

1   quite a superficial one (we thought), that credit card interest is quoted as a *monthly* rate, 1.5% say (equivalent to more than 18% annual rate), but mortgage interest is quoted as an *annual* rate, say 7%. We found that employees had a poor grasp of how to relate monthly and annual rates;
2   uncovering some of the psychology around credit card repayments, which are made to seem 'easy' (by setting a minimum payment as a percentage) but which lead in reality to extremely long and expensive pay-off periods. The customer tends to look at the size of the monthly repayment *right now*, not the total amount of interest that will eventually be paid.

Our TEBO was (like those in Chapter 4) a template spreadsheet, which participants had to fill in with several formulas (under the guidance of the researchers) with information from the scenario of a person who had built up a large debt on a credit card, then stopped using it to make purchases, and wanted to know the different options for repaying the debt and how much each option would cost. The different options were paying a fixed amount per month, or paying a percentage amount per month.

Figure 5.4 illustrates these two repayment scenarios. Since our aim was to stress graphical thinking by exploring with the TEBO, we drew attention to the different shapes of the graphs and linked these with the different modes of repayment.

The TEBO was further used to answer questions about comparing the total costs of borrowing using a credit card or a CAM. This could be done simply by replacing the monthly credit card interest rate (1.8%) with the monthly Current Mortgage rate (0.46% per month). It was at this point that we observed employees' considerable difficulties in relating monthly and annual interest rates. Few had any notion that there was a relationship, let alone what it might be.

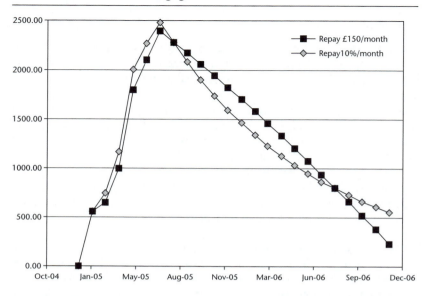

Figure 5.4   Graphs generated by a spreadsheet model. (a) Repayment of credit
card debt at £150 per month. (b) Repayment at 10% per month

TEBO 2: model of the mortgage illustration tool

This TEBO reconstructed the mortgage illustration graph in a spreadsheet (as in Figure 5.2), so the graphs could be reproduced with all the
input variables and calculations made explicit. All the input variables could
be varied according to different customer scenarios on the repayment
graphs. The whole structure was potentially modifiable by simple changes
that could lead to models of more complex situations. For example,
in Figure 5.5, a lump sum of savings of £20,000 was temporarily put
into the account, which reduced the mortgage interest and the overall
time to repay it. The convenience of the spreadsheet was that the £20,000
could be literally dropped into the formula in the month 60 row
('. . . – 20000') and taken out again in month 90 ('. . . + 20000'). A small
shortening in duration of the mortgage was visible in the graphs. The
spreadsheet (not shown) also calculated the amount of interest saved by
this offsetting.

The next activity started with the graphs, and asked participants to
match a given set of graphs against a given set of customer scenarios – see
Figure 5.6. An example scenario was:

> Miss Taylor is a self-employed landscape gardener. She has an annual
> tax bill that usually amounts to £3,000. She has a savings account into
> which she puts £250 regularly each month to pay her annual tax bill.
> After looking at a CAM she thinks she'd like to use her monthly savings

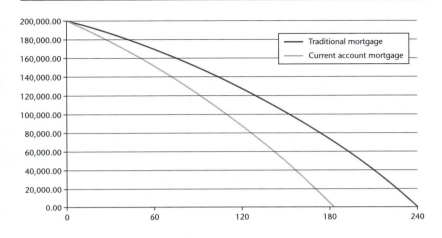

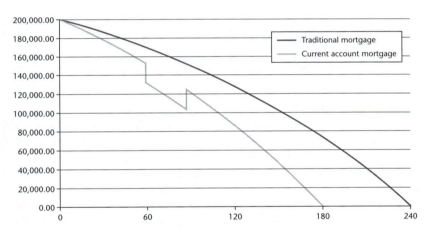

Figure 5.5 A spreadsheet model of complex situations, such as offsetting. Graphs (a) and (b) show the value of outstanding loan in £ versus months, and illustrate what happens when a lump sum of £20,000 is put into the CAM between months 60 and 90

to offset against her mortgage and to take £3,000 out of her CAM annually to meet her tax liability.

The participants had to read the graph and match it to the situation – in fact, graph (b), top right, is the correct solution.

TEBO 3: CAM Visualiser for day-to-day transactions

The final TEBO presented the most complex spreadsheet, which calculated the operations of a CAM on a daily basis but allowed the user to zoom out

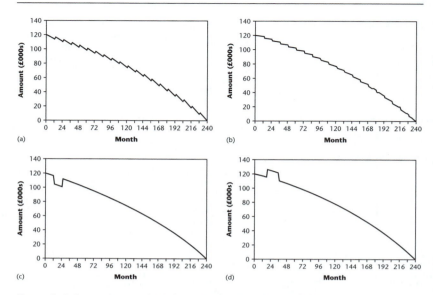

Figure 5.6 Scenario matching activity – each of a set of given graphs had to be matched against a given set of customer scenarios

and look at how daily decisions would influence the long-term repayment of the mortgage. It was developed in response to our observations in the Retention Department, where it was evident that customers could not easily connect short-term changes in their CAM with long-term consequences. For example, one question we were curious about was short-term offsetting: a salary is paid in at the start of the month, and held unspent whilst all daily expenditures were made on a credit card. These bills are then repaid from the CAM at the end of the month. What would be the cumulative effect over a period of years of doing this every month? Answer: it saves several hundred pounds over a five-year period, significant but questionable whether it is worth the daily spending discipline.

TEBO 3 was not completely successful in the final version we could produce. The reasons were similar to those described in Chapter 4, the With Profits/MVR TEBO. The spreadsheet proved difficult to use – the sheer volume of numbers necessary to show daily transactions meant that the spreadsheet became unmanageable; yet simply hiding that daily detail defeated the goals of the activity. Nevertheless the basic need for such a tool remained. It could have been developed as a visual tool, similar to the compound interest and present value tools described in Chapter 4, but this was not possible given the constraints of time and resources.

Role-play scenarios

The final learning opportunity consisted of two role-play scenarios for which the participants had to use the TEBO spreadsheets to model and understand the scenario, and develop explanations to convince a prospective customer, in a simulated telephone call with one of the research team posing as the customer. Each scenario was attempted by one of two groups, so that each group could then observe and critique the performance of the other group in role-playing. Here is one of the scenarios:

Scenario: Consolidating debt – Credit card and CAM

Mrs Jones has run up a credit card debt of £6,000; she has stopped making purchases on the card and is paying off the debt at 5% of the card balance per month. Mrs Jones is proposing to re-mortgage her flat with Current Mortgage, for £90,000 over 15 years, and the property value is sufficient to allow her to consolidate all of her credit card debt into her CAM mortgage. However, she is very confused by the information about interest rates – she knows that her credit card interest rate is 1.25% *per month*, but has no idea how to compare this with the CAM 'borrowing rate' of 5.7% *per year*.

She would like to know how much money she can save by moving her debt to Current Mortgage. She would also like to know if she could pay less back each month than her current debt repayments and still get a cheaper deal than her credit card.

Mrs Jones does not want to be paying back her debt for the entire 15-year term of the mortgage, and she has the idea that consolidation will mean that she will have to do this.

The employees worked quickly with the 'credit card' spreadsheet – TEBO 1 – to calculate the costs of repaying the debt in the credit card or the CAM, and as requested they checked what would happen if the CAM monthly repayment was reduced compared with the credit card payment (£150 instead of £300). They articulated all this information confidently in the customer conversation, significantly including the relevant technical details as part of the information:

C[ustomer]: . . . my credit card charges me 1.25% per month, but you will charge me 5.7?

Jack: That's an annual rate, so for your credit card you need to multiply roughly 1.25% by 12, which is 15%. So you're comparing 15% against 5.7%.

C: I see. But I still don't get – if I put the debt with my mortgage how is that going to help me?

Jack: Straight away you'll be paying at a lower rate, less interest, so it will be cheaper for you.

C: Well, how much difference are you talking, pennies or pounds? Will I have to pay my debt for another 15 years?

Jack: OK, you're paying about £300 per month. So if you carried on like that then after four years you'd have a remaining balance of £928, and you'd have paid £1,590 in interest. . . . With 150 per month in the CAM you could pay off all that debt in three years and eight months, and the total interest you would pay us is £645. So that's £944 less than you would pay the credit card company and the debt would be clear whereas with the credit card you'd still have a thousand quid left to pay.

C: How is that possible?

Jack: Because the interest rate is lower.

What was evident here, as well as in the other scenario (and see also Chapter 4) was that having a good personal understanding of the scenario was only one step towards being able to explain it to a customer. The participants tended to put across all the information they had calculated (see transcript above), making it hard for any customer to follow the explanation. The CML trainer analysed this as follows:

> I thought first that their explanations were more complicated than I hoped they would be [i.e. lots of numbers being talked at the customer]. I expected them to digest more what they had learned and communicate it in a more simplistic way. If I was a typical customer I would have switched off within 30 seconds. . . . So what caused the explanations I heard is that they were thrown out of their comfort zone. Now, it was extremely beneficial to present them with scenarios they had never been posed before, because they certainly challenged me. By being taken out of the comfort zone they tended to go into auto-pilot, using the things they know how to say as best they could. Whereas it would have been better for them to take a step back, and say OK let's use the spreadsheet to think about this.

These post-activity reflections suggested that more time was needed for all the participants to reflect on what they had taken from the spreadsheet-based activities, and perhaps develop more scenarios for themselves.

Outcomes for learning and practice

Impacts on practice

As with other companies, there was very limited scope to gain access to employees after the learning opportunities, in order to assess any impacts of our work on their practice. For CML, we did manage to organise a one-hour group discussion session, held four weeks later.

The employees remained positive about the value of the activities and the TEBOs. They reported several instances of changes in how they had engaged with customers following our interventions. However, a major problem from their point of view was that the new ideas they had learnt were based on the use of the TEBOs, which could not actually be used in practice. They were not approved as 'compliant' by the Compliance Department, and in fact, could not have been made so, given their openness of structure – perfect for a learning situation, but not so appropriate to the error-critical nature of practice.

> We did a lot of things in the spreadsheet that you could just not do on a normal form and normal illustration. I suppose that is difficult to talk around that when the customer gives you a situation where you can't actually do that. But at least having seen it you can go back and think I can see they *can* do that. Like the credit card issues and the things we talked about where the credit card rate is normally worked out on a monthly rate. Sometimes the customers will say 'well my rate is 1.8%' or something and . . . I never really thought about that . . . they have said 'oh no I have got a really good deal on my card'. I have always assumed that to be 'oh well they have 0%' when actually they might be thinking 1.8%. So now I would be able to say well hold on a moment what are you actually paying and is that a monthly or is that a yearly? . . . consolidating cards and giving a better monthly cost . . . might actually clinch a sale of a CAM.
>
> (Employee)

We cannot know for sure, but the fresh insights reported by these two employees suggest that their effectiveness at work had significantly changed.

Problems with interest rates

There were three notable findings. First, we noted in the explorations of TEBO 1, that most employees were unaware that paying off a constant percentage of their credit card debt every month – whatever value of the percentage below 100% – it was *never* possible to pay off the debt.

The second concerned misunderstandings around interest rates for compounding over different periods – as was also the case in the companies in Chapter 4. Here the impact of the problem on working practice was truly significant as employees saw little connection between credit card debt and mortgage loan.

The third finding was related to this. When invited to think about how a credit card debt and a mortgage loan could have the same underlying mathematical structure, we expected the employees to be able to relate, at least approximately by division or multiplication, the annual interest of a mortgage loan to the monthly interest of a credit card loan. To our surprise, five of the eight sales agents said they had never thought there was any relationship between monthly and annual equivalent interest rates, not even to the extent of 'approximately times 12'. Even the trainer working with us admitted that he had not thought about this issue before:

Researcher: There were things participants learnt which we would not have predicted. Some were stunned about the relationship between monthly and annual interest rates.

Trainer: I knew they would be. There is a complete misconception about this. And the only reason I picked it up is by having worked through your exercises myself, and realising that I had the same impression myself.

(Evaluation interview after the learning trial)

In the trainer's view, sales agents saw the different interest rates as labels for instruments (annual rates as labels attached to a mortgage arrangement or a savings account, monthly rates as labels attached to credit card or loan debts), without thinking through their mathematical meaning and the relationships that therefore exist between the values. The employee interview quoted above suggest the difference that our learning opportunities made in helping them to progress from pseudo-mathematical to mathematical thinking.

Reflections on design

In reflecting on the design and implementation of the TEBOs and associated activities, we registered some major successes. First, the interactions during the activities opened windows on relations that we had assumed were familiar, but turned not to be so. The most notable example was the relationship between annual and monthly interest rates for different types of loans, where the amounts were often nothing more than pseudo-mathematical labels without any underlying meaning. This meant that comparisons between different instruments could not be made. A second surprising result was that some employees were unaware that paying off a percentage of a credit card loan would always leave one in debt.

The learning activities with the TEBOs were successful in generating authentic interactions about the CAM. Some factors were made visible, such as the positive effect of being a higher-rate taxpayer, and the effect of re-valuing the property, thus adjusting the LTV advantageously. These were important selling points for specific types of potential customers that had been opaque to the employees prior to the learning opportunities. The learning activity of modelling the CAM with TEBO 2 was particularly successful in showing how the input of lump-sum amounts affected the shape of the graph, as well as the ultimate savings made. The learning activity with TEBO 3, the CAM Visualiser, was less successful, due to its complexity and the volume of numbers needed to show day-to-day transactions.

The scenario-matching activities, in which graphs of the outstanding balance had to be matched to different customer situations, worked well in terms of generating discussion and reflection, and all the participants experienced something which caused them to rethink how they worked.

We often were confronted with employees who displayed a discomfort with mathematics. One trainer commented: 'I saw people with heads in their hands, feeling uncomfortable – I tried to tell them, you feel uncomfortable because you are learning'. This discomfort was evident even among some trainers, who we noticed tended to divert attention during our interviews, to lifestyle issues rather than technical questions. For example, we found few who would engage with us about what the invisible interest rate could be behind the CAM illustration graphs used in company advertising.

The feedback we collected on the learning opportunities was generally positive and participants did, for the most part, come to realise that they needed technical arguments alongside soft ones, especially for communication with mathematically minded customers or their IFAs. The main challenge in the role-play activities was not the role play itself, which was a familiar learning tool for these employees, but how to make the dialogue with the customer more structured and quantitative around a mathematical model of the CAM and the customer's situation.

Conclusions

Our work at Current Mortgage Limited was broadly successful in identifying gaps in work performance related to TmL and the co-development of TEBOs and learning opportunities that were shown to work within existing modes of company training. This applied both to initial induction and continuing development – in fact, a better outcome than in pensions and investments companies, where there was less of a fit to existing training. Indeed, the CAM trainer with whom we were involved most closely was interested in the new possibilities and keen to take control of the prototype learning opportunities himself and to try them out in different training courses.

There was also an effective fit between the TEBOs that we developed and the needs of working practice to play a complementary role to the central IT system. However, making this work in practice would have required developing TEBOs that were compliant with company regulations and this was not straightforward to achieve. That said, the learning activities with the TEBOs were promising for use more widely in the mortgage sector of financial services as all of the spreadsheet models we developed were generally applicable to any current account mortgage or repayment mortgage.

Chapter 6

Summary, reflections and conclusions

This chapter summarises our key findings, draws some overarching conclusions concerning the nature of the mathematical skills gap in workplaces, and the approach we have taken to its resolution through engaging with TEBOs.

Key findings

In Chapter 1, we identified three ways by which symbolic artefacts and their mediation of the communication process across boundaries played a central role in structuring our research. These were:

- as an analytical description of how techno-mathematical literacies can become integrated within working practices;
- as a methodological strategy for conducting workplace research into the nature of mathematics used in workplaces;
- as a principle for the design of software-based mathematical tools to support mathematics learning at work.

These three themes around the use of symbolic artefacts at work also provided us with a framework for the presentation of our findings in this chapter. Overall our research shows that there is a major skills deficit among intermediate-level employees, which is the understanding of systems, not the ability to calculate. Calculation and basic arithmetic are of subsidiary importance compared to a conceptual grasp of how, for example, process improvement works, how graphs and spreadsheets may highlight relationships, and how systematic data may be used with powerful, predictive tools to control and improve processes. This skills gap needs to be systematically addressed by employers, working together with educators. It needs a commitment of time and resources on the part of researchers to appreciate how mathematics is actually expressed and needs to be communicated in particular workplaces. At the same, it requires employers to come to terms with the need for this new kind of mathematical understanding and to develop new pedagogical approaches for training, so as to make TmL more visible and available for exploration and development.

We elaborate this overarching conclusion in the five points in Box 6.1.

Box 6.1   Key findings

1   It is not true, as is often claimed, that the presence of IT systems in workplaces removes the need for employees to have a technically based understanding of products and processes. On the contrary, our research has characterised new kinds of 'literacies', techno-mathematical literacies (TmL) that are required for effective work that involves IT systems.

2   The growing use of process improvement techniques in industry involves the development of another kind of system, consisting of tools (some of which are IT-based) and methods for using process data as a basis for making improvements to processes. This creates situations where TmL becomes necessary for employees at all levels.

3   It is difficult for managers and trainers to recognise the nature and scope of the TmL that impact on their business. Even in sites that were most active in widescale technical changes (e.g. as part of process improvement), we found that the need for new knowledge involving TmL was insufficiently recognised. Moreover, there was often limited capacity amongst trainers and managers to communicate with companies' own technical experts to develop appropriate training.

4   Artefacts comprising symbolic information in the form of numbers, tables and graphs were often understood by employees as 'pseudo-mathematics': that is, as labels or pictures with little appreciation of any underlying mathematical relationships. Symbolic information thus failed to fulfil its intended role in facilitating communication across 'boundaries' between communities within and beyond the workplace.

5   The prototype learning opportunities developed in this research proved to be an effective means to deal with the problem of pseudo-mathematics, by making symbolic artefacts and work-process models more visible and manipulable through engagement with TEBOs (technology-enhanced boundary objects). This required determined efforts, involving the complementary expertise of employers and educators, in iterative co-design of TEBOs and activities that were authentic in the work setting.

The core of our ethnographic research involved identifying situations in the workplace where symbolic artefacts were intended as a means to share technically expressed information between different communities. Often, this failed to happen because of a critical skills gap in one or more of the communities involved, or equally important, the lack of an effective means of mediating the knowledge to be communicated between all those involved: for example, the largely implicit understandings of processes of shop-floor employees that need to be made explicit for communication as part of process improvement activity (see Figure 6.1 for a schematic diagram of the role of symbolic boundary objects).

Skills gaps can exist and not be critical for business performance. We found that it was usually the need to communicate with technically expressed information that made them critical, and this occurred in workplaces that were under pressure to become more efficient or effective in communicating with their customer base. The clearest examples of failure of symbolic artefacts to serve their purpose as boundary objects were the cases of the personal pension statement (Chapter 4), and the process capability indices in the automotive sector (Chapter 3).

Articulation work as an element of communication was common to all the sites of our research: it is a central feature of customer service and sales work for financial products, and is central for carrying out process improvement in a manufacturing context, since process improvement is concerned with employees working together to analyse and improve parts of the work processes.

In Boxes 6.2 and 6.3, we summarise the results of the ethnography that identified the main TmL needed in general in manufacturing and finance, along with additional specific requirements in the sub-sections we studied.

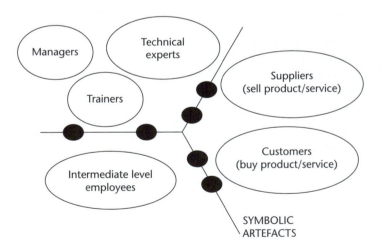

Figure 6.1 Boundaries of social worlds in a workplace: general diagram of the place of symbolic artefacts intended to serve in a mediating role, between workplace communities, and between employees and customers or suppliers external to the company

Box 6.2   TmL at stake in the manufacturing sector

General: Understanding systematic measurement, data collection and display; appreciation of the complex effects of changing variables on the production system as a whole; being able to identify key variables and relationships in the work flow; reading and interpreting time series data, graphs and charts.

Packaging: Appreciating key variables of processes – for example, the target mean and the variation allowed in the manufactured object – and communicating about these values with other employees and with management; acknowledging the role of *invisible* factors not evident in computer-generated data.

Automotive: Distinguishing mean from target, specification from control limits; knowing about the relation between data and measures, process and model; understanding and reducing variation; appreciating the basis of process capability indices and how they are calculated.

Box 6.3   TmL at stake in the financial services sector

General: Appreciating the existence of a mathematical model underlying financial products; understanding the influences on models of key variables and relationships; understanding percentage interest rates and their effects over time.

Pensions and investments: Understanding growth (compound interest) and the present value of money (including the effects of frequency of interest payments, management charges).

Mortgages: Interpreting graphs and charts; making estimates and predictions of costs of loans based on customer requirements and personal details.

In this book, we have described and exemplified our approach to dealing with the TmL skills gaps and the failure of communication of symbolic information. This has been based on the development of learning opportunities including interaction with authentic symbolic artefacts that have been modified to take a technology-enhanced form, which we termed TEBO (technology-enhanced boundary object). The aim of the learning opportunities and TEBOs was to develop flexible resources that would be adaptable by companies and organisations for incorporation into their own forms of training (both formal and informal) and, potentially, for use in workplace practice. In fact, Classic Motors (Chapter 3) was the only case in the research where this full trajectory was achieved. We also intended that individual employees should be able to adapt learning opportunities and TEBOs to their own needs. This happened again widely in the case of Classic Motors but was constrained in the regulated practices of other workplaces, particularly in financial services, where the use of any information and software had to be 'compliant', i.e. satisfy statutory regulations.

Figure 6.2 gives a schematic diagram to show how our research was intended to interact with different workplace communities, and, through TEBOs, to have an influence on working practices. Our approach to evaluating learning outcomes was guided by the idea of articulation work and communication across workplace boundaries. We therefore decided that we should include in the outcomes we needed to measure any changes, actual or projected, in the use of TmL within the practice: that is, how the employees made TmL part of their work of communicating with colleagues, customers or suppliers. We therefore set out to collect data on

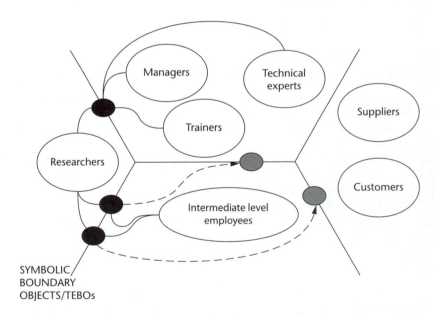

Figure 6.2 Boundaries of social worlds in a workplace, and the intervention of our research: general diagram of the research intervention using boundary objects. Black dots indicate symbolic artefacts and TEBOs introduced (or adapted) by the researchers; the intention was these boundary objects may be adapted into roles within the organisation (i.e. the dotted lines with arrows leading to the boundaries), to support training, practical engagement with customers or suppliers, and engagement between intermediate-level employees and technical departments within companies

this longer-term impact, alongside the immediate evaluations of employees and trainers.

Understanding systems with models: pseudo-mathematical and techno-mathematical

> People are part of the system; they need help. In spite of the fact that management is responsible for the system, or for lack of the system, I find in my experience that few people in industry know what constitutes a system. Many people think of machinery and data processing when I mention system. Few of them know that recruitment, training, supervision, and aids to production workers are part of the system. Who else could be responsible for these activities?
>
> (Deming, 2000: 366)

The range of workplaces considered in this book is quite broad, including various forms of manufacturing and the financial services industry. From our perspective, the important issue at stake in all cases was the need for intermediate-level employees to understand, at some level, the mathematical model behind a given symbolic artefact. Where employees were unable to deal with these models, or were not even aware of them,[1] the tendency was that they would arrive at *pseudo-mathematical* interpretations of the symbolic information – a form of fragmented understanding in which there was only superficial engagement with *meaning* of the mathematical symbols (e.g. numbers, graphs) so they were seen as labels or pictures with little if any appreciation for the underlying mathematical relationships. We provide some examples in Box 6.4.

Box 6.4   Pseudo-mathematical interpretations

Automotive sector: Process capability indices, simple numerical statistics, were mainly understood as labels for 'good' or 'bad' performance without meaningful connection to their basis in the manufacturing process.

Financial sector: Interest rates were often conceived as labels attached to a financial product ('a 5.9% APR mortgage'), rather than as elements of the underlying financial-mathematical models. The main consequence of this was a failure to appreciate the existence of any relationship between, say, annual and monthly interest rate.

Pseudo-mathematical interpretations arise, in part, because of the way systems are designed. There is often a decision that users of the system do not need, or are not able, to understand the mathematical models present within the system so their needs are not considered. The limited employee appreciation of mathematical models can also be at least partly attributed to the models just being too difficult mathematically (as in the case of the calculation of an annuity, Chapter 4). Additionally, algebra has been until recently the only language for expressing mathematical relationships for modelling. But algebra is a cut-off point for most intermediate-level employees (who typically do not study mathematics after 16) and they have limited algebraic fluency. We do not believe however that there is a simple equation between educational level and how mathematical understanding is mobilised in the workplace: it is the techno-mathematical understanding that matters, as is evidenced by those employees with limited mathematical backgrounds who were able to develop and interpret models using spreadsheets, or by tweaking different functions of the company IT systems. For example at Filmic, Chapter 2, some of the operators had a quite sophisticated quantitative understanding of how different parts of the complex production process inter-related. Additionally, we observed (in financial services) that *effective* algebraic understanding in workplace practices was rather weak amongst employees having A-level mathematics qualifications.

It was crucial for the research team to address the issue of pseudo-mathematics in our learning opportunities, since these interpretations immediately rendered invisible how any symbolic measure was derived with two consequences. First, employees did not *recognise the existence of crucial variables* (e.g. the transverse stretching of the film in Filmic, Chapter 2, which very few knew about simply because the machine controlled it automatically). Second, the measure tended not to be judged as an *objective abstraction* of the workplace, but was construed as nothing more than a management tool (see Felstead *et al.*, 2009).

Our approach with TEBOs was therefore to seek alternative forms of mathematical symbols that avoided conventional algebra by introducing a visual and interactive functionality. This was the basis for *techno-mathematical models*. Actually, this point is nothing new for those (minority) expert employees who are employed to develop models for IT systems, and who use algebra and computer programming to build computer-based models. The point here is that the majority of intermediate-level employees need now to develop a similar kind of understanding.

Spreadsheet software proved to be a powerful basis for developing TEBOs in the financial services sector. Spreadsheets are ubiquitous and familiar to employees, who therefore did not require any specific preparatory training about the spreadsheet itself, and were comfortable with its use. Spreadsheets also provide a comprehensive symbolic language for expressing relationships (between different cells of a spreadsheet), and using these relationships to do calculations. The novel aspect for the majority was constructing and entering formulae for themselves.

A major limitation of the use of spreadsheets for our purposes was, however, that it proved difficult for users to manage large numbers of cells and formulae while maintaining a global picture, particularly when values needed to be tracked over a long period. This led us to develop alternative sets of tools with visual and manipulative interfaces. These visual tools certainly enabled employees to interact and come to appreciate the key variables. This was particularly successful in the case of the SPC tools (Chapter 3). In finance, the visual tools played a role that was complementary to that of spreadsheets – providing the big picture while the spreadsheets focused on the formulae (Chapter 4).

An issue that we had to face was the choice of software in which to build our TEBOs. For the statistical models, we developed early prototypes based on the commercial educational software, TinkerPlots (Konold & Miller, 2005); see Hoyles *et al.* (2007) for more details. Although this has a well-designed manipulative interface, and proved accessible for learners and trainers, we judged that its commercial status and explicit educational agenda made it ultimately unsuitable for use in workplaces. We therefore then wrestled as to whether to develop the visual tools in a general-purpose programming language so it would be possible to design the interface exactly as we required it, even if the costs in programming time and expertise were high. We decided to go down this route and developed our visual tools in Flash. The iterative design process allowed us to test and re-design successfully. However the limitation is that it is unlikely that expertise would exist within companies to modify the tools to fit their own purposes.

In Table 6.1, we summarise the mathematical models investigated in the research, their pseudo-mathematical interpretations, the design criteria for the TEBOs to be used within our learning opportunities, and the TEBOs themselves.

Successes and challenges

> Telling the customer, 'I've used a spreadsheet and the answer is correct', doesn't go far enough. It is the explanation which tests you. Because, does the customer understand?
>
> (Interview with actuary, Lifetime Pensions)

Our approach to understanding the learning outcomes for our research in the workplace context was first to collect data on immediate impact and then to seek to identify any changes in work practice, and to see if and how employees would indeed manage to integrate their newly developed TmL into their normal routines at work. Thus our intention was that employees would carry through their learning from the training session into practice. Likewise, we anticipated that trainers and managers would regard the learning opportunities and TEBOs as a resource that could be developed for company training programmes.

Table 6.1 Summary by sector of symbolic artefacts, pseudo-mathematical interpretations, TEBO design and TEBOs

Sector/Sub-sector	Symbolic artefacts and models	Pseudo-mathematical interpretations	TEBO design focus	TEBOs
Manufacturing / Packaging	Process control system.	(Filmic) Using tactile feed-back to measure product conformance to specification, not the precise measures of film thickness. Lack of appreciation of cause and effect, and feedback control loops within the process.	Identifying critical variables and relationships of work process including, e.g., the effect of feedback loops.	Simulation of packaging production process.
Manufacturing / Automotive	Control charts and process capability indices within Statistical Process Control (SPC). Statistical sampling of data, normal distribution, measures of average and spread.	Process capability as good/bad numbers, invented by management and not measures of relative performance; disconnection between the production source data and these measures.	a. Using coloured bars dividing into each other as metaphor for algebraic relationships; layers where arithmetic calculation is performed, and algebraic relation-ships progressively revealed. b. Using visual metaphor of distribution measured against specification limits.	a. Visual manipulation tools for process capability indices; b. simulation of SPC analysis of a process.
Manufacturing / Pharmaceuticals	System monitoring and Overall	Key performance indicator as 'management tool', not	(not developed)	

	Equipment Effectiveness (OEE) as a key performance indicator.	direct consequence of process data.		
Financial services / Pensions	Pension projection and statement. Compound interest and present value of investments.	Not seeing connections between specific cases and general mathematical relationships.	a. To allow users to construct formulae and generalise relationships; add new variables; b. visual software that allowed direct manipulation of key variables (e.g. time, frequency of payment).	a. Spreadsheet models of pension projections, large fund reduction, smoothing and market value reduction; investment for future value; b. visual tools for compound interest and present value.
Financial services / Mortgages	Mortgage illustration / Compound interest for savings and loans	Monthly and annual interest rates as product labels, not in mathematical relationship; invisibility of calculations behind key factors (e.g. how much money have I saved?); mortgage repayment graphs as pictures of customer behaviour, not measured representation of a mathematical model.	To allow users to construct formulae, generalise relationships and build graphs of different scenarios.	Spreadsheet model of credit card loan for comparison with CAM; mortgage illustration tool and graphs produced as illustrations; CAM visualiser for day-to-day transactions and long-term consequences.

Thus we followed through to assess learning outcomes by revisiting workplaces between one and two months after the learning opportunities had been trialled, and interviewed employees to assess the impact of their learning experiences on practice. In a number of cases, we could point to significant improvements that had occurred in the integration of technical information into articulation work. We highlight some examples in Boxes 6.5–6.8.

Box 6.5   Impact in manufacturing/packaging

Process engineer involved in training:

If every operator and shift leader went through training using the tool there would be a base-line level of understanding that we risk not getting with the observational style training we currently use. I think the tool also helps identify people's strengths and weaknesses not only in terms of film-making process understanding but also logical problem solving ability. I didn't expect this. After going through the training activities with him, I now know far more about William [a shift leader] and the way he thinks about things than I knew before. Speaking as someone who hates open-ended tasks, I'm pleased I can now give them all to William!

Shift leader about the simulation:

I like it – I'm impressed. This will be good for training shift leaders, because there are scenarios you can't give them unless it all goes wrong – you don't want it to go wrong, but you do want it to go wrong because otherwise they won't have learnt anything to help them if such a scenario happens. So this is exactly a simulator – it's not exactly like what is in reality. It will get people's heads thinking.

Box 6.6   Impact in manufacturing/automotive

SPC specialist engineer:

One of the hardest things we have to get across is what the Cpk means – once you're familiar it becomes trivial, but to translate that to someone who doesn't know is really difficult, the tool enables you to show in a dynamic way – if I move this then this moves. It's like creating a cartoon from a load of slides. When the operators chart data they are taking little snapshots in time and your tool brings it all together like a cartoon, animating it.

Process engineering manager:

The operators know now if the figures go out of kilter, they know where the range is gonna be, where it's gonna end up, what effect it will have downstream. Before it was just a load of numbers, and what does Cpk matter anyway? Now they can see it moving out of spec, they can see now what they need to do to bring it back in. With numbers, they don't understand what's going on. The graphical representation shows them, and now they understand what needs to be done.

Box 6.7   Impact in financial services/pensions

Sales support manager:

I was concerned that people would find it interesting but would think it had no practical use. But the comments I got were that people had learnt stuff about Excel that they didn't know, but also that they had understood some of the processes behind the pensions products which they could use [with customers] . . . The overall feedback has been excellent, in lots of ways: content, pace, support – I thought there could be a lot of theory work, people sitting and not interacting with each other, so that was a surprise the level of debating exercises. There was debate and that challenged people, more than I thought there would be.

Sales support employee:

I think in this day and age we seem to rely on technology a bit too much without questioning as to how, why and where we get the answers from, so to see how to put it into practice, the actual formulas and the way we use them – I found that surprising in a way, it was something that I could do . . . it certainly opened my eyes to a few things.

Sales support employee:

When I'm talking to people on the phone now, it makes more sense in your head, how the calculations are arrived at. . . . Rather than reading from a script, as if that was in German, just pronouncing the words but I wouldn't have a clue of what it means in English . . . . It then means you can understand your speech as well sometimes, rather than sounding like a dummy, and saying to them, oh we'll get someone to ring you back, or write to you about that. Now you can more or less satisfy the caller's queries, at that first point of contact sometimes.

Box 6.8   Impact in financial services/mortgages

Trainer:

I knew they would be [referring to how many sales staff had been 'stunned' about the relationship between monthly and annual interest rates]. There is a complete misconception about this. And the only reason I picked it up is by having worked through your exercises myself, and realising that I had the same impression myself.

Sales staff:

We did a lot of things in the spreadsheet that you could just not do on a normal form and normal illustration [using CAM tools]. I suppose that is difficult to talk around that when the customer gives you a situation where you can't actually do that. But at least having seen it you can go back and think, I can see they can do that. Like the credit card issues and the things we talked about where the credit card rate is normally worked out on a monthly rate. Sometimes the customers will say 'well my rate is 1.8%' or something and . . . I never really thought about that . . . they have said 'oh no I have got a really good deal on my card'. . . . So now I would be able to say well hold on a moment what are you actually paying and is that a monthly or is that a yearly? . . . consolidating cards and giving a better monthly cost . . . might actually clinch a sale of a CAM.

As well as assessing how employees used what they had learned to change their practice, exemplified in the quotations in Boxes 6.5–6.8, we also have seen several companies adapt our learning tools for their own purposes. The most significant case of this concerned how the tools developed for statistics in process improvement were subsequently actively used in the automotive companies, with one company engineer demonstrating and disseminating them amongst international audiences of 'master black belt' process improvement engineers in Europe and the USA.

We can also report that most of the employees who engaged in our learning opportunities expressed a strong wish to undertake more learning of this kind. Given the overwhelmingly negative reaction to mathematics in most work-based training, we regard this as a very positive outcome. As we have observed, mathematics is a troublesome area for employee development, with both employees and trainers fearful of it. Mostly, this results in companies either avoiding mathematical training altogether (e.g. Current Mortgage, Chapter 5), or adopting lecturing approaches to mathematical teaching that fail to connect adequately with employee experience. We would criticise the SPC training that we saw in companies (see Chapter 3) on these grounds: introducing statistical ideas through formal definitions (using algebraic symbols that most employees cannot understand) and practice exercises may 'tick the box' that employees have been exposed to the ideas, but it does not translate into a practical understanding of how to use those ideas. The impressive worldwide response from trainers to our SPC visual tools suggests the extent of dissatisfaction which exists towards such traditional approaches and the thirst for new approaches.

Training cultures in workplaces: implications for research

We were interested to observe differences between sectors where there were strong training cultures, and those that had none. In fact, in most of the industrial sectors in which we worked, strong cultures of training did exist, and inevitably these companies were more able to collaborate with us in the different phases of the research. Nonetheless, we note a persistent problem of undertaking research in workplaces and this concerns achieving any *sustained* collaboration with companies and sectoral organisations (employer-representative bodies, and national training organisations). It is of course only through sustained engagement that research about workplaces can be valid. We experienced numerous false starts and delays. Initial contact was often enthusiastic yet frequently cooled when individual key contacts moved away to different roles, or when company priorities shifted at short notice (often due to directives coming from global headquarters in another country). Sadly, we found that initiatives to do with training and employee development are often the first to be cut or reduced when business conditions are difficult.

These difficulties significantly shaped the sample of companies with which we were able to do any work, let alone complete the full cycle of sustained engagement from ethnography to learning intervention. We had to be ever-resourceful in making use of personal contacts and serendipitous connections; for example, our whole engagement with the automotive sector was due to a chance encounter with a senior technical manager at a conference.

So far as we can tell, the problem of sustained engagement goes with the territory of workplace and vocational learning in the UK: many business organisations seem to give low priority to training and employee development (Westwood, 2004; Leitch, 2006), and the post-compulsory/ vocational education sector has been the subject of frequent major restructurings by central government. We would, however, like to emphasise that where companies and individual employees *were* able to sustain their engagement with our research, the partnerships proved extremely productive, yielding both excellent results for the purposes of our research, and significant benefits to the employees, and their companies. This has been evidenced in feedback from managers concerning changed practice, and by the take up of the TEBOs and their customised adaptation to achieve company goals.

We tried hard to offer our learning opportunities in a form that could be flexibly integrated into workplace cultures, and we achieved some success in this respect. This was evidenced at Classic Motors, for example, where the employees reported exploiting the learning activities and TEBOs in formal training sessions, as well as in a range of informal situations (e.g. employee analysing a process problem on the shop floor, technical manager presenting improvement proposals to general and financial managers). The example of Filmic (Chapter 2), where we had the enthusiastic collaboration of a few individuals, demonstrated that positive results were possible in situations where company training support was limited. In fact, we would conclude overall that enthusiasm of individuals (employees, managers and technical specialists) to try new ideas in training is as important as the existence of formal training structures – particularly so where mathematical skills are involved.

A note on differences across sectors

We have, so far, provided an overview of our findings in the two major sectors, which were broadly convergent. In this section, we note some important differences between them. Workplaces of course differed in the sophistication of processes, as reflected in the degree of automation through IT-based systems. But there is a major difference between manufacturing and financial services sectors in that the latter's products are in essence virtual and therefore can be entirely swallowed up within IT systems, which is of course not possible for any physical product. Additionally, process improvement, the common feature of all the manufacturing cases that we studied, is yet another kind of system, consisting of tools (some IT-based) and methods for using process data as a basis for enhancing quality and efficiency.

In terms of mathematical knowledge required in the different sectors we have observed that statistics are extremely important in manufacturing, for example, for a sense of how data are distributed and how their centre and variation can be measured. In finance, a core mathematical idea is that of compound interest ('interest on interest').

Another important distinction between the sectors concerns the role of the customer, which is immediate and dominant in financial services. This foregrounds issues of communication about financial products, but also the observed tensions around sales and advice. There is also a critical skills gap amongst customers that we did not research but cannot be ignored. In order for a customer not to be 'mis-sold' a financial product, the customer needs to understand what product they need for their own circumstances. This takes one into consideration of the developing area of 'financial literacy', that is of crucial importance but beyond the scope of this book.

Finally, we think it relevant to point to the different role of regulation in the two sectors. In manufacturing there are, of course, 'regulations' in the form of specification, health and safety concerns and so on. But these constraints operate at a rather general level. In financial services, regulations constrain interactions in very direct ways: what can be said, written, or even considered as a possible strategy. For us, these constraints needed careful consideration when designing learning opportunities and TEBOs, and in our trials, we became acutely aware of the understandable importance and prioritisation attached to the regulatory framework by employees.

Conclusions and implications

The overarching theme of this book has highlighted a problem concerning perceptions of mathematics, in general but also in workplaces. Long-established preconceptions are deeply ingrained about what mathematics is, with the subject most often described in terms of numeracy (arithmetic) and algebra (symbols and equations), with descriptions shaped by the relics of school experience with its emphasis on procedure and calculation. We argue that the major skills problem for workplaces is the understanding of systems, not an ability to calculate or manipulate. Employees need to be able to appreciate models of how IT systems work, or the methodological systems such as those that are used to implement process improvement in workplaces. It is however hard to appreciate the mathematical models in IT systems, as they become invisible behind 'user friendly' interfaces. Our work has shown that TmL is most evident in workplaces that are involved in changes in working practices. Yet, even in sites where the need for change was recognised and supported, we did not find the need for TmL *explicitly* recognised, although we found that when it was pointed out, it often resonated with managers and trainers.

There is a general problem of inadequate training of the UK workforce at intermediate level (Westwood, 2004; Leitch, 2006), so the problems of mathematical skills are not unique. But we have argued that the consequences of inadequate mathematical skills are of great economic significance because of the general drive in industry towards greater efficiency, and the changing modes of production where there is an increasing degree of customisation that involves responding to the needs of individual customers.

The two areas of industrial practice that we considered in this book, process improvement, and customer services, are of course not confined to manufacturing and finance and are of general importance across all industries, with the consequence that TmL, we could also predict, are of general importance. The requirement for TmL does not apply to all employees; only those who engage in situations where there is a need both to use technically expressed information or to communicate such information, either to fellow employees or to customers/suppliers outside the company. This we have argued is a requirement frequently of intermediate-level jobs, which are typified by shop-floor managers in manufacturing and customer sales/service agents, such as in financial services.

Effective training for mathematical skills is hard, not least as there is much fear of mathematics amongst both employees and trainers. Also, our research suggests that UK training practices are dominated by pedagogical approaches that mitigate against effective training: we observed very traditional approaches to mathematics based on the principle of teaching general techniques and definitions of mathematical concepts and then practising applying these, ignoring the whole richness of the workplace context in which employees are working, and the expertise that they have which can offer a huge potential for meaningful learning.

Fortunately, we suggest that more effective training of mathematical skills that gives voice to employee skills is a feasible option, and that technology can make this possible if three key principles for learning design are taken into account:

- *authenticity*, in which situations derived from actual workplace events can be the subject of discussion and reflection;
- *visibility*, in which hitherto invisible relationships become visible and manipulable through TEBOs;
- *complexity*, in which relationships are represented in non-trivial ways that reflect real situations, but alternative representations are explored for use so as to avoid the pitfalls associated with the use of conventional algebraic symbolism.

However, developing learning opportunities requires pedagogical and software expertise that is unlikely to exist in companies, and the role of employers in developing mathematical learning materials must not be underestimated. However there is a commonality of mathematical models for process improvement, and financial services, such that learning opportunities once developed in one company have potential for more widespread adoption.

The sustainability of the type of learning intervention we have developed requires an emphasis not only on co-design with workplace trainers and managers, but also, where possible, on co-teaching. Companies must be engaged to transform learning opportunities so that they will remain useful as part of the company's internal activity. This was difficult to achieve, not because of the participation of trainers (which was often excellent) but because of the lack of priority accorded to upskilling their workforce by many senior managers. We have become increasingly aware of a gap between rhetorical commitment to process improvement or improved customer engagement and the reality of employee development in practice.

Finally, we briefly consider some of the possibilities for future research along a number of directions. We see potential for co-developing comprehensive sets of learning opportunities around authentic, visible and complex learning opportunities supported by TEBOs. Subsequent research by Bakker and colleagues, building on the TmL project presented in this book, currently (2007–2011) explores the viability of this approach in vocational education.[2]

Another example of such a development is a related short research project that the authors undertook,[3] 'Workplace personalised learning environments for the development of employees' technical communicative skills' (November 2006 to April 2007). We looked in detail at the 'information advice and guidance' sector (comprising careers guidance services in universities, colleges, lifelong learning, etc.) where there was a recognised growing need to develop employees' techno-mathematical literacies. The purpose was to increase the effective use of statistically expressed 'labour market information' in providing careers guidance to clients (e.g. estimates for future trends in numbers of workers required in different job sectors in a specific city or region), and to develop tools to support the financial modelling of careers choices (e.g. looking at the potential for enhanced salary income to pay off study loans for education). The research scoped the development of a 'personalised learning environment' that was technically ambitious in that it would have features of virtual learning environments, combined with Web 2.0 social networking and information sharing, and intelligent adaptation for making automated decisions in response to a user's known profile and his/her real-time interactions with the system. One of the arguments we put forward in support of this technically complex software system was that, now and even more in the future, employees may find themselves in a position where employers become less willing to provide training for skills gaps when work could be outsourced to other countries (already a major trend in financial services), or individuals with necessary skills sets could be imported from elsewhere. Thus there is potential for employees to exploit specially designed social networks in order to develop themselves.

Other important research directions would involve investigating the evolution of techno-mathematical knowledge as it moves between formal education and the workplace. The relationship is problematic, since all the evidence points to the extreme difficulty of developing authenticity within formal settings. In vocational and further education a major challenge is to teach mathematics that students experience as relevant *and* that is general enough to be applicable in many future workplace situations. When mathematics is a separate subject in the curriculum, many students consider it pointless; when taught as part of authentic projects, little attention tends to be paid to it as it has become invisible.

Long-established preconceptions about mathematics are deeply ingrained, both in the world of work and the world of education. One way these reveal themselves is where employers complain about 'poor numeracy skills' in practices, such as financial services, where employees have little need to do arithmetic, because of the total computerisation of work processes. A central research challenge for skills development, therefore, is to educate both employees and managers about important mathematical models and relationships that are rendered invisible by IT within workplaces.

Underlying the complexity of this work is the need for sustainable co-working between educators, workplace trainers, managers and employees. We conclude with our best example of such collaboration. The TmL project ended with an event involving 60 invited participants from industry, education and policy organisations. We were privileged to be able to present our research in the form of joint presentations between the research team and the co-developers from three of our partner companies, an indication of the depth of the impact of the research on these companies.

At this event, the CEO of one of the major industrial companies drew our attention – not only to our success in developing TmL – but to an area that we had up to then, relatively ignored. This was, he told the meeting, in the area of job satisfaction and empowerment – giving voice and autonomy to the expertise of employees (an issue raised in fact by another TLRP project – Wolf and Evans, in press). It was especially gratifying to us that this comment was offered in public for all to hear and consider. It gave us pause for thought, as we had not seen mathematics in this more general and potentially powerful light.

> I think that the projects are absolutely excellent, the work that has gone into this has been outstanding . . . I think there is one part of this that goes a bit beyond the mathematical side, which has been the focus that has been sort of the soft side – of what the end user gains, the empowerment that the end user has, the knowledge that the person has when all is said and done, the job satisfaction that the operator has . . . So I think that is really one of the great parts of this entire project and all the work that has gone into this.
>
> (International business manager, Filmic)

Details of fieldwork

Companies and organisations which participated in the research

Please refer to the Tables on pages 188–193.

Table A.1 Fieldwork in packaging sector

Company	Phase 1 (Observation, ethnography)	On-site visits (person days)	Phase 2 (Development of learning opportunities)	On-site visits (person days)
Company A (adhesive papers) LABELEX	Eight interviews with senior managers, personnel in charge of process improvement, quality control, stock control, shift managers and team leaders in several shop floor areas.	10	No follow-on development activities with company. But prototype learning opportunities were trialled as part of one course at the Institute of Packaging.	4
Company B (wrapping films) FILMIC	In three manufacturing departments: interviews with department manager, supervisory managers. observation of work; interviews with senior production and technical managers.	7	Co-development of a computer-based simulation tool and associated learning activities, and testing the tool and activities with employees in four trials.	16

Company C (bakery) MASTER CAKE	Observations of the work of supervisory managers in production (four managers), and interviews done with senior production and technical managers; the work of the packaging design team (packaging managers, technologists and technicians).	10	No follow-on development activities.	
Company D (pharmaceutical packaging) [NOT IN BOOK]	Observation of the work of shop floor supervisory managers in production (tablet packaging), and the work of the packaging design team.	4	No follow-on development activities.	
Packaging Centre of Excellence, Leicester [NOT IN BOOK]	Exploratory visit to site.	2	Learning opportunities trial (based on Labelex and Filmic prototypes).	4

Table A.2 Fieldwork in automotive and pharmaceuticals manufacturing sectors

Company	Phase 1 (Observation, ethnography)	On-site visits (person days)	Phase 2 (Development of learning opportunities)	On-site visits (person days)
Auto company A (luxury car maker) CLASSIC MOTORS	Initial interview with senior analyst. Two visits for observation and interviews with senior/middle management and shopfloor team leaders. Observation of SPC training day. Documentary analysis of company training schemes.	9	Two one-day trials of learning opportunities as part of SPC course. Follow-up interviews. Co-design of training video.	9
Auto company B (sports car maker) SPORTING MOTORS	Visit to shop floor and brief observation of SPC in use.	1	One visit observation and interview with trainers and one day trial of learning opportunities. Follow-up interviews.	4
Auto Company C (design and manufacture of acoustic parts for cars) [NOT IN BOOK]	Direct approach came from company interested in using SPC TEBOs. Site visit and interviews with middle management.	1	No development activities.	

Pharma Company A (ethical manufacture and packaging) [NOT IN BOOK]	Observations of tablet-making and packaging; interviews and observations of two supervisory managers. Senior managers of two areas were interviewed, as well as the human resources manager. Documentary analysis of company training schemes. Interviews of process improvement staff. Attendance at statistical methods (SPC) course.	9	No development activities.
Pharma Company B (packaging) TOP GENERICS	Observations with supervisors and machine operators in two shifts; interviews with managers.	7	No development activities.

3

Table A.3 Fieldwork in financial services sector

Company	Phase 1 (Observation, ethnography)	On-site visits (person days)	Phase 2 (Development of learning opportunities)	On-site visits (person days)
Company A (Credit cards) [in Chapter 1]	Interviews with four staff in product marketing and data analysis to investigate how statistical information about customers is communicated between data analysts and marketing employees	2	No development activity.	
Company B (Pensions and life insurance, investment products) LIFETIME PENSIONS LTD	Interviews with actuary, training managers. Investigation of back office teams in pensions, investments and other areas. Documentary analysis of company training schemes.	15	Learning opportunities trial in pensions/ investments; follow-up interviews with participants and managers. Learning opportunities trial with customer enquiry employees; follow-up interviews.	23

Company				
Company C (Mortgage provider) CURRENT MORTGAGE LTD	Observation and interviews with several departments of company: telephone sales, retention, IFA interaction. Follow-up interviews with trainers (who also conducted survey of training needs).	15	Learning opportunities trial with telephone sales employees; follow-up interviews.	8
Company D (Pensions and life insurance) NATIONAL MUTUAL PENSIONS LTD	Investigation of back office teams in pensions sales, at two sites.	3	Two learning trials with sales administration employees. Follow-up interviews with participants and office managers in two sites.	14

Further reading on the Techno-mathematical Literacies research

Bakker, A., C. Hoyles, P. Kent and R. Noss (2006). Improving work processes by making the invisible visible. *Journal of Education and Work*, 19(4), 343–361.
Case study data: Master Cake
This paper contains a detailed report on the case study at the Master Cake bakery, with an analysis of the techno-mathematical literacies involved in the work done by the process improvement team (see Chapter 2).

Bakker, A., P. Kent, J. Derry, R. Noss and C. Hoyles (2008). Statistical inference at work: Statistical process control as an example. *Statistics Education Research Journal*, 7(2), 130–145.
Case study data: Classic Motors, Sporting Motors
This paper analyses techno-mathematical literacies in terms of the statistical concept of 'inferential reasoning', and connects it with the philosophical literature on inferential reasoning and the 'space of reasons' idea proposed by the philosopher, John McDowell.

Bakker, A., P. Kent, R. Noss and C. Hoyles (2009). Alternative representations of statistical measures in computer tools to promote communication between employees in automotive manufacturing. *Technology Innovations in Statistics Education*, 3(2). Online publication. Retrieved from: www.escholarship.org/uc/item/53b9122r.
Case study data: Classic Motors, Sporting Motors
This paper presents a detailed report on the case study at Classic Motors and Sporting Motors, focusing on the use of process capability indices, and the learning opportunities and TEBOs that were developed.

Hoyles, C., A. Bakker, P. Kent and R. Noss (2007). Attributing meanings to representations of data: The case of statistical process control. *Mathematical Thinking and Learning*, 9(4), 331–360.
Case study data: Labelex
This paper considers the role of graphical information, particularly SPC charts, in statistical process control, and discusses some early research on learning opportunities that was carried out prior to the developments described in Chapter 3.

Hoyles, C. and R. Noss (2007). The meanings of statistical variation in the context of work. In R. Lesh, E. Hamilton and J. J. Kaput (eds), *Foundations for the Future in Mathematics Education*, pp. 7–35. Mahwah, NJ: Lawrence Erlbaum Associates.
Case study data: Labelex
This paper describes the origins of the project's research methodology in relation to issues in mathematics education, and presents a detailed report on the case study conducted at Labelex (as mentioned briefly in Chapter 3).

Kent, P., R. Noss, D. Guile, C. Hoyles and A. Bakker (2007). Characterising the use of mathematical knowledge in boundary-crossing situations at work. *Mind, Culture, and Activity*, 14(1–2), 64–82.
Case study data: Lifetime Pensions
This paper contains a detailed report on the case study at Lifetime Pensions, as presented here in Chapter 4.

Kent, P. (2009). In the workplace: Learning as articulation work, and doing articulation work to understand learning. In G. Vavoula, N. Pachler and A. M. Kukulska-Hulme (eds), *Researching Mobile Learning: Frameworks, Methods and Research Designs*, pp. 61–76. New York: Peter Lang.
Case study data: Lifetime Pensions
This paper describes the idea of articulation work in relation to the research methodology of the TmL project.

Noss, R., A. Bakker, C. Hoyles and P. Kent (2007). Situating graphs as workplace knowledge. *Educational Studies in Mathematics*, 65(3), 367–384.
Case study data: Filmic
This paper contains a detailed report on the case study of Filmic, examining in particular the nature of the problem-solving approaches, and the use of the graph-based information, adopted by different employees.

Notes

1 Introduction

1 This sub-section is based on Hoyles & Noss (2007).
2 At the time of writing (2009) in the midst of the credit crunch, it is interesting to note how ignorance of how financial products work – on the part of managers, employees, and customers – has been identified as a major factor in the financial crisis. The trend towards complexity and ignorance was recognised by those managers back in 1994, and accelerated significantly over the intervening years.
3 The definition in official UK skills terminology is 'level 2' (equivalent to the higher grades of GCSE, the English national academic examinations at age 16), and 'level 3' (equivalent to A-levels, the English national academic examinations at age 18).
4 It is worth observing that the debate about mathematics and numeracy still continues, with an added dimension of the growing use and incorporation in curricula of what is termed 'functional mathematics'.
5 But not quite, as there are some sophisticated details which we could not include in the TEBO, and in fact some of these details were confidential company information.

2 Manufacturing 1

1 This case study is described in detail in our paper, Bakker *et al.* (2006) – see Further Reading.
2 This case study is described in detail in our paper, Noss *et al.* (2007) – see Further Reading.

3 Manufacturing 2

1 SPC is also used in the manufacture of high volume, low value products (e.g. packet foods or processed drinks), where automation and process control tend to be pursued to a greater level, and different means of sampling are required (Caulcutt, 1995) but we did not do research in these sectors.
2 On the shop floor, calculations were not done, but left to the SPC department to do remotely.
3 0.3% [about 1 in 300] of data points can be expected to appear outside of the control limits.

4   Cp is still a useful measure however, for example if the process mean is known to be too high or too low and there is work going on to change it.

5   For details of the work at Labelex, see Hoyles and Noss (2007) – see Further Reading.

6   The observations at Classic Motors and Sporting Motors are described in our paper, Bakker *et al.* (2009) – see Further Reading.

7   For additional detail on the development and trials described here, see our paper Bakker *et al.* (2009) – see Further Reading.

8   Actually, the idea of manipulating a distribution is quite an odd idea from the viewpoint of formal statistics – the logic is that the distribution arises out of the sample data set, so to modify the distribution independently of any change in data does not make sense.

4 Financial services 1

1   There have been proposals to change the regulations so that selling with commission is not allowed and thus eliminating the distortions that arise from it. (See 'Retail Distribution Review' on the Financial Services Authority website, www.fsa.gov.uk).

2   It appeared that IFAs had quite frequently advised buying such a product, despite the fact that the With Profits fund was intended as a long-term investment.

3   It is pertinent to ask why compound interest should be relevant to a pension, which is equity-based and not a cash investment; the answer is that, looking back over 40 to 50 years, the historical performance of equity-based investments had consistently averaged around 7% per annum, though in any short period it could be well below (or, in prosperous times well above) this average.

4   This case study is described in further detail in our paper, Kent *et al.* (2007) – see Further reading.

5   SMILE Mathematics was developed by London teachers in the 1960s and the resources are now widely available online.

6   The third option was not part of the original school activity, and was introduced as a result of a design discussion after which we decided that the original task was too mathematical (with its mathematical focus on functions as being linear or exponential, etc.) and too far from practice to be engaging for employees.

7   This is not in fact exactly the correct data, as it should have been data about the market value of units in a With Profits fund, which would be less volatile than the stock market index but we decided interacting with this data set would provide an adequate idea of the smoothing process and MVR.

8   Mathematically, what is happening is that $Vg = Mg \times ((1 + I)^N - 1)/I$, where $I = $ (percentage interest rate)$/100$ and there are N payments. Then, $Vg = c \times Mg$, and $T = c \times M$, with the same constant c.

9   Another participant applied this same heuristic to the New York Shopping question: Suppose the discount was 50%, tax was 10% and the price was $100; then it becomes much clearer that you pay $55 either way.

10 In fact, it took us some time to appreciate all the complexities of financial practice: some rates are precisely set by division/multiplication, whereas others require compounding. For example: If a savings account has a 'nominal rate' (aka 'quoted rate') of 5% annual interest, but interest is paid monthly (or quarterly or daily or whatever), then the monthly rate paid out is 5/12 %. Then the AER is the equivalent annual rate as if interest were paid annually, thus AER $= 5.116\% = 100 \times ((1+0.05/12)^{12} - 1)$. It's interesting that the AER is always

called a 'notional rate' in financial literature (because it assumes that all interest earned monthly is left in the account to compound, and that the rate does not change during the 12 months, etc.), yet mathematically we might say it is a 'true' rate, or at least a 'truer' rate than the quoted rate of 5%.

11 Accessibility can sometimes be at the expense of visibility.

5 Financial services 2

1 An added complexity is that interest is usually calculated daily, but paid monthly by the customer.

2 A good sales agent had to be able to identify the clearly inappropriate cases and put off further enquiry since it required several years of mortgage repayments before the company started to make a profit on each customer. Agents told us that high-profile 'simple message' advertising campaigns used by the company, especially on television, tended to generate high volumes of calls from people who were not likely to be appropriate customers.

6 Summary, reflections and conclusions

1 We saw cases of both intentional absence of education (financial IT systems), and ineffective teaching of statistical concepts (manufacturing).

2 The project is called 'Boundary crossing between school and work for developing techno-mathematical competencies in vocational education' (funded by the Programme Council for Educational Research, Netherlands Organisation for Scientific Research) and is based at the Freudenthal Institute, Utrecht University; see the website: www.fi.uu.nl/~arthur/mbo .

3 See the final 'scoping reports' for details, at http://www.workplace-ple.org.

Bibliography

Alwan, L. C. and H. V. Roberts (1995). The problem of misplaced control limits. *Applied Statistics*, 44(3), 269–278.

Anis, M. Z. (2008). Basic process capability indices: An expository review. *International Statistical Review*, 76(3), 347–367.

Ben-Zvi, D. and J. Garfield (eds) (2005). *The Challenge of Developing Statistical Literacy, Reasoning and Thinking*. New York: Springer.

Bessot, A. and J. Ridgeway (eds) (2000). *Education for Mathematics in the Workplace*. Dordrecht, The Netherlands: Kluwer Academic Publishers.

Bicheno, J. (2004). *The New Lean Toolbox: Towards Fast, Flexible Flow*. Buckingham, UK: PICSIE Books.

Bowker, G. C. and S. L. Star (1999). *Sorting Things Out: Classification and its Consequences*. Cambridge, MA: MIT Press.

Caulcutt, R. (1995). *Achieving Quality Improvement: A Practical Guide*. London: Chapman & Hall.

Clayton, M. (1999). Industrial applied mathematics is changing as technology advances: What skills does mathematics education need to provide?. In C. Hoyles, C. Morgan and G. Woodhouse (eds), *Rethinking the Mathematics Curriculum*, pp. 22–28. London: Falmer Press.

Cobb, P., J. Confrey, A. diSessa, R. Lehrer and L. Schauble (2003). Design experiments in educational research, *Educational Researcher*, 32(1), 9–13.

Coben, D. (2003). *Adult Numeracy: Review of Research and Related Literature*. London: National Research and Development Centre for Adult Literacy and Numeracy.

Deming, W. E. (2000). *Out of the Crisis*. Cambridge, MA: The MIT Press.

diSessa, A. (2000). *Changing Minds: Computers, Learning, and Literacy*. Cambridge, MA: The MIT Press.

Eraut, M. (2004). Transfer of knowledge between education and workplace settings. In H. Rainbird, A. Fuller and A. Munro (eds), *Workplace Learning in Context*. London: Routledge Falmer.

Felstead, A., D. Gallie, F. Green and Y. Zhou (2007). *Skills at Work, 1986 to 2006*. Oxford: SKOPE (ESRC Centre on Skills, Knowledge and Organisational Performance).

Felstead, A., A. Fuller, N. Jewson and L. Unwin (2009). *Improving Working as Learning*. Abingdon, Oxon: Routledge-Falmer.

Finzer, W., T. Erickson and J. Binker (2005). *Fathom!* [Computer Software]. Emeryville, CA: Key Curriculum Press.

FitzSimons, G. E., D. Coben and J. O'Donaghue (2003). Lifelong mathematics education. In A. J. Bishop, M. A. Clements, C. Keitel, J. Kilpatrick and F. K. S. Leung (eds), *Second International Handbook of Mathematics Education*, Vol. 1, pp. 103–142. Dordrecht, The Netherlands: Kluwer Academic.

Gal, I. (2002). Adults' statistical literacy: Meanings, components, responsibilities. *International Statistical Review*, 70(1), 1–25.

George, M., D. Rowlands, M. Price and J. Maxey (2005). *The Lean Six Sigma Pocket Toolbook*. New York: McGraw-Hill.

Gravemeijer, K. P. E. (1994). Educational development and developmental research in mathematics education. *Journal for Research in Mathematics Education*, 25(5), 443–471.

Hall, R. (1999). Following mathematical practices in design-oriented work. In C. Hoyles, C. Morgan and G. Woodhouse (eds), *Rethinking the Mathematics Curriculum*, pp. 29–47. London: Falmer Press.

Hall, R. and R. Stevens (1995). Making space: A comparison of mathematical work in school and professional design practices. In S. L. Star (ed.), *The Cultures of Computing*, pp. 118–145. London: Basil Blackwell.

Hall, R., R. Stevens and T. Torralba (2002). Disrupting representational infrastructure in conversations across disciplines. *Mind, Culture, and Activity*, 9(3), 179–210.

Hampson, I. and A. Junor (2005). Invisible work, invisible skills: Interactive customer service as articulation work. *New Technology, Work and Employment*, 20(2), 166–181.

Hand, D. J. (2009). Mathematics or mismanagement: The crash of 2008. *Mathematics Today*, 45(3), 106–107.

Handel, M. J. (2003). *Implications of Information Technology for Employment, Skills, and Wages: A Review of Recent Research*. Arlington, VA: SRI International. [Retrieved 18 December 2009 from http://www.sri.com/policy/csted/reports/sandt/it/]

Handel, M. J. (2004). *Implications of Information Technology for Employment, Skills, and Wages: Findings from Sectoral and Case Study Research*, Arlington, VA: SRI International. [Retrieved 18 December 2009 from http://www.sri.com/policy/csted/reports/sandt/it/]

Hoyles, C. and R. Noss (2007). The meanings of statistical variation in the context of work. In R. Lesh, E. Hamilton and J. J. Kaput (eds), *Foundations for the Future in Mathematics Education*, Chapter 1, pp. 7–35. Mahwah, NJ: Lawrence Erlbaum Associates.

Hoyles, C., R. Noss and S. Pozzi (2001). Proportional reasoning in nursing practice. *Journal for Research in Mathematics Education*, 32(1), 4–27.

Hoyles, C., A. Wolf, S. Molyneux–Hodgson and P. Kent (2002). *Mathematical Skills in the Workplace*, London: The Science Technology and Mathematics Council. [Retrieved 18 December 2009 from www.lkl.ac.uk/research/technomaths/skills2002]

Hoyles, C., A. Bakker, P. Kent and R. Noss (2007). Attributing meanings to representations of data: The case of statistical process control. *Mathematical Thinking and Learning*, 9(4), 331–360.

Ishikawa, K. (1990). *Introduction to Quality Control*. New York: Productivity Press.

Joiner, B. L. (1994). *Fourth Generation Management: The New Business Consciousness*. New York: McGraw-Hill Professional.

Kent, P. and R. Noss (2002). *The Mathematical Components of Engineering Expertise: Final Project Report to the Economic and Social Research Council*. [Retrieved 31 December 2009 from http://www.lkl.ac.uk/research/MCEE]

Kent, P. and R. Noss (2003). *Mathematics in the University Education of Engineers: A report to The Ove Arup Foundation*. London: The Ove Arup Foundation.

Kent, P., R. Noss, D. Guile, C. Hoyles and A. Bakker (2007). Characterizing the use of mathematical knowledge in boundary-crossing situations at work. *Mind, Culture, and Activity*, 14(1–2), 64–82.

Konold, C. and C. Miller (2005). TinkerPlots: Dynamic Data Exploration [Statistics software for middle school curricula]. Emeryville, CA: Key Curriculum Press.

Kotz, S. and N. L. Johnson (1993). *Process Capability Indices*. London: Chapman & Hall.

Lave, J. (1988). *Cognition in Practice: Mind, Mathematics and Culture in Everyday Life*. New York: Cambridge University Press.

Lave, J. and E. Wenger (1991). *Situated Learning: Legitimate Peripheral Participation*. New York: Cambridge University Press.

Lee, C. P. (2007). Boundary negotiating artifacts: Unbinding the routine of boundary objects and embracing chaos in collaborative work. *Computer Supported Cooperative Work*, 16(3), 307–338.

Leitch, S. (2006). *Prosperity for All in the Global Economy: World Class Skills: Final Report (Leitch Review of Skills)*. London: Her Majesty's Stationery Office.

Magajna, Z. and J. Monaghan (2003). Advanced mathematical thinking in a technological workplace. *Educational Studies in Mathematics*, 52, 101–122.

Masingila, J. O. (1994). Mathematics practice in carpet laying. *Anthropology and Education Quarterly*, 25(4) 430–462.

Mathews, J. (1989). *Tools of Change: New Technology and the Democratisation of Work*. Sydney: Pluto Press.

Millroy, W. L. (1992). An ethnographic study of the mathematical ideas of a group of carpenters. *Journal for Research in Mathematics Education*, Monograph 5.

Montgomery, D. C. and W. H. Woodall (2008). An overview of Six Sigma. *International Statistical Review*, 76(3), 329–346.

Nakajima, S. (1989). *TPM Development Program: Implementing Total Productive Maintenance*. New York: Productivity Press.

Nardi, B. and Y. Engeström (eds) (1999). A web on the wind: The structure of invisible work. Special issue of *Computer Supported Cooperative Work*, 8(1&2).

Nathan, M., G. Carpenter and S. Roberts (2003). *Getting By, Not Getting On: Technology in UK Workplaces (Report by The Work Foundation iSociety Project)*. London: The Work Foundation.

NCETM (2008). *Mathematics Matters*. London: National Centre for Excellence in Teaching Mathematics.

Noss, R. (1998). New numeracies for a technological culture. *For the Learning of Mathematics*, 18(2), 2–12.

Noss, R. (2002). Mathematical epistemologies at work. *For the Learning of Mathematics*, 22(2), 2–13.

Noss, R. and C. Hoyles (1996a). *Windows on Mathematical Meanings: Learning Cultures and Computers*. Dordrecht, The Netherlands: Kluwer Academic Publishers.

Noss, R. and C. Hoyles (1996b). The visibility of meanings: Modelling the mathematics of banking. *International Journal of Computers for Mathematical Learning*, 1(1), 3–31.

Noss, R., C. Hoyles and S. Pozzi (2002). Abstraction in expertise: A study of nurses' conceptions of concentration. *Journal for Research in Mathematics Education*, 33(3), 204–229.

Nunes, T., D. W. Carraher and A. D. Schliemann (1993). *Street Mathematics and School Mathematics*. New York: Cambridge University Press.

Oakland, J. S. (2003). *Statistical Process Control* (5th ed.). Amsterdam: Butterworth-Heinemann.

OECD (2003). *PISA 2003 Assessment Framework*. Paris: Organisation for Economic Co-operation and Development.

PACKMAP Project (2003). *PACKMAP 2003: The Packaging Industry Mapping Project*. Melton Mowbray, UK: The Institute of Packaging.

Pyzdek, T. (1991). *What Every Manager Should Know About Quality*. New York: Marcel Dekker.

Reich, R. B. (1992). *The Work of Nations: Preparing Ourselves for 21st Century Capitalism*. New York: Vintage.

Scribner, S. (1986). Thinking in action: Some characteristics of practical thought. In R. J. Sternberg and R. K. Wagner (eds), *Practical Intelligence: Nature and Origins of Competence in the Everyday World*, pp. 13–30. Cambridge: Cambridge University Press.

Shaughnessy, J. M. (2007). Research on statistics learning and reasoning. In F. K. Lester Jr. (ed.), *Second Handbook of Research on Mathematics Teaching and Learning*, pp. 957–1009. Charlotte, NC: Information Age Publishing.

Smith, J. and L. Douglas (1997). Surveying the mathematical demands of manufacturing work: Lessons for educators from the automotive industry. In R. Hall and J. Smith (eds), Session 10.39, AERA (American Educational Research Association) Annual Meeting, Chicago, IL, USA.

Star, S. L. and J. Griesemer (1989). Institutional ecology, 'translations,' and boundary objects: Amateurs and professionals in Berkeley's Museum of Vertebrate Zoology, 1907–1939. *Social Studies of Science*, 19, 387–420.

Strauss, A. L. (1993). *Continual Permutations of Action*. New York: Walter de Gruyter & Co.

Steen, L. A. (ed.) (1997). *Why Numbers Count: Quantitative Literacy for Tomorrow's America*. New York: The College Board.

Suchman, L. (1996). Supporting articulation work. In R. Kling (ed.), *Computerization and Controversy: Value Conflicts and Social Choices* (2nd ed.), pp. 407–423. Orlando, FL: Academic Press, Inc.

Treffers, A. (1987). *Three Dimensions: A Model of Goal and Theory Description in Mathematics Instruction – The Wiskobas project*. Dordrecht: Reidel.

Victor, B. and A. C. Boynton (1998). *Invented Here: Maximizing Your Organization's Internal Growth and Profitability*. Cambridge, MA: Harvard Business School Press.

Wake, G. D. and J. S. Williams (2001). *Using College Mathematics to Understand Workplace Practice: Final Report to the Leverhulme Trust*. Manchester: University of Manchester.

Westwood, A. (2004). Skills that matter and shortages that don't. In C. Warhurst, E. Keep and I. Grugulis (eds), *The Skills that Matter*, pp. 38–54. Basingstoke: Palgrave Macmillan.

Williams, J. and G. Wake (2002). Metaphors and models that repair communication breakdowns and at disjunctions between college and workplace mathematics. Paper presented at the Annual Conference of the British Educational Research Association, September 2003.

Wolf, A. and Evans, K. (in press). *Improving Literacy at Work*. Abingdon, Oxon: Routledge.

Womack, J. P., D. T. Jones and D. Roos (1991). *The Machine That Changed the World: The Story of Lean Production*. New York: Harper Perennial.

Zuboff, S. (1988). *In the Age of the Smart Machine: The Future of Work and Power*. New York: Basic Books Inc.

Index

eBooks – at www.eBookstore.tandf.co.uk

A library at your fingertips!

eBooks are electronic versions of printed books. You can store them on your PC/laptop or browse them online.

They have advantages for anyone needing rapid access to a wide variety of published, copyright information.

eBooks can help your research by enabling you to bookmark chapters, annotate text and use instant searches to find specific words or phrases. Several eBook files would fit on even a small laptop or PDA.

NEW: Save money by eSubscribing: cheap, online access to any eBook for as long as you need it.

Annual subscription packages

We now offer special low-cost bulk subscriptions to packages of eBooks in certain subject areas. These are available to libraries or to individuals.

For more information please contact webmaster.ebooks@tandf.co.uk

We're continually developing the eBook concept, so keep up to date by visiting the website.

www.eBookstore.tandf.co.uk